ACCLAIM FOR TRAVELERS' TALES BOOKS
BY AND FOR WOMEN

The Best Women's Travel Writing 2008
"The authors here know how to spin a tale."   —*Body+Soul*

The Best Women's Travel Writing 2007
"Some of the best travel writing—well, writing, period—this year lurks among the pages of *The Best Women's Travel Writing 2007*."
                                            —*Dallas Morning News*

100 Places Every Woman Should Go
"Will ignite the wanderlust in any woman…inspiring and delightful."
          —Lowell Thomas Awards judges' citation, Best Travel Book 2007

Women in the Wild
"A spiritual, moving and totally female book to take you around the world and back."   —*Mademoiselle*

A Woman's Path
"A sensitive exploration of women's lives that have been unexpectedly and spiritually touched by travel experiences…highly recommended."
                                            —*Library Journal*

A Woman's World
"Packed with stories of courage and confidence, independence and introspection; if they don't inspire you to pack your bags and set out into the world, I can't imagine what would."   —*Self Magazine*

A Woman's Passion for Travel
"Sometimes sexy, sometimes scary, sometimes philosophical and always entertaining."   —*San Francisco Examiner*

Sand in My Bra
"Bursting with exuberant candor and crackling humor."
                                            —*Publishers Weekly*

A Woman's Europe
"These stories will inspire women to find a way to visit places they've only dreamed of."   —*The Globe and Mail*

The World Is a Kitchen
"A vicarious delight for the virtual tourist, as well as an inspiration for the most seasoned culinary voyager."   —Mollie Katzen

Family Travel
"Charming stories about taking the kids along…should give courage to any wary mother who thinks she may have to give up on her love of travel when she gives birth."   —*Chicago Herald*

T R A V E L E R S ' T A L E S

THE
BEST
WOMEN'S TRAVEL
WRITING

2009

TRUE STORIES
FROM AROUND THE WORLD

TRAVELERS' TALES

THE BEST
WOMEN'S TRAVEL
WRITING
2009

TRUE STORIES
FROM AROUND THE WORLD

Edited by
LUCY MCCAULEY

Travelers' Tales
an imprint of Solas House, Inc.
Palo Alto

Art Direction: Stefan Gutermuth
Cover Photo: © Duncan Walker
Interior design and page layout: Melanie Haage using the fonts
  Nicolas Cochin, Ex Ponto, and Granjon
Author Photo: Gail E. Atwater

ISBN 1-932361-63-4
ISSN 1553-054X

First Edition
Printed in the United States
10 9 8 7 6 5 4 3 2 1

For my wise-women mentors

Susan Jampel,

Lonia Winchester,

and Helen Bacon Landry (1924–2007)

…there isn't a train I wouldn't take,
No matter where it's going.

— EDNA ST. VINCENT MILLAY

Table of Contents

Editor's Preface

My family and I spent the better part of 2008 in Tübingen, southern Germany, where my husband, Charles, was on sabbatical. As I struggled with getting to know a new culture, place, and language, I learned that German has several words, in fact, for the verb "to know." Like Spanish speakers, among other people, Germans use a different word if they're talking about knowing a person (*kennen*), for example, as opposed to knowing a fact (*wissen*).

But it wasn't until near the end of our stay abroad, my language skills increasing little by little, that I learned yet another German nuance of "to know." *Begreifen* means to "grasp" something, to take hold of it—to understand, comprehend, embrace it. Significantly for me, *begreifen* is sometimes how Germans speak about knowing a *place*— of coming to know it intimately, beyond where maps will take you, beyond the things that guidebooks can indicate. Yet it can also be understood as a way of letting ourselves be grasped by the possibilities of a moment, of being formed and informed by what we encounter.

By the time we left Tübingen, I realized I had come to know our temporary home, in the *begreifen* sense, by many means. I knew it through walks with my daughter, Hannah, who turned five there and attended a German kindergarten for seven months. One of our after-school rituals in that picturesque little university town was to visit the sheep and goats housed in a fenced-in shed nearby. We would save up our bread all week to feed them (that is, until the *"Bitte Nicht Füttern!"* sign appeared on the gate...oops!). Or sometimes we'd climb high to the top of the wide green hill near our house and sit on a bench, gazing at the town below. We'd take turns picking out our house, our friends' houses, the steeple of the church in the *Altstadt* (old city).

But I also came to know Tübingen through our friends Karin and Rolf, who would take us with them into the *Altstadt* for the ritual of Saturday shopping, introducing us to their favorite cafés and vendors in the market square. We'd inevitably bump into other Tübingers who would be out too, walking the cobbled streets, all of us trying to get our shopping done by 2 P.M. when everything shut down for the weekend. Karin also helped me to know Germany through food, eating and cooking always according to season and what was available in the open-air Friday market. With her I learned to prepare homemade potato salad, *wurst* and *spätzle*, and the particularly rich brand of *kuchen* (cake) that only Germans can concoct. Meanwhile, Rolf took it upon himself to instruct me in the intricacies of the German language while plying me with dark German chocolate.

Later, when our friend Christian presented Charles and me with bikes to use during our visit, suddenly I came to know Tübingen in a wholly new way. I was free at last to traverse the red bike lane on the sidewalk, moving swiftly past the gardens and ancient buildings of Tübingen, the wind billowing my skirt.

As I peeled back the layers of the town, its people, and language bit by bit, it struck me that this kind of "knowing," of grasping the nature of a place in the *begreifen* sense, is exactly what the stories in Travelers' Tales books uniquely describe.

When James O'Reilly and Larry Habegger started their press in the early '90s, there was little else like Travelers' Tales on bookstore shelves (apart from a few standalone, single-author travelogues). Among the maps and guidebooks that could tell you where to stay, what to do, and how much it would cost, the would-be traveler found little that offered a sense of the places themselves—of what it would actually feel like to *be* there, to take hold of and be embraced by the myriad possibilities therein. But then Travelers' Tales came along, with its books of personal essays collected by country and, later, by topics such as nature, humor, spirituality, and women's writing. These books helped revive a lost art—the travel story—which had gone virtually uncelebrated in the English language since the nineteenth century and the spate of travelogues inspired by American and British ventures abroad during the Grand Tour era.

This year's *Best Women's Travel Writing* marks my fifth year as editor of the series, and fifteen years since I began work on my first anthology for Travelers' Tales (*Spain,* published in 1995). One of my favorite aspects of the job is doing events at bookstores each year with some of the authors from these volumes. I love reading with these women and interacting with live audiences, usually filled with travelers with fascinating tales of their own. Over the years, as I've listened to and read women's travel stories, I've come across tales that quite literally changed my life and the way I approach the world.

I heard, for example, a story about a woman volunteering on an archaeological dig, and I felt emboldened to try it too, in Turkey. I read about women traveling alone with their children and felt encouraged to do the same, starting the year my daughter was born. I became so inspired reading stories of women going on spiritual pilgrimages that I eventually walked part of the Camino de Santiago in Spain. And when I faced some difficulties in my relationships, I remembered stories I'd heard about women who traveled as a way to heal from emotional pain, and soon found myself hitting the road.

So when at bookstore readings I sometimes get the question, Why a *women's* travel book?—the answer is clear: As a woman, especially one who often travels alone, I think there is value in learning about how other women move in the world. How do we use our wisdom, strength, and vitality to navigate new territory? And how do we handle the vulnerability we might occasionally feel where, in the same situation, a man likely wouldn't? From reading stories of women's wild and adventurous spirits, of their acts of daring, I draw inspiration and the courage to try new things.

A friend once told me that reading the stories in these books is like getting to eavesdrop on other women's conversations, vicariously enjoying the juicy details and learning from the nuggets of wisdom. I'd like to invite you now to listen in on the stories of travel in this collection, ranging from the rhapsodic to the humorous and the harrowing: to learn, for example, how Alexis Wolff came to know South Africa through the purchase of a pet chicken; how Jenny Williams connected with Kenya through a game of soccer; how at Easter Island Catherine Watson struggled with a desire to go native and never leave; and how Nancy Vala Michaels spent two weeks following the bends of the Mississippi River and her own inner compass.

May the stories in this book set you on a path toward your own experience of *begreifen,* of traveling in a way that allows you to truly know a place, to gain a sense of it, and become transformed by it.

—LUCY MCCAULEY

Introduction

Faith Adiele

A few years ago when my travel memoir was released in paperback, a San Francisco bookshop invited me to return to do a follow-up reading. I'd been touring steadily ever since the hardcover had come out sixteen months earlier, so by then I was tired of hearing my own voice (and suspected that others might be as well). As an excerpt from the book had just been reprinted in that year's *The Best Women's Travel Writing*, I proposed a group reading of local contributors instead. The good folks at Travelers' Tales circulated the idea in the Bay Area, and after a round of enthusiastic emails, three other writers signed on. I planned to come to town early so that we could all meet beforehand for drinks.

Our meeting at a bar across from the bookstore was like a reunion of old friends. Perhaps it was because we are already members of the same "club"—virtual neighbors in an anthology, sisters in the Travelers' Tales family. Or perhaps it was because we instantly recognized each other as sister travelers/writers, recognized that both writing and traveling can be solitary ventures and adventures that (ironically) isolate us from kindred spirits. We hadn't traveled to the same places or in the same way or for the same reasons, but we recognized each other nonetheless. And when the time came to cross the street for the reading, we lingered, reluctant to break up our new community.

A nice group of friends and strangers had turned up that summer evening, and I watched them listen to the three readers. The audience was so attentive and well behaved that I thought of my Nigerian family. It amuses them how we Americans go to public spaces to sit quietly next to each other like little islands, motionless, hands in our laps, peering intently ahead. Any connection we feel is likely to be with the performer alone, directed in a straight line from our seat to the podium or stage. As I listened, I pondered if and how I could bend that line and spark an instant community like the one we'd formed in the bar across the street, not unlike those that spring up among travelers on the road. (And frankly, since the audience had already sat through three readings and mine was supposed to be the longest, I figured I'd better do something drastic if I had the slightest chance of holding their attention!)

When I took the podium, I asked myself what question would I most like to be asked by a stranger. It came to me. And so I suggested that folks get up, approach someone they didn't know, and share their favorite place in the world. To my amazement (and probably because they *weren't* my students) they did. They gave little trills of surprised laughter, glanced around brightly, hopped up from their seats, and really did it. In fact, they wouldn't stop doing it! Long after my little icebreaker had served my own selfish purposes, people leaned in towards each other, the room buzzing with laughter and exclamations and chatter. Clearly I had tapped into something with the idea of a favorite place, and clearly such places came with every writer's dream—*details*.

As I wandered among the pairs, eavesdropping under the guise of "facilitating," I overheard snippets of everything I love most about travel writing: here were setting and story; there were characters and culture; strangers confessed personal histories to each other, colored with image and emotion. It reminded me of Don George's definition of the genre in his Salon.com "Wanderlust" column: "At its best, travel writing is extraordinarily complex and fulfilling—encompassing person and place; history, art and culture; food and philosophy; essay and reportage." I'm always telling my writing students that studying travel literature can teach them everything they need to know about good writing in general (and that in the process they will get the added bonus of becoming better readers and world citizens).

And why not? Can't it be argued that literature begins with *The Odyssey*, the departure from the familiar, the real and metaphorical voyage through hardship, the return home? The first time I heard the story, I recognized it: the arc was satisfying; it made sense. In "Against Travel Writing," Robyn Davidson puts it beautifully: "The metaphor of the journey is embedded in the very way we conceive of life—movement from birth to death, from this world to the next, from ignorance to wisdom." The minute I read this statement, I was relieved. At last I understood why every story I write, be it a spiritual coming of age in the Thai forest or an investigation into family history in Nigeria and Finland or a meditation on the terrors of public speaking for *O Magazine*, felt to me like a travel tale. Not necessarily the kind of travel where you venture out from the safety of home armed with nothing more than a Swiss army knife and tampons, or the kind where you wander into a remote village that's never seen anything quite like you and stand surrounded in the plaza, or the kind where you spew the contents of your stomach onto the ground and have your sense of self shaken to the core in the process. But

travel perhaps as Frances Mayes puts it: "journeys when
the traveler is moved from one psychic space to another."
Or as Susan Orlean says: "getting lost...losing yourself
in a place and a moment...feeling yourself lifted out of
your ordinary life into something new."

Then, not unlike with travel, along with recognition
and relief came fear. How pathetic and limiting as a
writer to have only one story! Once the word was out
about Faith's single plot, assignments would dry up! But
again a woman traveler/writer came to my aid—Mary
Morris paraphrasing writer and critic John Gardner
in her classic *New York Times* piece on women's travel
writing: "[T]here are only two plots in all of literature:
you go on a journey, or the stranger comes to town."
Her argument was that for years women have been
"denied the journey, we were left with only one plot to
our lives—to await the stranger." And so, as a result, our
travel writing has been more about people, less about
place. According to Morris, "Women need and want to
be connected, to be joined to other human beings. We
don't easily go off alone into the wild, to the North Pole
or in search of elusive beasts."

Now, some twenty years after she wrote that, the
stories in this rich collection—perhaps Travelers' Tales'
most diverse yet—make clear that we certainly do.
Women do go off easily and alone into the wild, to
the North Pole and Antarctica, to Easter Island and
Ethiopia, to Albania and Laos, in search of elusive beasts
of all sorts. (And then, yes, we gather in bars and book-
shops afterwards to connect with other women—and
men—around the journey.) But even if "male travel" is
adventure and hardship, and "female travel" is connecting to others, that's fine by me. I believe that the best
travel writing—by anybody—combines both, the inte-

rior journey with external quest, the yin and the yang. And though, as a woman, I do still have to consider my personal safety, I also have to consider my race and nationality and economic status, both when traveling and when writing about it. As Jamaica Kincaid has said, "The travel writer: She is not a refugee. Refugees don't do that, write travel narratives. No, they don't. It is the Travel Writer who does that."

Many of us, who travel because we care about the world, share Kincaid's ambivalence about what our travel does to that world. How do we negotiate the politics of tourism and travel responsibly? How do we negotiate the politics of who gets to travel, that is, who gets to look and then paint the picture for those who cannot? How do we describe foreign worlds when it could be argued that the imperialist origins of travel taint the very language we use to talk about difference?

I, for one, relish the challenge. Travel writing seduces, and for that reason I believe it is potentially the most subversive and most important of literatures. Friends and family imagine a glamorous life of drinks with tiny umbrellas by the pool. Literary critics tend to dismiss it. And yet, if done properly, it's a literary bait-and-switch, the political detail of journalism and the social detail of history wrapped in the drama of fiction and the lyricism of poetry. An entire world in its beauty and ugliness, its triumphs and failures, goes down easily. If done properly, travel writing forces us into someone else's eyes, gives us the context to understand what we're seeing, and adds a bit more to our understanding of the world. We emerge changed, perhaps ready at the slightest suggestion from a stranger in a bookstore to open ourselves up, recognize others, form community.

℘ ℘ ℘

Faith Adiele is the author of Meeting Faith, *a travel memoir about becoming Thailand's first black Buddhist nun, which received the PEN Beyond Margins Award for Best Memoir of 2004; writer/narrator/subject of* My Journey Home, *a documentary film aired on PBS about growing up with a Nordic-American single mother and then traveling to Nigeria as an adult to find her father and siblings; and lead editor of the international anthology,* Coming of Age Around the World: A Multicultural Anthology. *She is a contributor to* O Magazine, *and her travel essays and memoirs have been widely published and anthologized. The recipient of numerous awards, including fifteen artist residencies in four countries, a UNESCO International Artists Bursary,* Best American Essays *shortlist, and the Millennium Award from* Creative Nonfiction, *she currently resides in Pittsburgh, where she is Assistant Professor of Creative Nonfiction at the University of Pittsburgh. Her current project is* Twins: Growing Up Nigerian/Nordic/American, *a social/cultural memoir that will complete the story begun in the PBS documentary.*

CATHERINE WATSON

♫ ♫ ♫

Where the Roads Diverged

On Easter Island, a traveler finds her home and heart.

I was in Ecuador, on my way to a folklore performance, sharing a ride with two other tourists—a middle-aged Canadian woman and a young computer guy from California. They started comparing notes on their Latin American travels. I didn't join in. I'd seen the continent edge to edge over the previous twenty-five years, but I didn't want to interrupt their conversation by saying so. I just stared out the window, only half-listening.

Then I heard something that snapped me alert—something that made me feel as if I'd been kicked in the chest, as if my heart had stopped, as if I couldn't breathe.

"You know the place I liked best?" the young guy said. "Easter Island!"

The Canadian gushed in agreement. There was *so* much to do there! New hotels! The new museum! All

1

the tours there were to take! And they've put so many of the statues back up....

My God, I thought, suddenly strangled by memories. My God, my God. They're talking about Easter Island as if it's a *place. Just another place.*

At the folklore show that night, I applauded when the rest of the audience did, but I wasn't there. I'd been thrown a quarter century into my own past, back to a forty-five-square-mile triangle of black lava and wind-blown grass in the middle of the Pacific Ocean, 2,200 miles from Chile, 2,400 miles from Tahiti.

La Isla de Pascua. Rapa Nui. *Te pito o Te Henua.* The navel of the world. "The place farthest from any-where...."

By any of its names, Easter Island felt like home to me, the only place in the world that ever truly did.

I had been under its spell since before I could read, ever since my father first showed me its pictures in books—haunting pictures of giant stone heads perched on grassy slopes, lips pursed, eyes blank, staring out to sea.

I was a shy child then, and I grew into a shy adult, ill at ease with people, lonely but most comfortable alone. I took refuge in daydreams—always about somewhere else, somewhere distant and strange, where a stranger like me might better fit. When I was old enough, I started traveling, trying to make my dream world real.

By the time I got to the South Pacific, I was in my early thirties, and I'd been looking for home all my life—for the place I really belonged, the place where I should have been born. I felt I'd found it on Easter Island, the instant I stepped off the plane. It was as if the island had been waiting for me, all that time, the way I'd been waiting for the island.

Yolanda Ika Tuki met me at the airport. Actually, she just met my plane, she and a pickup truck full of other island women, all hoping to rent out rooms to tourists. There were only a couple of flights a week from mainland Chile and not many visitors. Most of them were already booked into the island's only formal lodging, a six-room motel, but the local women met the plane every time anyway, crowding up to the stairs before passengers had a chance to get out, piling luggage into the pickup and pleading for guests.

Yolanda met the plane, met me, met my eyes. It felt like fate.

Her small house stood on a shady, sandy lane on the outskirts of Hanga Roa, the island's only village. She had one room to rent, a sunny, recently added annex that felt instantly familiar. The walls were varnished plywood, like a summer cabin up north, and the furniture looked like the stuff in the government clinic where my father worked—chrome tubing, green leatherette cushions.

The reason made me smile. Everything in that room—walls, furniture and louvered windows—was indeed U.S. government issue, liberated by the locals after our Air Force abandoned a satellite-tracking base on the island in the 1960s. Even the varnish smelled like home.

Yolanda was short and thick-bodied, like most of the older island women, with dark skin and black hair. She might have been forty or fifty or even sixty. I never knew. Yolanda cooked for me, interpreted the island for me, introduced me to her neighbors and friends, included me in her household. It felt like a family but wasn't quite, so I fit right in.

There was a quiet man I assumed was her husband, whom I saw mainly at dinner. A pretty little girl who was a neighbor's out-of-wedlock child—Yolanda said the mother's new husband didn't want the girl around. And the child of another neighbor, a slender boy of about eleven whose history had a different twist.

He was half-American, one of about thirty youngsters that the U.S. airmen had managed to father while they were here. It was a noticeable number, out of a population of less than 2,000, 600 of them kids. The islanders loved children—people joked that babies were "our biggest product"—but this boy wasn't happy. He yearned to find his father and go live with him in the States.

"I know my father loves me," he said, "because he wrote to my mother once." One day the boy showed me the precious letter. The American man had promised nothing, hadn't included his address or even his last name. He was just saying goodbye.

This is what outsiders have always done in Polynesia, starting with the first European explorers and their crews—love 'em and leave 'em, down through the centuries. It made me feel ashamed, but the islanders didn't seem to mind. All good stories, in fact, seemed to begin, "When the Americans were here...." They had brought the modern world with them—electricity, piped water, Coke in cans, movies, the airport. "We *loved* the Americans," one islander told me.

Islanders didn't feel that way about people from Chile, which has governed Easter Island since 1888. They said Chileans couldn't be trusted, were lazy and given to stealing. Chileans said the same things about them.

Among themselves, the islanders spoke their own language; it was soft, rounded and full of vowels, like all its cousins across Polynesia. With me, they spoke Spanish, the island's second language and mine as well. But while I heard about local problems—feeling discriminated against by mainlanders was mentioned often—no one dragged me into them. I think it was because I was under Yolanda's wing—not a part of the community, but not an ordinary tourist, either. She treated me more like a daughter.

Sometimes, when she called me for breakfast, she would come in and perch on the foot of my bed and chat. She also gave me advice. It wasn't always wise, but it was always the same: *Disfrute su vida, Catalina,* she said. Enjoy your life, Catherine. And I did.

I began to exist in the present tense, as if I had no past regrets and no future fears. It was something I'd never done before. That, and the incredible distances surrounding us, lent me an exhilarating freedom. I likened it to hiding in a childhood tree fort with the rope pulled up. "No one knows where I am," I kept thinking. "No one can find me."

My days quickly fell into their own gentle rhythm: Go out walking after breakfast. Explore a cave, a volcano, a vista. Take pictures. Talk to people. Go home for lunch. Nap or write or poke around Hanga Roa. And in the late afternoon, walk over to Tahai—the row of giant statues, called *moai,* that stood closest to town—and watch the sunset paint the sky in the direction of Tahiti.

After supper, the island's only TV station went on the air, and I joined Yolanda's household around the set. The programs, flown in once a week, would have been odd anywhere, but here in the uttermost corner of Polynesia, the mix was especially peculiar: decades-old "Beanie and Cecil" cartoons, a British-made series of English lessons ("Why are there no onions in the onion soup?"), a quiz program on Chile's fishing industry and American reruns, subtitled in Spanish—"The Six Million Dollar Man," "The Rockford Files."

"Is there a lot of that in the United States?" an adult asked reasonably after one of Rockford's chronic car chases. The children thought the Six Million Dollar man was real. I couldn't get over the station's signature logo: three dancing *moai,* wiggling their world-famous bellies on the screen.

One evening I stayed in my room, writing. Between gusts of wind that rattled the trees, I caught snatches of soft music. In the church down the lane, people were singing Polynesian hymns. If I'd known nothing about this culture, that music alone would have told me they'd been seafarers. There was a canoeing cadence in it, like the throb of waves or the steady beat of paddle strokes.

There was distance in it too, and a touch of sadness. It made me think of the complicated, crisscross navigations that populated the Pacific in ancient times, and the vast emptiness that early voyagers sailed into without knowing what lay ahead, and how many must have been lost before others happened upon this tiny fleck of land.

"Wind and music and nothing to do," I wrote in my journal that night, "Sunday on Easter Island." But it didn't feel like Sunday. It felt like Saturday. Every day on the island felt like Saturday.

I knew what my favorite place would be before I saw it—Rano Raraku, the extinct volcano where the giant statues had been quarried and carved. They were already old friends. Face to face, they looked exactly as they had in the books of my childhood—an army of elongated heads frozen in mid-journey down the grassy slopes.

This was where, in the late 1600s, the ancient carvers put down their stone chisels and never picked them up again. The reasons aren't fully known, but shrinking resources likely led to warfare, devastating the old culture.

The heads at Rano Raraku were the ones that never reached their destinations, travelers stranded in mid-trip. Islanders said these *moai* were blind. They had not yet received their stone eyes or gotten their stone topknots, and they would never stand on an altar like Tahai's.

The cylindrical topknots—like top hats the size of corn cribs—were quarried at another volcano, Puna Pau, where the lava rock was rusty red instead of grayish black. Abandoned topknots lay on the ground like giant red boulders. They all had been hollowed out inside, the better to fit onto a statue's head. One afternoon, I curled up inside a topknot and spent an hour watching white clouds drift across brilliant blue sky, over a landscape of yellow grass; it reminded me of a Kansas prairie.

The weather reminded me of Hawaii—frequent showers, followed by clearing skies and rainbows. But the resemblance stopped there. The island was a big pasture edged by cliffs. It wasn't tropical, and it wasn't lush. Outside of gardens and protected valleys, there were almost no trees, and the beaches were black rocks.

Yolanda told me there was another American on the island, a woman about my own age. I ran into her one sunset at Tahai, and we struck up a friendship. She had visited the island before, drawn by its archaeology, but she was back this time because of a boyfriend, an islander. She wanted to see where that relationship was going to lead. I soon knew what she was wrestling with.

One night, Yolanda took me to Hanga Roa's little disco—about half the village was there—and I found an island boyfriend too. That meant I was swept into another extended family—parents, sisters, cousins and armfuls of little nieces and nephews. There were more gatherings in homes, lots of talking, loud card games that I usually couldn't follow. Their favorite was a complicated four-person game called "bree-hay"; it turned out to be bridge, pronounced in Spanish.

The most beautiful spot on the island was one I'd never heard of—Orongo, the place of the birdmen. My islander borrowed horses—much easier to borrow than cars, because there were more of them—and we spent a day riding up there and back.

Orongo was a fringe of low stone huts on the lip of a high, sheer cliff, with the blue sea crashing at its foot. Seabirds nested on the cliff front, and in the past, island men used to risk their lives to climb down and gather eggs each year. The rituals they performed at Orongo didn't die out until the 1860s, and the cliff was still dangerous. There were no protective guardrails, just the stone huts, a rim of grass and that sheer, dizzying drop to the limitless sea. Standing up there was like being on the edge of the world, or the prow of a ship.

From the beginning, Yolanda had been urging me to stay longer. I'd only planned on a week, but as plane day got closer and she kept talking, I weakened. Yolanda was right, I decided. There was really no reason to leave so soon. The only thing waiting for me was a small internship on a newspaper in Buenos Aires, and the start date was more than a month away. Besides, there was no penalty for changing my reservation. What harm could it do to wait?

I missed one plane. And then another. And another....

And while I waited, my newly simple life grew complicated. I was enmeshed in a love affair, all right, but it wasn't exactly with the man I'd met. It was with Easter Island itself. My island.

I could see a different future opening up for me there, and every time I cuddled one of the little nephews on my lap, it seemed more real, more possible. How many people, I wondered, get to live their dearest wish? How many people really find paradise? How many dare to stay once they find it?

That was the biggest question, and the longer I stayed, the harder it was to answer, and the less like paradise my paradise appeared. I loved the "wind and music" part but I was no longer sure about "nothing to do."

I watched the men and began to understand why every day felt like Saturday. It was because so few of them had real jobs. I watched their wives and noticed that the idle men didn't help them with all those babies. I saw how few options there were for everyone, even the children, and wondered how many options there would be for me.

Yolanda kept on telling me to enjoy my life. But my Minnesota conditioning had begun to kick in. *Be careful what you wish for,* it whispered in my ear. *Be careful....*

My American friend confided that she and her island boyfriend were having problems—sometimes he drank too much, and then they argued. It scared her. It scared me too, and I started to undermine myself with questions:

What would I do when the magic wore off? Who— what—would I turn into if I stayed? Could I really grow old here? Would days of childcare and evenings of bree-hay be enough? This wasn't just some other town—this was another world. It had taken me a lifetime to reach it. What if it took that long to get away?

I couldn't tell whether I was being realistic or just a coward, didn't know what I wanted to do, let alone what I should do. Maybe I preferred daydreams to reality, after all. Didn't I, on almost every trip, imagine what it would be like to live there? And didn't I always go back to normal, back to family, house, job, no matter how tempting the place was? Yes. Yes, I always went back.

And now I did again.

I made the final decision fast, on almost no notice so I couldn't be talked out of it by my boyfriend, by Yolanda or even by myself. I must have said goodbye to the people I was leaving behind, but I don't remember doing even that. All I know is that when the next plane left, I was on it, and when the clouds closed behind me over Easter Island, whatever future I could have had there vanished into mist.

Everything I have written since then has come from that decision. Leaving Easter Island broke my heart, but it also turned me into a travel writer.

It's a nutty way to live, really—a kind of paid home-lessness, a career dependent on permanent exile: Go away, have experiences, find stuff out *and then come back* to tell it to the folks at home. It means always being on the outside looking in, longing to stay and never staying. I was perfect for it.

I still looked for "home" when I was on the road, and sometimes—on other islands, in tiny towns—I found it for a while. But never again with the same foreordained, consuming clarity I felt on Easter Island. I wasn't sur-prised: All acts have consequences, and you can't defy destiny without paying some sort of price.

I have never gone back. I can't. When asked, I say it's because I don't want to see how the island has changed (all those hotels, all those tours...).

But the real reason is that I don't want to feel like an outsider there. I don't think I could bear being just another tourist in a place where once, however briefly, I belonged. And I don't need or want another look at the path not taken; I've been seeing it, ever since I caught that plane.

Over the years, people have asked me about what I do. One question comes up again and again, usually from women in full stride, doing the great American juggling act—husband, children, home, career: "Aren't you afraid," they say, "traveling around the world alone like that?"

No, I tell them. Leaving home's a cinch. It's the staying, once you've found it, that takes courage.

Catherine Watson was the award-winning travel editor of the Minneapolis Star Tribune *from 1978 to 2004. She is the author of* Roads Less Traveled: Dispatches from the Ends of the Earth *and* Home on the Road: Further Dispatches from the Ends of the Earth, *from which this essay was excerpted. This essay won the Silver Award for Travel Memoir in the second annual Solas Awards.*

ॐ ॐ ॐ

On Down the Road

Nobody said changing her life would be easy.

"You will be free to *not* be yourself." I liked the sound of that, my horoscope for July 15th, the day I left on a two-week trip down the Mississippi River. No, not on a raft. I know a few crazed individuals have done it, one of them named Huck, but have you seen the Mississippi? It's one of the most powerful big rivers in the world. It can move towns from one state to another; bend rails from their tracks. It can drown New Orleans.

I drove a car. From Minneapolis, skipping downriver like a thrown rock, darting here and there, hovering like a dragonfly over friends and family. I meant the river to be my focus and it was, in the way a large, continuous, natural presence will inform your thinking. I wanted to forget my life back home and I did, emptying my brain of the laundry, the bills, the troubles, the traffic.

The traffic. We are in a three-way tie where I live outside Washington, D.C. for the country's second worst road congestion. But along the river there just isn't any. No traffic, no road rage, and no clogged arteries. I rolled down the window and let the wind rearrange my hair. I could hear grasshoppers and smell sweet grass. I could see the Mississippi off to my left, roaring and frothing from a storm the night before. I listened to music and sang along. I drove down the Avenue of the Saints (so named because it connects Saint Paul and Saint Louis) and took the fall line. I mean I followed the curve and gravity of the road instead of crawling along in a parking lot of fumes.

And the troubles? My life had lately been a dizzying and exhausting swirl of changing feelings, situations, and angry, despairing words. I have a twenty-year marriage that counts for something, but not everything. I have children, almost grown. I know what I want but the way is not clear to getting it. I wish I could be like a bird whose eye sees everything in a telescopic grid pattern, see the patterns of my life, see the places where I sank down in mud of my own making, or ran a *parcours* of joy, or trudged along unwillingly. I wanted to follow that hand-lettered sign that says SNOW PEAS FOR SALE down a shady dirt road. I wanted to let my troubles slide by instead of being inhabited by them.

My horoscope continues: "You will be free to be aimless and clueless." I had planned the whole trip so that I knew where I would be and what I would do, who I would see every day. Which left my mind free to wander. It wandered all the way back to the past, to a town by the river and thoughts and obsessions that had stayed in my head. An old lover still lives there. He is the only man I could ever dance with. I ran down bluffs with him, swift and sure-footed. He made me swoon. I made

him cry. We danced some more. Then he refused to talk
to me and I didn't know why. I thought of him as either
my one chance at true love or a total jerk. It was finally
clear to me that he couldn't be both. I stood in front of
a pay phone, dithering. If I called him now, could I find
out which one he was? I dialed his number only to be
told by a digital voice that it would take more coins than
I had to make this call. I hung up. Exhausted by the
argument I was carrying on with myself, I decided to
just keep on moving down the road.

Minnesota Highway 43 runs along fields of corn and
sunflowers and Queen Anne's Lace and then plunges
suddenly down into cool green pine and white birch,
down towards the Root River. I had made a detour just to
travel on it. This road makes me forget about everything
but the sheer pleasure of driving. Curve after curve, perfectly pitched to let the car coast along with only a slight
touch of the wheel. It slips by a deep, green valley where
the air is fresh and cool. I have the feeling of being deep
in the bosom of Mother Earth. The road floats by a steep
hill dotted with three white sheep, crosses a bridge and
runs through a hamlet called Choice with a church and
one house. Then it starts to rise, the woods fall back and
we're up in the corn and sun again.

I slowed down for a small knot of road construction.
I was headed away from my past but the man at the
end, holding the SLOW sign, caught my eye. It was my
old lover, gone to seed. I passed by slowly and took him
in. His hair was a grizzled gray and white, badly cut.
His clothes looked slept in, his blue work shirt barely
covered a protruding gut. His expression was pained. I
wondered if beer played a large part in his life. I always
thought he would sense my presence but he didn't look
at me. I didn't stop. For miles I tried to convince myself

that it wasn't him, why would it be him, but I couldn't. Obviously, I wanted it to be him. It seemed my mind and heart had finally chosen: jerk. Horoscope: "You won't be plagued by the longing for someone to love you and see you for exactly who you are."

I took a photo of the Mississippi. This river is a bull snake making its muddy and muscular way down to the sea. The Indians named it Mississippi and it shakes its hips through the heart of America, carving out the boundaries of other Indian-named states. The river is wide with islands of green and inlets and sandbars and wetlands. It shimmers—silver, gray, black, and green— with the last rays of the sun. A mist is rolling in. A train on the far side of the river cuts a straight line through the trees while its whistle blasts a steamy chord that floats an echo all the way downriver.

"You will be free to be quiet and meek." I'm always defending myself and others even when they don't need it, even when I don't need it. As a child, I wasn't allowed boundaries. Now I erect flimsy barriers that I can't maintain. I have an aunt, a Dominican nun, who was always in my face, literally planting her tiny self inches from me, while she attempted to hammer God into my spiritual ambivalence. There is a video that shows me backing up and her leaning into me like a little yapping white dog.

Now I've come to terms with God and what that means to me. No religion, no superstition, no crazy rules, no fairy tales, only a few open questions. Is there an unseen power? Maybe. Will I have a life after this one? Maybe. Maybe not. I can't go any further than that. What remains is a life to be lived the best way I can. Be good. Be happy. I sit by my aunt's bed at the convent in the green hills of Wisconsin, where she has retired at ninety-three. She is leaving her life, quietly, slowly, peacefully. We sit together and look at photographs and talk. I see in her eyes how much it means that I am there.

I've been headed towards Hannibal all along. Hannibal, Missouri. The town is amazingly free of tackiness, retaining a slightly shabby charm and a real pride in their native son, Samuel Clemens, also known as Mark Twain. I climbed 244 steps up to the lighthouse, looked out at Jackson's Island where Tom Sawyer and Huckleberry Finn hid out, went through Mark Twain's house and museum, bought his autobiography. I caught a ride on a steamboat, chugging upriver at a top speed of ten miles per hour and listened to a skillful blend of history and malarkey: a barge can hold 1,500 tons of cargo, fifteen barges are equal to 900 semis and on your left is Lover's Leap where yet another Indian princess jumped off to drown in the river rather than be parted from her Indian brave, the son of her father's enemy. For one wild moment, I thought: "I could live here."

I took another detour on the way back to kayak down the Root River. I stayed overnight at a campground at the bottom of towering cliffs. In the morning, a big, surly guy smoking Camels took me up high to the source of the river. Because of the steep descent, there was a series of rapids over hidden rocks. It was an interesting challenge to see quickly where the water was moving fast and strong and therefore deepest and to follow that path in my boat. A young bald eagle flew down, looking for fish, right in front of me. I saw a muskrat. A blue heron flew with me down the river. It was wild and beautiful and I saw no one until almost the end where I met a father and son tubing.

"Did you fall in the water?" asked the boy, around eight years old. "Nope. Did you?" "Yeah. And we peed in the river!" That was so obviously the highlight it made me laugh. We waved good-bye and I kept going down-river, past an old mill and under a railroad bridge. There is something about traveling slowly through time—in a kayak, on a bicycle, by train, even walking—that is meditative. Thought is replaced by motion and scenery. Your body relaxes even while you are working it.

This trip has been a sabbatical of sorts, full of wander-ing, observing, absorbing knowledge from museums, peo-ple, music, and the landscape. I've seen primitive sturgeon at the bottom of an aquarium, a nun in full habit playing Mah Jong on the computer, and children learning how to cast a fishing line into the water. I've eaten Czech kolaches and four-star meals, walked a labyrinth, visited Indian burial grounds, slept on a tugboat, rested in the comfort of old friends and family, drunk a lot of wine including a bottle of "Pinot Evil," kayaked down rivers, climbed up hills, watched the Mississippi as it runs toward the sea. It's important to me to understand how to be on my own, to navigate, to test the current and the wind, to know where I'm going and how to get there.

The night before I left on the plane to fly back to my home, I sat at an outdoor café in Minneapolis, eating a dinner of figs and lamb and goat cheese. I had a sud-den thought: *I am the woman I imagined myself to be.* In being free to not be myself, I have somehow found myself, even amazed myself. I've been flexible, adapt-able, friendly, and open. I have been in a different town almost every night and loved it. I get a thrill every time I say the words, "Got to get back on the road."

But then I came back home, fell into the rut of my life and lay there way too long, staring up at the stars that were shining down on the Mississippi from a different angle, aching to go back.

"There is holy water in your tears." No one said changing the direction of my life would be easy but I see with a quick lift of joy that I might be lucky. It might be fortune's eye that is forcing me to look at my life and see that it's not really working. As if my soul is download-ing instructions that call in external circumstances that ask me to examine my beliefs and methods, look at the path I'm on, see where it may lead me. I must take all the advice I am given, sort through tea leaves and talk, and make a life that suits me. And then the tears will become a blessing.

So here, back home, I finally picked myself up, got my kayak out, threw it up on my car, and went to find some water. I paddled hard across the lake and then let the boat drift, watching a blue heron and three box turtles in a row on a log, letting the sun loosen the knots in my stomach. I thought of nothing and relaxed down to where I am free to not be myself and where anything may happen.

Nancy Vala Michaels is a freelance writer and artist living in Virginia. Her mind is frequently in a restless state which only travel can satisfy. She is currently working on a mystery novel set in Budapest and the north woods of Minnesota.

KARI BODNARCHUK

ഽ഼ ഽ഼ ഽ഼

Close Encounters

A kayaker goes in search of icebergs and whales off
Newfoundland's northern coast.

*A*fter adjusting the straps on my lifejacket and
giving the fishing village of Quirpon a final, wist-
ful glance, I announced, "I'm ready." Ready or not, it was
time to paddle out of the protected harbor and into a deep,
narrow channel between Labrador and Newfoundland,
where icebergs drifted past humpbacks and minkes that
had come there to feed.

Ed English, my guide, steered his boat up next to
mine and pulled out a chart so we could run through our
route one more time. We would paddle along the west
side of Quirpon ("car-poon") Island for several miles
and then around an exposed headland where the North
Atlantic battered two-hundred-foot cliffs that rose out
of the salty depths. Then we would duck into a sheltered

inlet on the north side of the island. Here, perched on a bluff, sat a renovated nineteenth-century light-keeper's house that served as a seasonal inn for anyone who managed to make it to this remote outpost. This would be our home base for several days, as we went kayaking around icebergs and whales in the Strait of Belle Isle.

"Once we pass Cod Cove, there's really no turning back," Ed warned, pointing to an "X" on our chart, which marked the last bail-out spot before we reached the headland. "I've seen perfectly calm waters on the west side of the island and then run into eight-foot swells after rounding the point. If that happens, we'll have to keep going because it's almost impossible to turn around in that kind of water."

"No problem," I said, my stomach tightening.

I had driven one thousand miles from Boston to Newfoundland's northernmost tip in hopes of kayaking around icebergs, and I did not want to turn back now. But I had never paddled in such a challenging place, even after years of kayaking. Water temperatures in the Strait of Belle Isle only reached the mid-forties in the summertime, and the fishermen wore insulated survival suits even on pleasant days. Paddling around icebergs was also dicey. A calving berg could let loose an avalanche of ice chunks the size of grand pianos and small houses. Even if I avoided getting hit by one, a falling chunk of ice could create a wave big enough to capsize my kayak. That's why Ed was with me. He had spent years paddling around icebergs and was certified in marine rescue and survival. He even traveled up to the Arctic to train the local Inuit in how to survive in the wild, so I trusted him completely. But I also knew that even with a good guide, disasters can happen, especially in extreme environments when the weather and conditions were unpredictable.

As we slipped out of Quirpon Harbour, a curious gray seal popped its head out of the water just several feet from my kayak and a falcon soared overhead. We pointed our bows north and stuck close to the island as we paddled through the steely-blue waters, which disappeared hundreds of feet beneath us, and by beaches covered in pebbles and driftwood. Small chunks of ice called "bergy bits" floated by, occasionally with a seagull perched on top. The water was moderately choppy, but the nippy breezes sent shivers through me, despite the added insulation from my wetsuit.

After passing Cod Cove, our point of no return, we kayaked by huge crevasses in the sea walls, carved out by the ocean over time. Suddenly, about fifty feet off to our left, a humpback slapped its tail on the water's surface.

"Whale!" I yelled.

"There's another one," said Ed, pointing straight ahead.

The whale surfaced, shooting a funnel of spray into the air, and then arched its back before diving into the depths and leaving behind nothing more than carbonated water and a fishy smell. I had seen plenty of whales on organized tours aboard large vessels, but never up so close and virtually at eye level. Next to these bus-sized mammals, I suddenly felt very small.

We counted eight, nine, ten humpbacks around us, sticking their fins out of the water, exhaling with a loud whoosh, or kicking up their enormous tails. Gannets circled overhead or plunged underwater in search of capelin left behind by the feeding whales. As we drifted and watched, a minke whale dove right beneath me. I could see its white belly pass within inches of my boat, so close I could have reached out and touched it. The whale was probably no longer than twenty feet, but

being that close to such a powerful animal, especially
while in a small, tippy boat, both awed and spooked me.
As it swam past, I braced myself in my kayak, pressing
my legs against its sides and pushing my feet down hard
on the foot pedals, just in case the whale bumped against
me. Within seconds, the minke slipped out of sight, as
silently and gracefully as it had appeared.

Meanwhile, Ed had spotted our first iceberg, tucked
in a bay to the west of us, but in the opposite direction
that we were heading. The flat-topped monolith had
grounded on a shoal and would stay there and melt, or
else get pushed out to sea by the strong winds and the
currents. Nearly all of Newfoundland's icebergs come
from the west coast of Greenland, Ed explained. There,
massive glaciers dump five square miles of ice into the
ocean each year. As these cathedrals of ice travel south
with the Labrador Current, along a water route known
as Iceberg Alley, they're carved into fantastic shapes
by the wind and the waves: giant horseshoes, mountain peaks, domes and wedges. Thousands survive the
sixteen-hundred-mile journey, picking up dirt and rocks
as they scour the seabed en route. By the time they reach
Newfoundland waters at least a year later, they average
the size of a fifteen-story building.

This berg looked enormous even from a few miles
away. I wanted to get a closer look, but there simply
wasn't time. That morning we had learned that Tropical
Storm Arthur was barreling up the coast and Ed wanted
to reach the light-keeper's house before the wind kicked
up or fog descended on us. We would have plenty of
time later, he assured me.

We rounded the headland and, as Ed had predicted, ran
into heaving six-foot swells. I had paddled in three-foot
waves before, but nothing this big. "Just keep paddling,"

I said to myself, as my stomach churned and the wind blew with a fierceness that didn't give me a second to rest my burning arms. Strong gusts nearly ripped the paddle out of my hands. Although Ed and I were only twenty feet apart, I lost sight of him for several long seconds at a time, as the waves rose between us and we dropped down into the troughs. I struggled to propel myself forward and keep my boat upright. My kayak tipped on edge, but I kept it from flipping with a quick slap of my paddle on the water's surface. It took about half an hour of hard paddling to finally clear the sea walls, a distance of only a quarter of a mile. Eventually, we reached an inlet by the light-keeper's house and dipped into the bay, where the ocean ricocheted off the steep rocky walls, creating small waves that assaulted us from all angles.

After a less-than-graceful landing, when a wave sucked my boat off the rocky beach and dumped me into the frigid water, we scrambled up an embankment to the light-keeper's house. Doris, a short, matronly woman who oversaw the inn with husband Hubert, met us on the front porch. She swung her arm over my shoulder in a motherly way and said, "How was your trip, m'dear?"

"Exciting!" I said, and then told her about the waves, the whales, and the iceberg sighting. "I hope we'll see more icebergs tomorrow."

Doris had grown up in Quirpon and told us wonderful stories about the area as she served us cloudberry pie and iceberg water. One time, a friend of hers who lived on the coast had woken up to a wall of white outside his bedroom window. A giant iceberg had drifted into the bay overnight. "Ice wranglers" lassoed the berg and towed it away, since it was a hazard to the fishermen and other boaters living there. Doris also had a cousin, Boyce, who harvested icebergs. When a berg calved, Boyce went out in his fishing boat and used a winch to hoist one-hundred-pound chunks of ice into his boat. When he got them back to shore, he hosed them off to remove any saltwater, melted them down, bottled the water, and made a bundle selling it as "pure iceberg water."

"He got twenty-eight tons of ice last year," she said. "That's about seventy-five-hundred gallons of iceberg water."

After fresh-baked cod for dinner, I bundled up and sat on a rock below the lighthouse watching humpbacks and minkes feeding in the channel. From there, I could see the coastline of southern Labrador and was reminded of a t-shirt I had seen: "Labrador: it's not the end of the world, but you can see it from here." Even Quirpon Island felt like the end of the world. It had taken me an entire day to drive up the Great Northern Peninsula from Corner Brook, the closest city about three hundred miles away. Only one road led up the peninsula and it wound along a coastline dotted with fishing villages, glacial lakes, and forests of tuckamores—windswept trees permanently bent from the ocean's strong breezes. Along this route, a town hall was about the size of a two-car garage, speed limits were suggestions not rules (at least, according to Ed), and the occasional shops told the story of ingenuity and survival: they sold boots and mittens made out of sealskins, intricate carvings made from whale bone, and jams and sauces made with wild berries that were unique to Newfoundland, like cloudberries and partridgeberries. Whom they sold these products to, I wasn't sure—I had barely seen a dozen cars on my drive. And by the time I had reached the island, I wasn't surprised to learn that we were the only ones staying at the inn.

The Labrador coast soon disappeared as a thick veil of fog from the tropical storm descended on the area. If the storm lingered, we could get stuck there for days. Our only chance for getting back to the mainland would be to abandon the kayaks, hike three miles down the island to Grandmother's Cove, and then hope to catch a lift across the harbor from a local boater. But in such a remote and barren place, where everything depended on the weather, there were no guarantees.

Socked in by fog, we spent the next few days exploring the island. Doris lent me her knee-high rubber boots one morning, so Ed and I could hike along the cliffs and across the desolate island, which was blanketed in spongy bogs and tangled underbrush. We hacked our way through the scrub and scrambled through patches of white fir and black spruce as we made our way up Great View Mountain, which, on that day, offered only a view of clouds due to the stormy weather. Another day, Ed and I paddled through fog and four-foot swells to reach Pigeon Cove, the next inlet to the east, where kittiwakes nested in cracks on the four-hundred-foot sea walls. Murres, eider ducks, and guillemots hung out on a tiny island in the bay or swooped overhead.

When we returned to the inn, Doris always flung her arm around my shoulder and asked, "How was your day, m'dear?" Then she would serve a big meal like fresh cod or roast beef with homemade bread. And when the fog briefly lifted, we would catch a glimpse of the flat-topped berg still grounded in the bay or see other bergs silently drifting past the island. I was dying to go out and explore them. Each morning, I stepped outside to see what glimmering ice castles had floated into view overnight.

The sun finally came out on the third day and the ocean's surface was mirror smooth. After a pancake breakfast of toutons—dense bread smothered in molasses—Ed and I hopped in our kayaks and set off in search of icebergs. As we paddled back around the granite headland, we spotted an iceberg in the middle of the channel. From about five miles away, it looked like a bar of Dove soap floating in a big bathtub, but as we got closer, I realized it was about as tall as a seven-story building and as big around as a city block. It loomed overhead and in my narrow, sixteen-foot kayak, I felt like a little piece of driftwood floating by.

Seeing an iceberg up close was more spectacular than I had imagined. I could see blue streaks running through the white ice, formed when melt-water refreezes in the cracks, and water pouring off the top or trickling down its sides, giving it a shiny glow. Seagulls perched on a jagged cornice high above us.

"If the birds suddenly take off, it's a good sign the berg is about to calve," said Ed. "They feel the vibration."

"How do you know how close you can get?" I asked.

"That depends on its size and shape. As a general rule, the distance between you and the iceberg should be about one-and-a-half to two times the height of the berg."

We paddled around the iceberg, staying a good hundred feet away. On the back side, sand, rocks, and shells clung to the ice, debris the berg had picked up as it scraped along the ocean floor. We also discovered another smaller iceberg that was shaped like a triangle and had a thin, translucent peak. We nosed our kayaks up against it and watched as the waves splashed onto the ice. The sea was so clear we could see the berg scoop down about fifty feet underwater.

We continued over to a cove along the mainland, where our flat-topped iceberg had collapsed in the middle like a fallen cake, so that its walls swept down to sea level. They were also covered with thousands of dimples, formed as the berg slowly dissolved. We stopped paddling and listened to the ice as it melted: a crackling, fizzling sound like Pop Rocks or seltzer water, created as millions of bubbles released air that had been trapped there since the Stone Age, when hunter-gatherers were still painting on cave walls and parts of North America were blanketed by glaciers.

I followed Ed around the iceberg and we found a gray seal sleeping on a floating chunk of ice that had recently broken off. The seal lifted its head and watched us quietly slip past. A pod of white-sided dolphins showed up shortly after and Ed began banging the sides of his boat with his hands, a trick for getting the dolphins to come up and investigate. They swam closer to us and as they did, Ed dropped a hydrophone in the water and handed me the earpiece. I could hear squeaking noises as the dolphins chatted to each other.

Floating around us were blocks of ice that had broken off the main iceberg. Since there was less of a chance that these bergy bits would roll or break apart, Ed suggested I climb onto one. He picked a berg that was wide and flat and rose just several feet out of the water. As Ed held onto my kayak, I carefully slithered up onto the chunk of ice, wondering just how much weight would cause a bergy bit to roll, and whether or not the toutons I'd had for breakfast were enough to do the trick. The bergy bit slightly dipped down on one side as I scrambled onto it, but it leveled off as I crawled to the middle of the ice and sat up. The berg had a corduroy-like surface, but in some areas it was covered with hundreds of little dimples making it look like a golf ball. Ed encouraged me to drink the melt-water from one of the indentations on the berg.

"It's the purest water you'll ever have," he said. "Better for you than what we drink out of the tap."

Since the iceberg was simply a block of compacted snow, it was made entirely of fresh water. It was perfectly pure, according to Ed, because when it formed thousands of years ago, "we didn't have air pollution or acid rain." Plus, it hadn't been treated with chemicals like our drinking water. I had tried Doris's iceberg water, but in my experience everything tastes better in the wild. I lay down, rolled onto my belly, and slurped the water out of a little pocket in the ice—and quickly spat it out. Instead of the world's purest water, I had ended up with a mouthful of saltwater that had washed up on the berg from the waves. "I think I'll stick with Doris's iceberg water," I told Ed.

Ed tied my boat to his so it wouldn't float away and went off to paddle around an iceberg that was shaped like a shark's fin, while I sat on the dining room-sized bergy bit and listened to it fizzle as it slowly melted beneath me. I could feel the berg swaying as the wind, waves, and current slowly pushed it across the bay. Sunlight lit up a towering berg about half a mile away and I couldn't help but wonder: If that berg calved right now, could the waves it created wash me off my little bergy bit? I pushed the thought away. A seal popped its head out of the water nearby, but something else caught my eye. Several chunks of ice were floating toward me. As they bumped up against each other, getting jostled by the waves, they created an eerie grinding noise. They were too small to tip me over or knock me off my berg, I was sure. Or reasonably sure.

I looked over to where Ed had paddled, but he had disappeared behind a berg. I felt both exhilarated and unnerved to be sitting on an iceberg in such a wild and remote setting. We hadn't seen another boat all day and there were no signs of life along the forested coastline. If anything happened to Ed, the best I could hope for was that my bergy bit would eventually float within swimming distance to shore—meaning within a few feet, since I wouldn't last long in these icy-cold waters. Or that maybe Doris's cousin Boyce would come out to harvest a berg and find me perched on the ice like a seal.

I was relieved when Ed finally reappeared and paddled back to me, towing my lifeline with him. I carefully slipped into my kayak and then we paddled several miles back to the inn, where I knew Doris would be waiting to hear all about our day—and I couldn't wait to tell her. Before rounding the headland, I gave one last glance over my shoulder toward the bergs and smiled, thrilled to have survived my first but I hope not my last iceberg encounter.

Kari Bodnarchuk is an adventure-travel writer who has written books on Rwanda and Kurdistan and earned many awards for her writing and photography, including two Lowell Thomas Travel Journalism awards. She writes for publications like Outside, Backpacker, The Miami Herald, *and* The Boston Globe, *and has contributed to numerous travel anthologies, including* The Best Women's Travel Writing *for five years in a row. She lives in Bellingham, Washington, where she and her husband have had several close encounters with orcas and humpbacks.*

✂ ✂ ✂

Big Cats, No Guns

In Africa, life is good—
when you're not on the menu.

$\mathcal{T}$he first time I tracked lions, it was from the relative safety and comfort of a large—although open—Land Rover, with a loaded rifle situated handily next to the driver. At that time our guide had assured us that as long as we didn't wear brightly colored clothes, make noise, or stand up, the animals would perceive us to be part of the vehicle, and therefore not worth eating. His logic was not entirely convincing. Lions have been making their living—for, what, a couple hundred thousand years?—by figuring out what is, or is not, edible. And we were going to fool them by *sitting* instead of standing? I was sure the big cats were smarter than that.

But this safari was different. We were going on foot, and the strict policy at Camp Okavango was *no guns*. Big cats, no guns, traveling on foot…hmmm.

Adding to my trepidation, our guides, Robert and Rodgers, explained that if we saw lions this morning, they would be hungry, because big cats usually hunt at night. If they were still out stalking prey in the morning, it meant they hadn't found anything to eat the night before. A crazy thought wriggled into my mind: the guides were using us as lion bait. They thought we were clueless American tourists, foolish enough to follow them deep into the big cats' territory with no means of protection. We were.

Their plan was to travel from our camp by motorboat through the vast delta to another island, and from there to proceed on foot in search of the big cats. Many miles out, through the winding, papyrus-lined waterways, Robert announced excitedly that he had spotted dust in the trees. I didn't see it, even with my binoculars. And I didn't understand what dust had to do with lions. But I went along with the program. We anchored the boat, disembarked, and walked into the remote island's open forest.

This was no Sunday stroll: the tall brown grasses hid treacherous obstacles. Elephants had eaten the relatively tender bark and roots of trees, leaving dead branches and uprooted stumps scattered everywhere. Aardvarks had dug large holes in the ground. Thorns caught on our clothing, and greedy vines grabbed at our legs. And the dung! Everywhere we had to step over dung—all kinds of it, large and small, round and elongated, fresh and dry, in varying stages of decomposition.

I could tell the difference between rhino middens and elephant dung, and was learning to differentiate buffalo from giraffe. Then I saw a new kind of dung: smaller, rounder, fresher—glistening, in fact. Was it lions'? I wondered just how far away the lions actually were, and how close we intended to get. Checking my field guide, I

found that lion droppings "are similar to that of the leop-
ard, but larger." This was only marginally more helpful
than the entry for elephants, which read, "A good way
of testing the freshness of dung, is to thrust your hand
into the centre of it. If the dung is fresh, it will be warm
inside." Right. Like I'm ever going to employ this meth-
odology. They didn't even provide a chart correlating
temperature to time elapsed to distance traveled.

We were a noisy bunch of Americans, and Rodgers
admonished us to "do *shhh*" and to "talk silently." I
noticed that Rodgers and Robert did indeed talk silently,
communicating with their eyes and hands that they had
heard a noise in this direction, or that they wanted us to
walk that way. They reminded me of a TV SWAT team,
moving swiftly and efficiently through the bad guy's
hideout just before the big shoot out. Our group, on
the other hand, moved like a bunch of Keystone Cops,
zigzagging randomly, tripping in the aardvark holes,
backtracking around fallen trees, and fighting back with
all our might when vicious vines attacked.

Robert reminded us to walk in single file, always
staying together. If we fell back or got out of line, he
warned, we'd look smaller and be "on the menu." As if
lions haven't had plenty of experience in picking individuals out of a herd. As if they would look hungrily at
a line of humans hiking single file and think, "That's
just some big, nasty-tasting giant caterpillar, seriously
overburdened with indigestible cameras and binoculars,
stumbling slowly and vulnerably through my sovereign
territory. Forget it—no chow there."

Most important, Robert said: if a lion did come
towards us, "Don't run! Stand your ground!"

Stand my ground? In the face of a charging lion? What
kind of instruction was that? My heart pounded at the

thought of it; my legs stiffened, and I wondered whether it would be a good thing to be frozen with fear. My hands began to sweat, and I remembered reading somewhere that humans, dogs, and other mammals whose paws sweat with anxiety do so because the sweat increases friction between the paws and a substrate, allowing for quicker getaways. I was built to run then, *not* to stand my ground!

I stayed near the front of the line, just behind Maureen, a psychiatric nurse from Pittsburgh. Maureen walked with her shoulders slightly hunched, took each step slowly and deliberately, shaded her eyes from the sun as she scanned the distance. I thought she looked like a professional tracker, except for her bright white Asics Gel running shoes—obviously bought new for the trip—and hot pink windbreaker. I had chosen my place carefully: surely the hot-pink-windbreaker variety of meal would be most tempting. If a lion charged, I would simply maintain my position behind the primary bait.

Maureen's left shoelace was untied. Should I tell her? If I did, she'd stop to tie it, and the whole single-file line would crash into us like a row of dominoes. I would be trampled by my fellow travelers, and perhaps sprain my ankle or fall into a pile of warm dung in the process. If I didn't, Maureen might trip and fall, and be eaten alive. I kept my mouth shut.

A large, lone bird circled the sky above us. Robert identified it as a White-Backed Vulture (*Gypus africanus*). Our guides had amazing eyesight. Born and raised in the delta, they could identify all the birds and animals from far away. Soon a second vulture appeared, and then a third. Apparently they knew something we did not.

As we hiked deeper into the forest—way too far in to run for the boat—Robert still saw dust. We kept walking, single file, assiduously staying together, not falling back or getting out of line, doing *shhh,* going deeper into the forest.

At one point I was tempted to stop and photograph a Little Bee-Eater (*Merops pusillus*), a tiny, brilliantly colored and exquisitely beautiful bird, as it caught insects in the tall grass. But when I considered the possibility of "death by lion," I decided to stay with the group.

"Listen!" Rodgers and Robert both heard the lions. We kept walking. At first we didn't hear anything, but a ways farther in we heard a low rumbling sound. "It's the lions! Yes, and they are chasing buffalo!" The rumbling, our guides explained excitedly, was the sound of a thousand hooves. We proceeded, still in line, straining to get a look through the trees at a buffalo or a lion. Suddenly Robert hurried back into our midst, eyes wide and round, and bulging so the whites showed around their whole circumference. "They are coming this way!" he shouted hoarsely. *"We are too close! Go back! Go back!"*

Finally I saw the dust, a huge cloud of it, about two hundred yards away and coming towards us fast. It was swirling above a herd of several hundred Cape Buffalo, and they were coming towards us fast, too. Stampeding, actually.

We had been told to stand our ground in the face of a charging lion, but what was the protocol for a buffalo attack? There was no time to ask. Our careful, single-file line disintegrated into chaos as we ran back—hats, cameras and binoculars flying. No more zigzagging to avoid holes or backtracking around fallen trees; we leapt them all heroically. Several of our group turned out to be talented sprinters, and I personally tested the freshness of five or six piles of dung in the space of twenty seconds.

As suddenly as the stampede began, it was over. It's interesting, what goes through one's mind at a time like this. As soon as *"Escape, escape!"* had run its course, I was overwhelmed with the perfection of Nature's Grand Plan: elephants knock down large trees, allowing grasslands to develop, which attracts grazing animals, which provide food for the lions. The aardvark holes create natural traps for the lions' prey; the elephants' monumental, nutrient-rich droppings fertilize the tall grasses.... Lost in the beauty of the Grand Plan, it was several minutes before I remembered Maureen. How did her untied shoelace fit in? Had I been homicidally remiss in not mentioning it earlier? Or was I simply playing my predetermined part in the "survival of the fittest"? Did Maureen stand, or did she run? Had she been trampled by stampeding buffalo, eaten by a hungry lion?

I came to my senses, surveyed the scene, and saw Maureen's hot pink jacket halfway up a small tree, with Maureen still inside it. Apparently it had not provoked the lions. We began to regroup, and everyone seemed to have survived. The Cape Buffalo—still about seventy yards away—had also survived. They had all stopped running and were now milling about restlessly. They seemed to be more afraid of *us* than of the charging lions. This did not strike me as an effective adaptive behavior, but what do I know about the life of a buffalo? And what did they know about humans? At any rate, they kept their eyes on us *and* on the lions, which—conveniently—made it easy for us to observe the five adult lions that were now in our immediate vicinity.

Make that five *hungry* adult lions.

I had heard that female lions form hunting bands, and that the males don't bother to assist them. But this was a group of four females and one large male with an impressive golden mane. What was *he* doing there? He was probably so famished that he couldn't even wait for the females to make a kill. He was big, that was for sure. I couldn't see his teeth, but I know they were long and sharp, and I'll bet he was salivating.

I smelled the dust. Dust, and a sweat-like smell. Was it the buffalo, or the lions? Was it me? Was it fear? The lions were not yet attacking, so I had a moment to contemplate: should I turn and run, or stand and scream? Would it make a difference? Did I have a choice? I would like to report that Rodgers and Robert were unfazed, but that would not be entirely true. Actually, they looked anxious. They had no guns. They were responsible for a dozen travelers. And we were seventy yards away from five hungry lions.

The big cats paced around the edges of the buffalo herd, eyeing one individual, then another. What if one looked at me? Should I make eye contact, or avoid it? I began to feel panicky. Robert's words echoed in my mind, "If a lion does come towards you, *don't run!*" Legs locked, I stood my ground, and felt proud of myself for having the presence of mind to follow instructions in a crisis. But then it occurred to me: if I stood my ground, and everyone else retreated, did that make me clever? Or did it make me lion food?

Fortunately, my survival did not depend on my own cleverness: Rodgers and Robert took control, instructing us to remain facing the lions and walk slowly backwards, away from them. We did so. Soon, it was safe to turn and walk—a bit more quickly—back to the boat. When we were safely on board, and motoring back to camp, I marveled at the beauty of Nature's Grand Plan, at green papyrus against intense blue skies and the exquisite deliciousness of a bottle of cold beer. Life is good, when you're not on the menu.

Laurie McAndish King has chased lemurs through the mountains of Madagascar, fought off leeches in tropical Queensland, and trapped raptors in the Marin Headlands. Her award-winning essays have been published in Travelers' Tales and Lonely Planet anthologies and in the San Francisco Chronicle Magazine. *She coedited two volumes of Left Coast Writers'* Hot Flashes: sexy little stories & poems, *and is currently at work on a third volume in the series. See her online newsletter for travel writers at www.travelwritersnews.com.*

෯෯෯

Risen

Artichokes, goat meat, bread sublime enough to raise the dead—it must be Easter in Sicily.

While back in the States the day before Easter they were soaking eggs in pastel pink, yellow, green, and blue baths, we were rolling into the small Sicilian town of Partanna to see the Crucifixion up close. We found parking on a street with the enticing name Via Circeo—that powerful witch—and walked the curving roadway past a bakery, a tobacconist, a grocery. Drifting through the green plastic strands which shielded a doorway floated the distinct presence of cheese—maybe *bel paese* or *taleggio*—pungent, clean, and salty.

"I love this, Maia," I enthused to my cousin once removed. "At home, everything comes sealed in plastic." Here foods were properly worshipped, displayed on marble stands, their holy essences sifting through the air. Here, the cheese stood alone.

A sign read *Macelleria*—butcher store. Oh-oh. We were eyeball to glazed eyeball, face to muzzle with twelve furry baby goats, killed and hung in a row along the outside wall, their abdomens split open, intestines stolen away.

"*I capretti*," Maia informed me. "Eaten at Easter time."

"We don't see this at home," I stammered. They were hanging by their necks, for Christ's sake. Their delicate hoofs dangled, purplish-gray, little feet of Pan. And their heads, with tiny budding horns.

"It makes the meat more tender. We eat them only once a year." Maia kept up her steady clip along the street. "Ehh, *cara mia*, one way or another, animals are killed so that we can eat. It's just that way."

"I know, but…"

We'd turned into a crowded piazza where an outdoor stage had been erected. Loudspeakers blasted a warped recording of a Handel oratorio to get us in a melodramatic mood. Two palm fronds like green parentheses framed the Doric-columned facade at stage rear. Whitewashed walls reflected brilliant morning light. The sound grew more and more distorted each time the piece played, three, four, five times on a loop. Everyone milled around and chattered, the adults and the kids using hand gestures. I laughed aloud at a three-year-old looking up at her parents and protesting something with both her hands flying.

"The play we will see derives from secular theater originally performed in the street: the annunciation, the birth of Gesu, or in this case, the tribunal," explained Maia.

"Mm-hmm. I'm grateful that you are such a historian."

"Historian, *boh*. I have lived my whole life here, naturally I take an interest in the past."

Eventually *Il Spettacolo* began. The cast of dozens, young men, mimed the action while a booming, disembodied voice narrated. Jeering Hebrews in floor-length woven robes, headdresses and sandals; glowering Roman guards wearing metal breastplates and helmets; the Jerusalemites straining to listen, brows wrinkled, then loudly protesting; the Apostles huddling to one side. Pontius Pilate delivered his speech, stabbing the stage with his spear, gold robes glistening in the sun. Carl Orff's Carmina Burana pounded from the speakers.

Jesus appeared, manacled, dressed in a white robe, long blond hair, head lowered. They condemned him. The stage crowd showed no mercy, shrieking, hurling styrofoam rocks which bounced off his chest. Some spectators cried out, "Traitors, traitors!" Kids ran around playing tag. The guards stripped off Christ's robe to reveal him pasty and naked except for a demure white loincloth. They tied his wrists to the wall and two henchmen came forward to whip him. His body snapped with each lash. During one spasm the blond wig flew off, exposing the actor's close-cropped black hair. Oh Christ. The audience guffawed. Maia shot me a bemused look. Jesus continued to recoil with each blow, enduring this new humiliation. A pre-recorded rooster crowed three times. An extra in a red costume climbed down off the stage, retrieved the wig from outstretched hands and rushed over to fit it back on him.

They pushed the Crown of Thorns onto his head, which began dripping stage blood. ECCE HOMO. He groaned, heaved the full weight of the cross on his shoulder and began to drag it, haltingly, out of the square.

Mary Magdalene followed close behind, nearly horizontal with grief. The stage crowd formed a line after him. Electronic cymbals crashed.

"He carries the Cross and Life. He carries the Cross and Suffering. He carries the Cross and Humanity," intoned the tremulous narrator.

We filed after the procession out of the piazza down a long path, which truly seemed dispirited, the powdery earth having no color to it. We ended up on a broad field, littered everywhere with trash. At a distance we could see the action continuing on a hillside. Halfway up the slope two crosses had already been erected, two figures pre-crucified—not statues, but men—and between them, blond Jesus was being nailed to the cross. The hammering went on and on.

"They're not using real spikes, are they?"

"No, we would never actually crucify anyone. What a notion!" Maia gaped at me.

"They do in the Phillippines," I countered. "I read it somewhere."

"Well, maybe there, but here, it is an honor to simply share in the pain, to relive the agony of the Savior," she whispered, "in a metaphorical sense."

For long, excruciating minutes Gesu Cristo leaned at forty-five degrees while his tormentors struggled to keep the cross from tipping over. Next to me a mother unwrapped a prosciutto sandwich and handed it to her child. He grabbed it and, never taking his eyes off the Passion, sank his teeth in. Finally they hoisted the crucifix vertically. The crowd murmured, the music swelled. Maia motioned to another part of the hill where Judas hung by his neck from a tree. Shrubs hid his feet. The loudspeaker droned on. Picnics were produced all around, salami sliced with pocketknives, olives chewed and pits spit out, the lazy hiss as Arancina bottle tops were unstoppered.

Maia shifted from one foot to the other. "Would you like to stay a little longer?" She shielded her eyes from the sun.

"What happens next?"

"He doesn't die till three. They will remain crucified on the hillside all afternoon, until a certain time tonight when the body will be taken down, and placed in a secret cave in the mountain."

"Let's go then, shall we?"

"Oh-kay." She enjoyed using the popular American expression.

While returning to the square, two actors in Hebrew costumes passed us, nonchalantly carrying a huge cross back to the stage. To props? They didn't struggle at all with its weight, for it was made of balsa wood. They passed so close that a splinter snagged a wool thread in Maia's jacket and I carefully unhooked her while the Hebrews held still, apologizing to the *signora*, chatting in Sicilian. A Roman guard on a motorcycle buzzed by with his skirts flapping, spraying us with dust from the road. We returned down Circe's street of the goats. I kept my eyes fixed on the sidewalk when we passed the butcher's.

Two days later, Pasquetta, Little Easter, dawned delicate pink, dainty as the inside of a seashell. Our final day of itinerary had us heading west for the hills to a festivity at a monastery, San Martino delle Scale. The outskirts of Palermo fell away; stone buildings here and there dotted the road. So when I spotted way up near a rocky summit a zigzag of new buildings—chunky boxes—teetering, I pointed.

"What's that?"

Maia shook her head. "A government housing development. No one lives there. They haven't completed it and they won't."

"Why's that?"

She hesitated. "Mafia."

"They look strange, wrong."

"Oh yes. They are."

"They don't fit."

"No."

"They're out of scale. Weird."

"Yes."

"Why would anyone want to live in such a place? So hard to get to up there."

"No one would."

"But then why build it?"

She rubbed her thumb and fingers together, a muscle in her jaw pulsing. Maybe I'd get the hang of not asking upsetting questions one of these days. The twisting road dipped into a pine forest. Wisps of bluish smoke floated through the trees.

"Look. Do you see?"

"A forest fire?"

"Not at all. It's picnickers stoking fires to roast artichokes, another of our traditions. Hours are required to prepare the coals, to heat them red hot, to let them cool to white before burying the *carcioffi*."

Wow, getting up in the dark to do a choke justice, now that's devotion. "I've tasted them cooked so many different ways, but never from underground."

"Then you shall, today."

"Primo dug a pit?"

"Primo has the day off. We'll be eating out today."

"Ah."

Maia left the car next to a cream-colored stone wall which enclosed the monastery. We followed a path alongside, her walking shoes clacking against the caked earth. As if someone had suddenly turned on the volume, we rounded a bend and came upon a slew of folkdancers, singers, musicians in a clearing. Accordions bellowed, tambourines shimmied, mouth harps twanged. Someone kept spinning a painted vase high into the air and catching it, again and again.

"What does the vase signify?"

Maia gave it some thought. "Happiness," she finally replied.

Compared to the somberness of the previous celebrations, this was all gaiety and frolic. The resurrection had occurred, the weight lifted, Lent ended, and vases flew. We heard a song about a donkey—*Lu me' Sciccareddu*—each time the singer heehawed the audience went wild. I had a little donkey, very dear, and then they killed him, my poor donkey. What a beautiful voice he had, like a great tenor, donkey of my heart, how can I ever forget you?

The dancers cavorted along the road we'd followed, beckoning us onlookers toward a piazza where a brass band and blastula-like bunches of red and yellow balloons bobbed in the breeze. Antique wooden horse carts painted in every bright color—the famous *carretti siciliani* that my grandmother of course had a two-inch version of on her windowsill—stood in a circle. The workhorses, all gussied up in magenta and green plumes, mirrored cloth, tassels and fringes, stamped and shook their heads, ringing little bells, raring to go. We moved in closer. Scenes of fierce battles and angelic visitations, dragons and steeds, paisleys and dots and portraits of saints, crowded every inch.

"Look underneath, Natalia, at Hell." Carved devils, monsters with dangling tongues, winged beasts clung below.

"Fantastic." I bent down to see the detail up close. Hell had no vacancy. Creatures jammed every possible spot.

The drivers, wearing black caps and red pompons at their throats, cracked their whips and the wheels began to creak. Children in day-glo parkas, pinned in next to their grandfathers, peered over the sides. One cart, festooned with wildflowers and shafts of rye, carried a cage of songbirds and a wooden wine cask. A man following behind turned the spigot to dispense white wine into plastic cups a little bigger than thimbles, which he offered to everyone. "Made at home," he smiled. "Good for the stomach. Don't refuse it."

Maia licked her lips. "*Buono, no?*"

And powerful as all get out, especially at 11:30 in the morning. The cart circled around again. We each accepted another thimbleful. This one went straight to the brain. All daytime wine drinking had to stop tomorrow, I affirmed. The circle being of modest size and the cask being full, we had a few more refills.

A priest wearing black-rimmed glasses clambered onto the cart, blessed the birdcage, reached inside and grabbed a few frantic, petite birds. He released them to the sky. They chirped deliriously and fluttered above our heads. He clutched another wriggling handful, and more birds swirled up into the sunshine. The crowd let out a cheer.

"I want to show you the Benedictine Abbey," Maia announced. I followed her lethargically, heated up from five tablespoons of super-concentrate. Mass was in progress. Maia motioned that we squeeze in along the back wall onto the dark wooden benches. The congregation, mostly women, mumbled in response to the hypnotic Latin. Then a Gregorian chant, which fell and rose like a tide, reverberated from wall to wall. I sat marinating in the Gregorian scale, trying to decide whether it was more major key with a minor overlay, or minor with major. Or neither. Could there be such a key, neither major nor minor? "Only Gregory knows for sure," I may have mentioned to the vibrating atmosphere.

Maia nodded along, hands folded, but then suddenly turned to me. "Time to eat."

The smell of something baked had swung out into the piazza like secular incense. Good thing we nabbed the last empty table at the trattoria.

"*Cameriere*," Maia raised her hand to a waiter squeezing by with three steaming plates of pasta balanced on each forearm. "A half liter of red wine, please."

"Right away."

"I've already had enough vino, Maia. Really, I'm kind of drunkish."

"Don't worry about it. Drink what you wish, if you wish, when you wish."

Pasquetta frolickers and all their relatives jammed three dozen tables which the waiter worked alone. After forty days of Lent, they were starving and clamoring for his attention. Feed us. Feed us now.

Even my stoic cousin sighed in relief when he finally showed up with the carafe and wineglass stems laced upside-down between his fingers, and leaned down to be heard over the din. "We offer holiday specialties today. *Capretto. Carcioffo. Pasta al Forno San Martino.*"

"Baby goat for each of us, and an artichoke to share?"

I shook my head, trying to prevent the sight in front of the butcher store two days ago from returning.

"It's traditional today," she lobbied, "you'll like it."

No goat. Never goat! I nearly hollered into the racket.
"I'm sure it's delicious, but an artichoke is what I'll have.
The kind roasted underground, right?"

"Certainly. My brother-in-law and I stayed up last
night making the pit. As a matter of fact, he's still out
there overseeing the operation. No first plates to begin
with for you ladies? No pastas?"

No, but Maia pleaded for some bread before he raced
off. We were grateful, desperate really, when he slid a
plate of rounded rolls onto the table. My cousin grabbed
one, tore it open. The crust cracked defiantly, curls of
steam exhaled.

"Crunchy," I broke open a roll. Its dough, stretchy,
gave way, smooth and moist, flecked with bran.

"Perhaps you didn't know that Sicily played bread-
basket to the Roman Empire."

"That's amazing. I did not." Two thousand years later
the basket hadn't emptied, Sicily kept giving of herself.
Two thousand years later the bread kept breathing, body
and soul.

"Here," Maia urged, "have a little to wet your throat
while we wait. *Salute.*"

"*Cin-cin.*" I took a sip against better judgment, then
bit into the crust. Golden durum semolina grown on the
broad breast of the island's interior, flung into last summer's air to separate out the chaff, and ground between
meter-wide stones; bubbly yeast kept teeming since
Roman times; sea salt in sacks hauled by painted carts
from the Tyrrhenian shore; water caught in a ceramic
jug from the always splashing monastery spring—I
tasted these immediate ingredients. How could a dough
kneaded from them not effortlessly grow? Punched
down—large and little gasps of air imprisoned inside—

would it not triple in volume? Beaten down again, yea vanquished, would it not rise a second, a third time? Brushed with oil of olives from sacred groves, would it not meet its mysterious destiny—raw to cooked, matter to spirit—sealed inside the fiery oven, the rock rolled into place? Snatched at the right instant from that infernal heat, would it not thrust forth, to be borne triumphant on platters by monks (who had just completed their morning prayers, thus imparting a heightened spiritual zest to the loaves) through gardens respiring with spiky rosemary under the morning sun, and be delivered unto the trattoria's back door wrapped in cloth? And here kept warm next to the oven, guarded near Vesta's sacred flame. This much you could—I did—taste in one mouthful. Everything alive. If a bite could bind a person to a place—to ensure becoming a part of it—this one bound me to the island. I was here for the duration. The reverse of Persephone, committed to hell because of the six pomegranate seeds she chewed, we bit into morsels of paradise.

"My *carcioffo* is probably still in the ground, down the mountain, miles away," I yawned behind my hand.

Maia was lost in studying the noisy room around us, consummate observer, anthropologist, cultural attaché to her own paesani. Every table had ordered before we did, and seated a full clan. Generations were crammed together, parents force-feeding toddlers, teenagers wolfing down pasta by the spoon and forkful, sleeping babies cradled by grandparents, everyone gabbing, laughing, eating, swallowing. The waiter oiled around the floor, delivering plates and platters, more bottles of water and wine. More bread and beer, bowls and bills.

So if artichokes took hours to roast, the brother-in-law, equipped with walkie-talkie, was probably just loading the baskets with the last of the blessed thistles onto a *sciccareddu's* back right now. I relaxed into my chair with more vino. Treat the donkey well, give him a handful of hay and a drink from a trough, sing him the donkey song, and take your time because, man, those tenors were tiny beasts of burden. I could wait—we had Bread and Wine. An excellent sacramental appetizer. An old favorite. A meal really. A religion. I refilled Maia's glass and added a few centimeters to my own.

The waiter was nowhere in the dining room. I took another roll, broke through the crackly crust stratas, pulled at the elastic, steamy dough, probed and pinched the warm mass. There must be a technical name for the meeting of crust and dough, brown and white, a baking term for the realm between exterior and interior...the body and spirit...the dead to the living.

"You know, both my sisters have an allergy to wheat. Can you imagine life without bread?" I asked, my mouth full.

"Why? What happens to them?"

"Oh, they get sleepy, lethargic, yawn a lot. I'm so lucky to have escaped it."

"I should say." She drained the carafe.

"They even get disoriented." I kept chewing.

The waiter stood over us with plates, trying to remember who ordered what: sacrificial kid goat and the huge vegetable, like a baked green crown. The *capretto* smelled sort of barbecued.

"*Buon appetito*, ladies."

I loosened the first outer charred leaf off the subterranean globe—rounded like a basilica dome—and nibbled its meatiness, bittersweet and mineral. Though seared in a mini-inferno, it hadn't given up any moist ghost. I plucked my way through complexity, spiraling in, the marinade of lemon and olive oil, mint, crushed garlic yielding up.

"Fabulous! So delicious I can't tell you."

"Would you care to taste the meat?"

"No, no. I've got this."

We savored without conversing, the best way to manage in such a loud room. A person achieves something engaging with an artichoke. Does any other vegetable in the world have a built-in goal? Leaf, leaf, leaf, leaf, leaf, leaf, leaf, thicker to thinner, exterior to interior, then the prize of the huge heart. All those roasting hours made this apotheosis. At the end I was just sated, full of Sicily's generous fruits. When the waiter set our bill down I grabbed it, but my cousin fixed me with a no-nonsense look and demanded the slip.

"Maia, you must stop treating me as a guest, or for sure I'll get on your nerves very quickly."

"We have to eat."

"Exactly, and here's my contribution to that effort."

"I don't want to hear another word about it," she stood, brushed the crumbs off her lap and firmly pulled the slip from my fingers. The woman was not to be messed with.

We crossed the empty piazza, strewn with plastic winecups, peanut shells, shreds of burst balloons and horse manure, and circled the cream-colored monastery walls to her Fiat. We were well on our way down to Palermo, past the Mafia-Nightmare architecture up on the crest when a herd of goats—leaping, stumbling, tripping and glorious—filled the road. The unruly carpet of fur and horns that maaa-ed insisted upon right of way. Maia turned off the motor and nodded. She knew the score.

Natalie Galli's articles have appeared in the San Francisco Chronicle *and* The Berkeley Monthly. *Her memoir,* Three-Cornered Island, *details her search for Franca Viola, the first woman in Sicilian history to publicly refuse the tradition of coercive marriage.* Ciao Meow, *her children's book about a free-wheeling cat, boasts illustrations by her sister. Look for her contributions in* The Best Women's Travel Writing 2007 *and* 2008, Travelers' Tales Italy, *and* Italy: a Love Story. *She lives in San Rafael, California.*

ぶ ぶ ぶ

Up a Creek without a Paddle

An intrepid traveler faces the Amazon—at night.

I should've said no. I should've said, "Perhaps a canoe jaunt down the mighty Amazon River in beastly darkness might land us on an episode of Stupid People, and the Crocodiles That Ate Them."

But instead, when Mark, an adventurous Hawaiian surfer dude I met at a jungle lodge in Xixuaú-Xiparinã Nature Reserve—a 172,000-hectare protected chunk of land 280 miles northwest of Manaus, Brazil, tucked deep within the Amazon rainforest—asked if I wanted to take a canoe ride with him at 2 A.M., I couldn't climb in fast enough.

"Um, could you get out of the canoe for a minute? I need to push it into the river first," Mark said.

Right. We were off to a rocky start.

Still, the first few minutes were quite pleasant, as Mark paddled down a maze of winding waters, squeezed between walls of lush green foliage studded with giant trees—some 200 feet tall—in a soothing silence sliced occasionally by the charming serenades of the birds inhabiting the jungle.

But then, when we reached a fork, our canoe drifted into a path that looked a little worse for a DANGER: ENTER AT YOUR OWN RISK sign. You know the one—the dark, creepy path that protagonists in horror movies invariably always choose over the bright, welcoming one as a prelude to their grisly, yet quite predictable, deaths.

"Um, Mark, should we really go that way?" I asked in a would-be panic-free voice.

"Don't worry, I know where I'm going," he answered in a relaxed tone, assuring me that he had canoed this very same route two days ago.

But I did worry, for even the moon seemed reluctant to penetrate that area. I flicked on my flashlight. The jungle had eerily trespassed on the river, with tree trunks drowning in the water, fallen limbs floating limply on the surface, and trees tantalizingly stretching out their skeletal branches over the river, like long fingers poised to strangle.

"Turn off the flashlight, we don't need it," Mark said.

I did, grudgingly. Our canoe cleaved the black water, when suddenly a loud roar that sounded like a dinosaur opening a creaking door thundered through the jungle.

"What was that?" I whispered, forcing my voice to sound calm but pinballing my flashlight beam wildly across the jungle.

"It's just howler monkeys in the trees, don't worry," Mark replied. "Turn off your flashlight."

Splash!

"What was that?" I whimpered, now abandoning all pretence of fearlessness. It was one thing for a creepy noise to issue from the upper stories of the jungle; it was a whole other story for it to emanate from right underneath my seat.

"It's nothing, probably just some fish," Mark said.

Probably? Just some fish? Is the piranha, rumored to attack ill-fated swimmers and leave behind nothing but clothes and skeletons, just some fish? And what if it wasn't a piranha? What if it was an anaconda, lurking around our canoe, waiting to slither its thirty-foot-long sinewy body onboard and strangle us? Or a black caiman, lying in ambush, ready to lunge and bite with its snapping jaws?

I reignited my flashlight. The waters looked serene, innocent even, but I knew they hid mysteries underneath. For centuries, the world's largest river—its 1,100 tributaries contain one-fifth of the planet's river water—had seduced adventurers, tantalizing them with the allure of the mythical country of gold, El Dorado. History tells us how in 1541, Spanish conquistador Gonzalo Pizarro launched an expedition east of Quito, Ecuador in search of this land. Along the way, he sent his lieutenant, Francisco de Orellana, to look for provisions. Instead, Orellana discovered the Amazon River, navigating its entire length. Upon his return, Orellana recounted tales of treasures of gold and encounters with fierce female warriors who reminded him of the Amazons of Greek mythology—that's how, rumor has it, the Amazon got its name. But when Orellana attempted a second voyage down the Amazon, his ship capsized and he drowned.

Absolutely positive that I would not fare too well against Amazon warriors of any kind, I timidly proposed that we head back. Mark gingerly rebuffed my idea with his usual "Don't worry. Turn off your flashlight and just enjoy the ride."

I would have enjoyed it were I not too busy trying to identify the creatures responsible for the blood-curdling noises around me and, consequently, fending off what I believed to be an imminent attack by them, awkwardly flailing my arms as though beating away a fly.

"Everything O.K. back there?" Mark asked. "You're rocking the canoe a little."

"Everything's fine," I lied. "What are those sounds, birds?" I asked hopefully, deeming this to be a fair guess, what with a third of the world's bird species living in the Amazon.

"Nah, I don't think so," Mark said, without offering any alternatives.

More mysterious shrieks, roars, and howls echoed from unseen nocturnal creatures. More pre-emptive swatting of phantom attackers ensued from me. Then suddenly, the ungodly racket snapped into silence— ominous silence—kicking my imagination into over- drive as to what horror might befall us next.

"MARK, WATCH OUT!"

CRASH!

Our canoe careened into a tree, touching off panic as Mark was knocked backwards, felling me like a Domino, rocking the canoe violently, nearly capsizing us, and flooding our boat with an alarming amount of water— which was now dragging us down into the netherworld of the piranha, anaconda, and caiman.

"We're sinking!" I cried out, bringing Mark back up to speed as he re-emerged from his knockout, a little dazed.

We started to fervently bail our boat, which most unco- operatively seemed to swallow more water than we could scoop out, until it finally bobbed entirely back up onto the surface.

"Are you O.K.?" Mark asked breathlessly, looking anxiously around.

"Yeah, you?.... Wait, where's your paddle?"

He glanced at the river with a hint of worry creasing his brow.

"Are you kidding?" I asked in disbelief.

He wasn't kidding. Evidently, Mark had dropped our one and only paddle into the river when he was ambushed by the tree. We looked all around us with the flashlight, but the paddle had disappeared.

Familiar flutters of hysteria started to flare inside me as I realized we were stranded in the middle of the Amazon, when I heard another splash! This time, it was Mark. He had jumped into the water and was towing the canoe with his sturdy frame. Just then, flashes of all the nature shows I had watched came flooding back... "Caimans hunt mostly at night. Concealed in the water but for their bright red eyes, they lie in wait, studying their prey. Then when the latter stumbles near, they lunge and drag the unsuspecting prey underwater."

"Mark, please get back into the canoe," I pleaded, scanning the water surface for a suspicious glow.

"Don't worry," he heaved, with a return to his typical carefree manner. "We're almost there."

Sure enough, a few tense minutes later, we reached our destination—a sprawling expanse of pristine sandy beach awaited us like an oasis in the middle of the jungle. Mark hauled the canoe to shore, and we both slumped into the sand, drenched and exhausted. Above us, the moon had finally decided to show, and a million stars twinkled. This had the makings of a beautiful night—were it not for the grim prospect of re-enacting scenes from movies such as *Lake Placid* or *Anaconda*. Oh, and there still was that little matter of being stranded up a creek with no paddle.

Mark and I regrouped and devised a crack, foolproof strategy: We would paddle back madly and swiftly with our bare hands, all the while praying that we didn't accidentally manhandle a seven-foot-long crocodile. And I would be granted an unprecedented, no-holds-barred access to my flashlight.

We had barely put our plan into motion when we heard the faint rumbling of an engine. Mark and I froze mid-paddle as the noise floated closer and closer. Finally a small motorboat emerged from the shroud of darkness, with a short, shady-looking Brazilian man at its helm. We offered him a sheepish smile to the effect of "Are you here to save us, kind stranger?" He shot us a dirty look that indicated he clearly was not. No words were exchanged as he cruised past us, with a lingering gaze that seemed to say, "I didn't see you, you didn't see me."

"That was odd," I whispered to Mark. "Now, quick, paddle fast and make sure you don't slap anything that's moving!"

Sound advice, for a nature show once warned that crocodiles are dangerous when taunted or irritated—and surely an unexpected karate chop to the nostrils would do the trick. And for that matter, I didn't think a piranha or anaconda would take too kindly to a whack in the head, either. So we paddled as gracefully as possible, trying hard not to splash—for everyone knows splashes attract piranhas—and hoping that our dangling fingers weren't waving a hungry croc over.

Suddenly I jumped as my hand grazed up against something soft and grainy, and our canoe lurched to a stop. We had hit a sandbank. Out went Mark to push the canoe, as I dug my hands and feet into the sand to propel us out à la Flintstones, all the while wriggling and jiggling. We finally managed to glide back out onto deeper waters but didn't make it out too far before river gave way to sand again. And then again. By our fourth sandbank, we were wriggling free faster than Houdini out of a straightjacket.

As we proceeded through the river, I tried my utmost to ignore the bone-chilling shrieks that rang out around me, but now they came with floating eyes that I could swear were winking back at me from the forest. I remembered what the locals had said: The jungle, home to more than a third of the planet's species, has more eyes than leaves. Just as I began to imagine what the bodies behind those eyes might look like, we saw it—the shoreline where our lodge was located.

"See, we made it back safely. I told you there was nothing to worry about," Mark announced triumphantly, as we sailed smoothly over two submerged trees—and their branches promptly ensnared us like Audrey II in *Little Shop of Horrors*.

It was as if the Amazon gods were teasing us. There we were, just mere minutes from our lodge, stuck in a canoe—perched, as it were, atop two trees. This required a little more skill than we'd needed on the sandbanks. I slowly tottered to the back of the canoe and wrestled with the twisted, scrawny branches that clasped us in their deathly grip. One of the limbs broke off, sending me into a precarious spiral. I recovered my poise and tried again, this time with some choice fighting words. Another branch came undone. At this point, I recalled yet another less-than-comforting nugget the locals had imparted: The jungle is haunted, and its spirits steal the souls of those who harm it. I couldn't help but feel, then, that all my swearing and depleting of their jungle was doing very little to appease the surely already-peeved Amazon spirits.

With this in mind, I proceeded with more tact. I chose a particularly hefty branch and pushed it with all my ninety-five-pound might, while Mark duplicated my attempt in the front. Little by little, the canoe broke free until finally the branches released us entirely from their freakishly Herculean clutches and set us on-course for home.

As Mark and I scrambled back to our seats and started to banish the water that had crept onboard, the Amazon finally relented, mercifully letting its current carry us back to shore, unimpeded and untouched by the mythical piranha, anaconda, or Amazonian warrior.

That night, as I lay in bed, I wondered, How could I have underestimated the power of the Amazon, the largest rainforest on earth—and one of the least-explored realms of the world? After all, many a swashbuckler hardier than I has ventured into the Amazon and been defeated by its bewildering jungle and unyielding waters. And who was I to face off against the creatures of the jungle, the stuff of legends, many of them living relics of prehistoric times? They've survived the ages—I barely survived a canoe ride. Truly no place on Earth conceals more mysteries and enigmas than the Amazon rainforest. And something tells me we should keep it that way.

Aah, it sure felt great to be back in the safety of the lodge, far from the creatures I heard in the jungle that night.

Are those bats on my ceiling?

❦ ❦ ❦

Line Abrahamian recently quit her job as associate editor for Reader's Digest Canada *to freelance for travel publications, having been greatly inspired by her expedition in the Amazon.*

❧ ❧ ❧

My Mexican Housewife

A student helps her host mother reclaim her youth.

My first morning in her house, the señora came shuffling around the courtyard to my bedroom, her little slippered footsteps rousing me from my dream-laden sleep. I turned my head to the noise at the window. My eyes opened to her maroon-tinted head struggling to reach the top window slat, the only one I'd left open. Her voice hissed a Spanish greeting over the wobbly hum of the ceiling fan.

"*Sí, sí,*" I answered groggily, as I so often did those first few weeks, never knowing what had been asked or said but always answering the same. As I rolled out of my squeaky twin bed, I saw that her maroon head hadn't moved but she was still straining, on tiptoes no doubt, to see into my room. I pulled the thin sheet around my naked frame and caught her eyes focused on me, with a mysterious gleam—whether disapproval or intrigue I didn't know.

"*Sí*, I'm up, uh...*bueno*...*gracias*," I said quickly, hoping that the head would soon disappear.

"*Oh, muy cansada*," she said with a grin.

I reached across to my suitcase for a sarong to cover my now awkward nakedness. "*Sí*," I answered again. I realized that she had no intention of leaving her perch. She muttered something else, too quickly, but I understood *desayuno* and again agreed, "*Sí, por favor.*" I stood up, quickly tying the sarong around my body as she opened the bedroom door, then followed her through the courtyard into the house.

Her kitchen was already filled with the smells of the day's food. The chicken for lunch was boiling in a pot of onions and peppers, tortillas were crackling in a cast iron skillet, and papaya peels lay in a heap next to the stove. She sat me at a little wooden table covered with a bright floral plastic tablecloth and poured me a glass of freshly squeezed orange juice. As I drank my first sweet gulp, she placed a steaming plate of food in front of me—black beans, rice, and fried plantains. Then she sat down right across from me, her eager eyes awaiting my next move. I looked down at the plate of food and glanced at the little line of black ants scurrying across the placemat. The señora followed my eyes and quickly reached across the table and with her slight, brown fingers, and squashed each ant, brushing them to the tile floor. She pushed my plate of food closer to me, urging me with her smile.

I took my first bite of beans and rice, warm and soothing, and smiled back at her. Then I scooped up a plantain, still dripping with grease, and ate it in one bite. The starchy sweetness melted into my mouth, and I closed my eyes for a second to savor it. "*Delicioso*," I said.

She leaned back in her chair, crossing her arms with satisfaction and widened her smile. She raised her arm, pointed at her bosom, and with a grin said, "Me," tapping her finger on her chest, "good cook."

Not sure if she was making a statement or asking a question, I nodded enthusiastically, "*Sí. Bueno. Muy bueno.*"

Her chocolate eyes crinkled up as her face broke into a broad smile. She began to laugh, a sweet rolling chuckle, and reached across to take my hand, laughing harder as she held it and patted it. I didn't know what she found so funny, but I laughed with her—a little nervously. But beneath I felt relieved that we seemed to be getting along. I thought of the transformation my life had just undergone. There I was, wrapped in a sarong, already sweating in the humid air, holding hands with my new Mexican host mother, swatting mosquitoes with my free hand and thinking, "What am I doing here in the Yucatán?"

I had once heard "the impulse to travel is one of the hopeful symptoms of life." Perhaps my hope had led me on this solo trek to the tip of Mexico. But that first morning, in the señora's house, I couldn't see why. The two of us couldn't be more different. Years and worlds apart. And yet here we were, holding hands in her kitchen, living under the same tiled roof. Two women with different stories, and me without the language to tell her mine.

It wasn't long after that first morning that I wisened to the señora's daily schedule. By the second week of my stay, I was up and dressed before the maroon head appeared to call me for *desayuno*. Our mornings didn't change. We sat together at the little table; she watched as I ate, and then watched as I waited in the street to catch the bus to my language school. As I learned more in my intensive Spanish classes, I was able to come home

in the afternoon and chat with the señora. I could tell
her about my day at school or what I was hoping to do
in the afternoon. The first time I tried to explain to her
that I wanted to go for a jog into town, she looked at me
as though I were *loca*. I quickly fumbled through my
dictionary, thinking I had replaced the verb *correr* with
some utterly absurd phrase. But I pointed to the verb in
the dictionary, and still the señora looked aghast.

"*¿Por qué?*" she asked incredulously.

Sure, it was hot and muggy outside, and the town was
about three miles away, but that wasn't much compared
to the hours I logged on the gym treadmill back home. I
tried to explain that I liked to run, liked exercise, but the
señora didn't seem to understand. How could I explain
my need for an exercise routine to a woman who rarely
left her house? She had her own routine. She spent most
of the morning cooking, washing, cleaning; but by each
afternoon she was reclined in her hammock, her little
rabbit-eared television humming with the chatter of
Mexican soap operas. She stayed in that hammock for
the rest of the afternoon and evening, coming out only
to bring a plate of food or glass of juice upstairs to her
ailing husband.

I never ventured upstairs to the mysterious second
floor where she disappeared at night, from where I
could hear the muffled sounds of his coughing. He had
come downstairs only once, on the night of my arrival,
to greet me with a kiss on the cheek. I could scarcely
believe the skeleton of a man before me was married
to the señora, who looked to be thirty years his junior.
His skin was yellowed and dotted with brown moles,
his gray hair not more than a few persistent strands, and
the skin from his neck sagged over the neckline of his
t-shirt. After meeting him, I looked back at the señora,

who at age fifty-five was still in good physical shape with beautiful olive skin and a shining head of dark hair (the maroon tint was no doubt added). It was hard to fathom that these two were ever a good match.

After about a month in the Spanish school, I came home one day for an early dinner and found the señora reading a newspaper at the table. She looked excited as she pointed to a small article with a photograph of a mariachi band. The men in the photo, all older, looked distinguished in their wide hats and sequined suits. She launched into rapid chatter, talking about the band and the music, telling me they were her favorite and very good. She pointed to the date and time, and I understood that the band was playing the next night in the town square. By her excited gestures, I knew this was no ordinary event.

I tried to ask her about the band, where they were from and how she knew of them, and then tried desperately to follow along as she told an animated story. I couldn't be sure as to all the details, but as she talked I imagined she was describing her younger days, when the band was at the height of its popularity. Back then, she'd sing all the songs and dance all the dances. The girls would dress in traditional *ternos*, paint their faces, and move to the *folklórico* rhythms. The señora claimed she could no longer sing or dance, but when she was younger she couldn't get her fill of their music. Then her face dimmed a bit, and she said in a lowered voice, "*Ahora, no hay música.*" There is no more music now.

I started to ask, "*¿Por qué?*" but before I could finish, she nodded silently up toward the stairs. I nodded back and didn't add another word.

As she cleared up the plate from my dinner, she encouraged me to go into town the next night for the concert. She suggested I find some other student from the language school to go with, so I wouldn't have to be alone—it seemed that many of my solo excursions concerned her. I saw my perfect opportunity and asked her if maybe she would like to accompany me. Her eyes flashed with the same mysterious glint—maybe offense, maybe curiosity. She laughed a little and said, "*No, no,*" while shaking her head and dismissing the idea by describing herself as *floja*, which my pocket dictionary told me was "lazy." And with that, she cleared the rest of the dishes and took off back to her small room, off the kitchen, and closed the door. I heard the click of the television, the actors' voices crackling through, then the soft creak of the swaying hammock. I went back to my room, closed the door and flipped on the ceiling fan, its windy drone my only solace from the humid air. I lay in the bed with my journal open, drifting in and out of sleep, faintly waking from half-dreams to hear the señora as she prepared to head upstairs for the night.

I heard her footsteps pause near my door, then continue down the tiled hall to the small altar tucked into the alcove. She stopped for her nightly prayer. I imagined her long, Catholic fingers clasped together as I heard her whispered pleas to *La Virgen*. She prayed for each of her children and grandchildren. I tuned my ears to hear her voice over the crackling fan, and heard her ask for protection, love, forgiveness. Somewhere in her murmurs I heard my name. I pulled the sheet closer around my body, turning away as she climbed the stairs, and dropped off to sleep.

The next morning over *desayuno*, I mustered the courage and the Spanish words to ask the señora about the concert at the town square. I smiled and added that I thought she should go, to which she again shook her head and laughed it off. Again she told me that I should find another student to go with me, and I tried to explain that I didn't know the other students very well. Since I didn't partake in their nights of drinking in the local tourist cantina, I wasn't close with any of them. Of course, my Spanish couldn't suffice, and my explanation seemed to confuse her more than anything. But, as she walked me out to the door of the courtyard to say good-bye that morning, she asked, shyly, in broken English,

"You want that I come? Tonight?"

I nodded enthusiastically, "*Sí, sí,*" and she grinned back at me.

"*Tal vez,*" she answered, which I knew was "maybe."

I came back to the house that evening, dripping with sweat from the humid walk home. The door to the señora's room was closed, the TV humming, and disappointed, I figured that she was settled for the night. I went through the courtyard to my room and then into the dark bathroom. I showered in the cold water trickling from the rusted shower head, wrapped myself in a towel, and went back to my room to get dressed. As I changed into my clothes for the evening, I heard a quiet knock on the door. When I opened it, there stood the señora, no longer in her faded housedress, but dressed in a skirt and blouse. Her maroon hair looked even brighter, probably just re-dyed, and I even thought I detected a shimmer of eyeshadow across her eyelids.

"*Eres hermosa,*" I said with a smile that couldn't contain my excitement.

She answered in a low, hushed voice, "*Gracias,*" then told me we should leave for the bus in twenty minutes. As she stepped out of the room I closed the door, my eyes welling up. I didn't know if I was more excited to spend the night with her or to see she had fancied herself up. I finished getting ready, sure to put on a hint of makeup as well.

We left the house twenty minutes later, both clutching purses as we walked down the dirt road to the main street. We had pesos ready in our hands as we climbed onto the rickety bus that stopped in the middle of the road, and we sat together quietly as the other passengers watched this strange duo. We got off at the cathedral in the town square and walked around the plaza. The señora showed me the best stores in the central plaza, where to buy souvenirs for the best prices, and where the best *heladería* was. I went into the little ice cream shop and bought us each an enormous cone. We giggled as we licked at the melting treat.

When we walked into the park where the concert was, the señora found us seats near the stage. She sat in a rusted, metal folding chair with perfect posture, as regal as a queen. She glanced around the crowd and smiled at familiar faces. When the mariachis took the stage, her eyes shone in the darkness, and I saw that they were wet.

As soon as the pulsing music started, I watched her sing along to the band. She knew every lyric to every song and sang it just loud enough for me to hear. She carried a tune well, her voice crackling with years, but still poignant and melodic. When the band played *La Jarana,* the chair could barely contain her excitement as she swayed to the beat with her arms and torso. I wanted to stand up, take her hand and dance with her. I wanted us to dance uninhibited, to shake our hips and sway to the crooning horns, but I couldn't muster the courage to grab her hand. Maybe she would have laughed, or been too embarrassed, or maybe she would have liked it. I'll never know.

Instead, I sat and watched her that night. From the corners of my eyes I watched her face light up with every new song, felt her squeeze my hand and say the names of the songs before launching into her whispery singing. I watched her knees bounce up and down in perfect time to the beat, and saw her youth revealed—as if her stories were emanating from the music.

We took the bus home together that night, she still humming songs and trying to teach me lyrics. As we walked up the dirt road to her house, she stopped in front of the courtyard and kissed my cheek.

"*Divertísima, mija,*" she said smiling.

She hugged me and then headed up the stairs to the second floor where her husband lay snoring noisily. I tiptoed into my room and shut the door behind me. Leaning with my back to the door, I took a deep breath and waited to hear their bedroom door close. Then I heard her footsteps come bravely back down the stairs. I heard her feet shuffle to her little side room, and then the door squeak shut. I envisioned her bare footsteps on the cold tile as she crossed the room and then heard the soft creak of her hammock as she settled into her place.

Stacey Lee Tuel lives on a farm in Northern California, teaches writing at Sonoma State University, and also works in environmental education. Her Master's program in creative writing was completed at Sonoma State University with her collection of travel essays and stories, The Collected Writings of an Aspiring Gypsy. *She has written for Rolf Potts's "Vagablogging." This story won the Gold Award for Travel and Healing in the second annual Solas Awards. She still aspires to be a gypsy.*

𝕤 𝕤 𝕤

Tosi and Me

Her stay in South Africa was different from all things
"home" —especially her choice of a pet.

*W*hen I was twenty, studying Zulu for a summer
in Pietermaritzburg, South Africa, I was stroll-
ing through a street market and decided it might be fun
to buy a chicken. I handed the vendor my eighteen rand,
less than three dollars, and in return I received a scrawny
animal in a cardboard box. Chickens must not enjoy
traveling in boxes, because as I walked home holding the
package by its makeshift twine handle, my pet crashed
against the insides so violently that the box swayed back
and forth, once even falling to the ground. Irritated, I
decided to name my chicken Tosiwe, the Zulu word for
"fried." It was only later when I discovered I actually liked
Tosiwe a bit that I nicknamed her Tosi. I made a home
for her on my front porch, and after my classes I would

sit with her on my lap, petting her as she released a series
of faint baaks that blurred together into something that
sounded to me like a purr.

Owning a chicken delighted me, mostly because it
was something I'd never done. After all, that was why
I'd ventured to Africa (why I suspect everyone first
does): to experience a way of living completely different
from anything I knew.

When I'd learned I was staying in a mansion across
the street from a horde of fast food restaurants, I
was disappointed. I was further disappointed when I
attended a supposedly traditional ceremony honoring
the Zulu rain goddess and found participants wearing
jean jackets and talking on cell phones, and then weeks
later when I realized I still hadn't seen a giraffe, lion, or
even a single monkey.

My South African life didn't feel much different from
my American one—not until I bought Tosi.

Tosi stayed on the porch through the several days
when I didn't realize chickens needed to be fed, through
invasions by street cats and large birds, through my
weekend trip out of town, and through the appearance of a woman making chicken soup on the sidewalk
beyond the fence. But then, the day before I would leave
for a weeklong home-stay, Tosi wandered off for good.

On the bus ride away from the city, everyone—and
especially my Zulu professor—poked fun at my loss.

"Don't worry," he assured me. "I'll assign you the
family with the most chickens."

My professor had been amused by my interest in Tosi
all along. Although I bought her hoping to feel more
South African, he knew that Zulu people who bought
chickens on the street took them home to slaughter for
dinner; they didn't keep them as pets.

Trying to ignore the teasing, I stared out the window. The bus kicked up dust as it climbed toward our rural destination, but through the haze I admired the imposing flattop mountain, its sides speckled with tall pine and plump marula trees as well as modest, trailer-like homes. Accustomed to the flat cornfields of the Midwest, I found the dramatic scenery mesmerizing.

Eventually the bus rolled to a stop in front of a rusty gate, and I followed my professor outside. A squat older couple approached us. They introduced themselves as Mr. and Mrs. Gasa, and as they spoke to my professor in Zulu that was beyond my level of comprehension, I looked behind them to the complex of a dozen weathered, tin-roofed buildings arranged to form a courtyard. Crude farming tools were scattered across the dirt, and goats and chickens wandered around them and then into the buildings around whose corners children were peeking, watching me. I smiled, maybe at the children, or maybe out of happiness to finally be in this place so far from cell phones and fast food restaurants.

That first night for dinner, Mr. and Mrs. Gasa fed me fried chicken. I can only assume that when my professor was speaking to them in Zulu he shared the story of Tosi, because later Mr. Gasa led me outside and pointed to the chickens wandering around the dirt courtyard. He asked if I saw anyone I knew, and when I told him I didn't, he pointed to my stomach and smiled mischievously.

But it didn't take long for Tosi to fade from my thoughts. I was busy practicing my Zulu and playing with Mr. and Mrs. Gasa's grandchildren. I accompanied neighbors to a game park where I finally saw a giraffe, and I even joined a *lobolo* ceremony, walking in a line of women carrying crates of oranges, sacks of sugar, and other offerings on our heads. Life felt different and exciting, but what I loved perhaps most of all was its simplicity. When we wanted warm water, we heated it over a fire. When we needed eggs, we fetched them from the chicken coop. When we needed vegetables, we picked them from the garden. This was precisely the "Africa" of my imagination—the sort of place I'd been so desperate for back in Pietermaritzburg—and yet, strangely, beneath the exotic languages and dramatic scenery, it wasn't all that different from my childhood home.

I could have spent summers detassling corn in my rural Midwestern hometown. I could have raised live-stock as 4-H projects. But I'd scoffed at such bucolic endeavors then. I was too busy bemoaning my slow-paced existence and daydreaming about places where I assumed things of consequence happened. So why in my quest for something different did I end up happy somewhere so much the same?

Years later, I would think of my stay with the Gasa family when reading about a world religions professor who observed something about his students. Most came to his classes feeling estranged from organized reli-gion. Studying lesser-known faiths gave them a greater appreciation for spirituality in all its forms; after a while, most returned with a new appreciation to the religion in which they had been raised. "To find yourself," the professor commented, "you sometimes must go to a stranger."

On my last day with the Gasa family, Mr. Gasa appeared at my doorway. Today we're going to *bulala* a chicken, he told me, holding a live creature by its neck. I got dressed and joined Mr. Gasa in an empty room. Holding the animal down with his knees, he extended a knife in my direction. I held it over the squirming and screeching animal, my hands trembling, until finally I passed it back. But I stayed and watched as Mr. Gasa sawed the chicken's neck. Its head fell back like an opened jewelry box, dangling by a thin flap of skin. Blood spouted out in bursts. The chicken convulsed several times and then lay still.

I was at the same time horrified and mesmerized.

Throughout the course of the day the chicken was beheaded, plucked and gutted, its insides sprawled across the floor; the children fought over who would eat its head. Mrs. Gasa cooked the creature that afternoon over a gas burner, and it arrived on a platter that night as my dinner.

Maybe I could have killed and then eaten a chicken back home, but it took being with the Gasa family in this seemingly strange land for the experience to feel exhilarating.

As I ate, I didn't think of back home, or Pietermeritzberg, or even Tosi. In fact, not a single time that day— that week—did I find myself wishing to be anywhere other than exactly where I was.

Alexis Wolff grew up in the rural Midwest and has since made it her mission to live anywhere else. After stints in Connecticut, Kentucky, Norway, Niger, South Africa, and South Korea, she now calls Brooklyn home. Her travel writing has appeared in The New York Times, *the* Los Angeles Times, The Best Women's Travel Writing 2008, World Hum, *and the* London Sunday Telegraph, *among others. She has a BA from Yale University and an MFA from Columbia University.*

KATHLEEN SPIVACK

ॐ ॐ ॐ

By Any Other Name: A Love Story

In the damp cellar of a Loire Valley château,
she deepened her sense of French language and culture.

*D*oes language birth the object named? Or is it the other way around?

The city of Tours shimmered from the other side of the river Loire. La Touraine, the region, gleamed with its stately chateaux, silvery rivers, and pensive gardens. All invited one to stay—forever. It was raining that year; the cows brooded, depressed, up to their knees in water, barely turning their languid eyes toward me. "Stay, stay."

Every day I walked from the adjacent small town of Saint Cyr into Tours. I crossed the garden, took a shortcut to the "one hundred steps," and crossed the highway and onto the vaulted bridge that spanned the

Loire between the little town and the city and university where I was teaching. The river was high that year, with dead wood drifting downstream. I passed by a desolate looking island, which was flooded more and more each day and disappearing into the surrounding water. The Université de Francois Rabelais fronted the wide river bank with its soggy paths and wet abandoned benches, and looked into the ancient medieval town of Tours on the other side. The rain slanted, sent its silver needles horizontally. I was soaked after this pedestrian commute. I soon abandoned thigh-baring oh-so-chic little skirts for a more practical uniform: slacks and many sweaters.

"Exceptionnel," the local inhabitants muttered as the rain, a solid sheet, continued all that academic year. The government declared the weather to be a national emergency, as they did every year at exactly the same time. The river Loire flooded its banks, carrying protesting trees downstream.

Nevertheless, every day, at whatever moment we had free, under useless umbrellas that flapped and creaked and turned inside out, the entire university stopped everything to live the famous "art de vivre." Lunch, coffee, aperitif: students and faculty thronged the medieval latticed restaurants, cafés. The smell of wet wool permeated unheated restaurants, cafés, and little pubs, the desolate museums and the splendid theaters. It was "La Douce France."

Was it my gaze, held breath, "Remember this, Kathleen," that stroked each sodden pastel moment? Was it memory that brought it into being? Or was it the delicate precision of that "purest French," the music of the language so clearly spoken that it gilded the entire region? Those rivers, the Loire, the Indre, the Vienne, stretched out their languid bodies under watching watercolor clouds. The sky changed constantly. The region was full of history, and especially of the history of women, their grace and taste and beauty: Diane de Pothiers, Catherine de Medici. The air tinkled, feminine and silvery with rain; each view, each moment was watery, pastel.

The director of my department had found me a place to live in Saint Cyr, not far from her. It was the huge vaulted cellar room of a small chateau—it even had its own name, and a poster in the town hall commemorated it. It was classic and forbidding as a chateau out of the novels of Balzac, and held all sorts of pent up secret passions. An impenetrable stone wall gated the entire property, with embedded shards of glass along the top.

A friend drove me down from Paris after his job one early evening just before my first teaching day. It was late January; the journey was gloomy and sunken in darkness. There were no lights in the streets and I was overcome with a sinking feeling of isolation. It was like being dropped off at summer camp; only I had never been to summer camp. "Don't leave me here!" Everyone had told me that people outside of Paris were "unfriendly," closed: how was I to manage a lifetime of nights alone in darkness?

The manor where I was to live loomed before us, a damp pile of stone. My friend was irritatingly cheerful. "But it is an adventure…." He was impatient to drop me off and get back to Paris. Listlessly, we tried to find a town center, somewhere with a bit of life and animation. He drove me into Tours; we looked at the usual quiet buildings squatting around the railroad station. The rain was falling, falling—as it would for months. We found a pizza joint, then retreated to the darkness and Saint Cyr.

The manor had been built centuries ago. In my room one bare light bulb, low wattage, flickering French thrift French thrift clanked from a rusty chain in the middle of the space. My room at street level had iron bars on all the windows. The bathroom and adjacent toilet were freezing, crawling with spiders. I was already prepared for French thrift in rented lodgings, with its few scratchy, carefully counted out brown squares of toilet paper. The kitchen—but I didn't look at the kitchen area too closely. A hot plate, and sink that was to fall apart the first time I tried to use it, a little refrigerator that didn't work. "La boheme" was clearly in evidence.

Most interesting, however, was to be the bed. Ancient, seeming as old as the chateau itself, sagging, it stood in the middle of the room, drooping on one side, the mattress always threatening to slide off the broken bed frame onto the floor. How many bodies had it contained, emerging crippled from their encounters; and for how many eons? That broken bed was to become the focus and center of unexpected moments. "Fixing the bed" became the object of multiple drop-ins from visitors from Paris, my colleagues in Tours—and their husbands. How we heaved that clumsy bed around, trying to make it level!

One broken chair also occupied the room. A magnificent fireplace, sealed up, that didn't work; perhaps this room had been the ancient kitchen of the manor. The plastered walls cracked and flaked. I shivered under several wet wool layers, could never get warm. My friend, it turned out, had cousins in Saint Cyr. Hastily, he introduced me to them and then headed back for the bright lights of Paris. I sat there under the dim bulb and wondered.

My new colleagues in the English department arrived en masse the next morning at eight o'clock and banged

on the iron-barred window of my street-level cellar
room. "Wake up, wake up!" I peered out into damp and
gloom and rain and strangeness. This was to be my first
day of teaching my classes, but the faculty had decided
to welcome me with wine tasting in the nearby village
of Chinon. Wine tasting? I was teaching my first class at
ten that first morning. What better time? "Exactly," the
department head explained.

The wine tasting involved a drive through foggy
roads to an even damper, colder place, a "troglodyte," a
cave hollowed into a limestone outcropping in Chinon.
Photographs show me smiling bravely, a shadowy figure
in wine-cellar gloom, holding aloft an untasted glass of
wine, in several borrowed sweaters and scarves, gritting
my teeth and thinking no doubt of only one thing, a hot
cup of coffee. I tried not to wince, not to think "headache, headache." But the wine of the Touraine, even in
the early morning, surprise, surprise, did not give one
headaches. That is, if one stuck to only the best wines,
and of course the best champagne. I was starting to get a
hint of what this year was going to be like. I was already
starting to write funny letters about it to my family back
home—in my head.

There was an active social life of dinners and parties.
Most of the department, faculty and students, lived in
the region, so the "art de vivre" was well developed. By
the end of my first week in Tours, I too was starting to
give parties. I tried to find recipes that would reflect my
own regional New England cuisine. For if I were to be
a visiting American professor, it would not do to pretend to be French; I could never match their style, their
cuisine. I served a version of improvised Boston baked
beans from the hotplate. Recipe: open a whole bunch
of cans, add things—browned bacon pieces, caramel-

ized onions, a bit of brown sugar, and maybe—this was inspired—a can of chestnuts. I also created "pot roast," i.e. boiled one-pot dinners on the same hotplate. Recipe: brown a lot of garlic, put in a hunk of meat. Add a little vinegar to soften it, some herbs, vegetables, a can of beer: find some sort of pot cover and boil the hell out of the thing. Remove cover—and voilà.

My friend drove back down from Paris with a radio and a saucepan, a halogen lamp and a plug-in pot that boiled water and didn't blow the fuses. I lived on food that didn't need refrigeration: bread and cheese of the region, and bouillon cubes dissolved in boiling water.

Using cans of creamed corn and an improvised version of Bisquik (a bit of flour, egg, baking powder, a dash of salt) I made "corn bread" in the saucepan. In an extraordinary fit of martyrdom I tackled stovetop carrot cake. Recipe: dice up many bunches of carrots; cut off their long leafy tails and shake the dirt off them first. Add that makeshift "Bisquik" again, put in lots of cinnamon and nutmeg and other spices to disguise it if anything goes wrong. Pour the batter, with the irregular shaped oblong orange bits into the frying pan, set on hotplate, turn on low, put cover on pan. Hope.

I found Coca-Cola in a supermarket. My hosts would have been disappointed if I had offered anything else. I had once seen an American man commit the unforgivable faux pas of bringing a bottle of wine to a Parisian couple's dinner. The host considered himself a foremost French wine expert and the poor overeager distinguished guest was made to understand that never, never should an American presume to do something so gauche again. Maybe they were joking, but I was terrified. Coals to Newcastle, but on a much higher scale, that sort of thing.

I didn't want to leave anyone out so I invited the entire department. The Cousins came and brought their own chairs. Most of the guests sat on the bed and held on to each other for lack of any other way to stabilize themselves. The bed lurched and the food slid from the paper plates they held gingerly on their laps.

My room became a Project. By the second week I had been given a card table, some cutlery and dishes, two bottles of good wine, and of course a full set of wine-glasses. The faculty and the Cousins, all with generous invitations, saved me from too many lonely evenings and cold meals. They introduced me to the area, to the markets. I bought a bright new light bulb, the bright-est I could find. My guests disapproved; they preferred dim lighting, and besides, the old kings, Charles and Francois, had been just fine in the dark.

But I never managed to accumulate a better bed. Sometimes one of the men I had met stopped by on his way to the outdoor market, a mattress strapped to the roof of his little car. "A new bed," involved much heav-ing and hauling, as we had first to nudge the sodden mattress off the decrepit broken bed frame. The frame was propped up with cinder blocks since it had broken so many times. Ingenious engineering and bed-architec-ture took place, only to achieve the same results as before. Then we had to "try out" the new bed. This might have been awkward, only to be solved by plonking the man's children—who had been waiting in the car during all this—between us in the middle of the new bed, insisting that we try it together. Carefully not touching sleeves, we found ourselves lying like dead bishop effigies, stiff as boards on a mattress that didn't work either. The bed eluded all attempts. In the dark, I slid from skewed mattress into long underwear and clothes, sweaters and raincoat. Scuttling toward the penetrating dampness of Tours on the other side of the river, like the arthritic bed, I developed a permanently tilted position.

Tours was a place of generosity, celebrations, great food and wine, theater, music, poetry and imagination. It was a place of History, all sorts. The Musée de Beaux Arts held paintings of the region, and portraits of its august personnel, carefully posed and dignified, aligned its halls and staircase. Its prize exhibit was a stuffed elephant, Fritz, who dominated the museum. Fritz had keeled over and died in Tours soon after descending a railroad car. He had been on tour (in Tours) with the Barnum and Bailey circus. Now the enormous gray stuffed pachyderm stood at the entry of the museum. He looked content, with fixed friendly eyes. In the garden an ancient olive tree, even older than Fritz, spread its drooping branches, the weight of its elbows propped up by pieces of wooden railroad ties.

That year the walls of the chateaux along the rivers took in so much water that they fell down or had to be propped up. In my own basement room, weird undersea ticking sounds began emanating from the region of the blocked fireplace. Animals, I thought, not wanting to investigate further. One solitary evening, in an earthquake of sound, the concrete that had been poured in to seal up the huge, heat-sucking cheminée crumbled under the rain's weight. Thunderous, it piled downward, filling the room: heavy, sodden, a huge cone-shaped mass of wet sand.

It continued to rain; I wore three sweaters. An American friend came to visit some of the chateaux of Tours. We took a little bus to Chenonceau and had the whole place to ourselves, a rare occurrence. The lovely chateau floated on water, its outlines almost obscured by the rain. The American took a hotel room in Tours. It had heat! My French friend drove down the next weekend from Paris bringing a portable electric heater. I plugged it in; it hissed and began to glow for about a second and blew the feeble fuses. I wrapped myself in another scratchy blanket—I had begged my landlady for extras—and tried to sleep.

And yet it was a most exquisite year. The vast grounds of the manor sloped through wet woodlands to the river bank. It was so wet that the lawns sprayed upward when one walked on them. That year I drank wines as they were meant to be: the nectar of the gods. Silver, golden, rose, and ruby—the wines of the region Touraine. The great chateaux brooded, misty and delicate, as they rose up from their rain sodden lawns, and parapets and lakes and misty overlooks. Blois, Chambord, Chenonceau, Langeais: each had her history, looming above their own little towns, the walls, the markets, the cobbled streets. The great rivers wreathed and wound like sleeping dragons carefully bridged from time to time. Chateaux parapets crumbled, the outer wall of the castle Saumur fell in stone heaps onto a café nearby, the day after I visited. The shadows of disappointed French aristocrats still trailed their garments through the tapestried great halls. Villandry, Azay-le-Rideau, and Ussé, the forbidding Castle of Sleeping Beauty, seen from afar.

Time passed in a wave of watery drops. The language of the region was watery too, liquid and musical. Although I had been teaching in France for a number of years, communicating in more-or-less French, hearing the language spoken in Tours, the purity and clarity of it, made me want to go more deeply.

My French teacher, Joelle Blot, was retired from the famous language institute in Tours. She arrived at my first lesson perfectly dressed in a little tweed suit, high heels, a large notebook in place. Her students came from all over the world, with a wide variety of professions and interests. For me, she had prepared a series of classes centered around French poetry. We would start with the poet Eduard de Ronsard, she told me, because Ronsard was the poet of her region. She pointed firmly to a line of French, and asked me to read it aloud. Panic set in immediately. I felt like one of my own students, struggling to pronounce English, and terrified at the prospect.

"Rose," I muttered. Mme Blot was not pleased. She pointed again. "Rose!" she gurgled, as if to encourage me. I tried again. But the combination of sounds, that "R" and that particular "oh" of the French "O" eluded my anglicized ears. We don't have those sounds in English, and they are particularly difficult to reproduce. I tried again. "Rose." Madame was not pleased. "Rose," she corrected me. She pointed again at the page. I tried, but this time no sound came out. I was seized with embarrassment and fear. An overwhelming urge to laugh came over me, a paroxysm of "forget it," but Mme Blot would have none of it. I was experiencing French pedagogy—stern, insistent, brooking no laughter or other attempts to deflect attention from the subject.

This was to be a long afternoon. I could not look at the word "rose" without the urge to giggle. Then close to tears, almost sobbing aloud. "Rose," what a detestable word! I would never be able to say it. As Madame waited patiently, sitting next to me, her legs neatly crossed, her perfect curled hair and tweed suit and little ruffled blouse, I yearned for the lesson to end. Already we had been sitting there over an hour and a half. Later I found that my lessons were to last approximately two hours, or until Madam deemed I had actually learned something. I was dying to get rid of her. Finally, as the afternoon light grew darker around us, I rallied. "Now or never," I thought, and like the elephant Fritz, threw back my head and trumpeted a sound of pure frustration: the word "RRRRRRROZZZZuhhh." That final drawn out "UUUH" was my triumph.

"Ooh la la," exclaimed my teacher, "Comme c'est beau! C'est magnifique!" Madame closed the notebook. She beamed; she exclaimed, she was as proud of me as if I were Helen Keller with her hand under the dripping spigot, and Madame, like famous teacher Annie, the patient self-sacrificing tutor. She offered me a little candy. The lesson was over.

Rose, the most important noun in the language. It stood for the mystic religious heart of French culture and history, as in Rose windows, a contemplation of the endlessly furled blooms. The Name of the Rose. And, in the outcry of Blake's, that shivery "O Rose thou art sick..." The bloom off the rose, the disease, the eating away, evanescent, menaced. But for now, the word "Rrrozzzuuh" was a caress, a recognition of beauty.

Next week Madame arrived in her little car. "We will visit the country of Ronsard," she said. And we did, touring the little roads and back ways that Ronsard had walked. This was Madame's country. I was to spend many happy lessons with Madame Blot, journeying further into the beauties of French poetry, she reciting in that lovely pure Touraine clarity and precision of language, and me trying vainly to imitate. I learned to speak French slowly, not rushing in nervousness to blur my pronunciation difficulties.

On wet cold weekends Madame invited me to her house which had central heating and huge working fire-

places. There was a long winding driveway, lush lawns
and gardens. Her husband was kind, courtly. On Sunday
afternoons, grateful students stopped in from all over
the globe, students who had studied French in Tours
with Madame, now professors or doctors from Japan,
China, Sri Lanka, Canada. We sat around the fireplace
drinking tea from beautiful porcelain cups that had
been in Madame's family for generations while Madame
led us in "cultural" conversation, gently choosing which
of our mistakes to correct and tolerating incomprehensible accents. Ever the teacher, she attempted to "bring
us out," making sure that each one had a turn—did we
have a choice?—to "converse." I was reminded, had to
smile inwardly, at the picture of the "teacher" that we all
carry, that I am sure I project also to my own students,
that ever encouraging smile, that effort not to wince at
a mistake.

Madame had been mayor of her little town during
various land reforms, was a fierce atheist and socialist.
A best-selling book came out that year, a first-person
account by a mousy French professor about her attempts
to pick up men in the Bois de Boulogne, a boastful "so
many men in one night" sex confessional. Madame was
outraged. "She is taking the bread out of the mouths of
our prostitutes!" she exclaimed. "She is violating their
union."

My friend Joe came to visit on his way to Romania,
put down his backpack in my dank room and fixed
everything. Suddenly the hotplate, refrigerator, and sink
were working. He cooked for me, his specialty being
rice and vegetables in various permutations. There were
more dinner parties. Only the bed stayed the same, stubborn, uncomfortable as ever, clinging to its tilted broken
bed frame long after Joe had gone on his way.

Finally spring came to the Loire Valley; there was sweetness in the air. The damp rising from the sodden countryside smelled fresh, green as the inside of child-hoods spent in the country. And finally the garden burst into flower; suddenly, late spring, the rain stopped, and the birds went crazy with song. The land sprang into bloom. Wisteria bloomed on the great lawn outside my windows, and I moved outside to write, meditating with a cup of coffee under the dizzying fragrance of those pendulous violet flowers, in a daze of perfume, over-looking the silver river.

The town of Saint Cyr created a "Jardin des Poetes" across the street from my walled chateau. I had watched it take shape all that muddy spring without knowing what was going on, the yellow praying-mantis bulldoz-ers bowing and digging beyond my barred windows. There was a Grand Opening, and the mayor and other officials made speeches. After long flowery toasts and plenty of champagne, the whole town toured the park; there were little sculptures and groupings of bushes along its carefully planned paths with quotes from notable French poets at every turn. There were quotes even on the carefully placed park benches. The "Jardin des Poetes" was only one of the many flowered parks in the town and region. Suddenly my Paris friends all came to visit. There was music, songs and poetry at din-ner parties outdoors.

Walking the "cent marches" to the banks of the Loire, down the damp one hundred steps before crossing the bridge to the university, I passed wisteria everywhere. The cold stone steps were fountains of spilling blossom.

In late May, the roses came alive. In la Prieuré de Saint-Cosme, a ruined abbé at the end of a country road, the outdoor music festival began. Among the mossed and fallen stone walls, roses dripped from every side, red, pink, yellow and white, dizzying in their heavy hot odors. We walked among them, spending afternoons in admiration for the roses, the pastel sky, the air, the land giving its bounty after a year of rain. At Saint-Cosme the scents of new mown grass, damp stones and flowers mingled at Ronsard's tomb. Sometimes I took a book with me and spent whole days there dreaming beside the spot where the poet lay. What better place to be commemorated? There were climbing vines of roses everywhere.

"Rrrrroooooozzzzuhh," the winds tickled the cypress trees. "Rose," the name of a flower, its endless varieties. "Rose," a word used delicately in French to refer to a woman's sex. "Rose," its petalled mysteries. Rose windows. The abbeys, the chateaux with their chapels and love secrets. That region, the Loire, that country, each vista, unfurling itself like the petals of a flower, drawing us into her history, her sweetness.

The large circular rose garden in front of Madame Blot's house came into bloom, flooding the front yard with delicate color. Her husband had built the garden under the window of her bedroom, one year when Mme. Blot was recovering from surgery, so she could look out and see something beautiful.

"Rose," the word, almost unpronounceable by us anglophiles, with its discrete layers of meaning beyond the word itself. The decisiveness of the "R." The glancing-off of the "oh." That lazy languid "S" soft, trailing toward the caress of the consonant "E" which follows. Wasn't the word itself the emblem for the Touraine, land of beauty and wetness and flowering, music and graceful buildings and gardens? "Rose," its mysteries like the irresistible lure of France, would beckon me for the rest of my life. "A rose by any other name would smell as sweet." Would it?

Kathleen Spivack's book, The Moments of Past Happiness Quilt *was published in 2007. Her other books include* The Beds We Lie In *(nominated for a Pulitzer Prize);* The Honeymoon; Swimmer in the Spreading Dawn; The Jane Poems; Flying Inland; *and* Robert Lowell, A Personal Memoir. *Published in over three hundred magazines and anthologies, her work has also been translated into French. She gives theater performances and master classes, and directs the Advanced Writing Workshop in Boston, an intensive coaching program for advanced writers. She is a permanent (one semester per year) Visiting Professor of Creative Writing/American Literature at the University of Paris (Sorbonne). This is her third publication in* The Best Women's Travel Writing *series.*

❧ ❧ ❧

Lines and Angles

She struggled with the poverty in India—
and with herself.

My husband's driver always called me Madame. No one in Seattle calls me that, but in India it fit the social geometry.

He was driving us to the airport for our flight home. It was near midnight in Mumbai. The crowd of vehicles at the red light split the two-lane road into four, five, six. Motorcycles and rickshaws wriggled through gaps like cattle seeking space in the herd. Beams from cars and trucks behind jostled the late-night dark of the backseat.

Green light.

Dubey hit horn, gas, brake, and we made a right turn from three lanes in, shot up the entrance ramp to a highway. He twisted the rearview mirror to find my eyes. "Madame, I must tell you something."

Why wasn't he watching the road? Why was he talking only to me? David was at my side.

"My son, Madame, he is seven and all he can say is
mama and dada."

Earlier that afternoon David had called Dubey's cell
phone from our hotel in Kochi: Our plans had changed;
we were returning to Mumbai on an earlier flight. No
problem. Dubey would meet us. He would be there with
his car.

As the jet climbed out of Kochi, the flight attendant
handed out lunch. He queried each row: "Veg? Non-
veg?" I asked if there were any window seats available,
so David could take photographs. "Let me see what I
can do." He led us forward from our seats at the back of
the plane to the first-class cabin. Cradled in the spacious
smell of leather, I leaned into the aisle and looked back,
checking for disapproval from fellow passengers. I saw
no other white faces, but the only reproof was my own,
even as we whispered of our good luck.

Getting through the airport in Mumbai was easy. No
passports to display, no customs to clear from our domes-
tic trip. We piled our baggage onto a cart. We stopped by
the Tourist Information counter to book a hotel, a place
to spend nine hours before our flight home. Dusty glass
doors slid open to the smells of a hot afternoon: sweat,
diesel, jet fuel. Shouts of "Taxi! Taxi!" burst from the
throng of men outside. I shifted my purse and squeezed
it close to my waist.

A white signboard with our names floated in front of
us. "Hotel Samar? Mr. David?" said the man with the
sign. Where had he come from? How did he know us?
Oh, the Tourist counter. A phone call. And this driver
assured of a fare.

"We already have a driver coming. No thank you."

"No sir, no, you must go with me Hotel Samar."

Where was Dubey? We scanned the crowd, didn't see him. David headed to a payphone as I stood gripping the cart. The man with the sign ignored me and followed David, repeating his orders. "Hotel Samar. You go with me."

No answer at the payphone. David teetered toward giving in to the other driver. I wanted to wait for Dubey. Then relief: he bustled out and was beside us. "Sorry, sorry Sir. Had to park very far away." He pulled a handkerchief from his pocket and poked at the sweat on his face.

He took the cart from me and began to push the luggage toward the lot. The man with the sign stepped in front of the cart to stake his claim on us. We started to explain, but were stopped by contentious tones of a language we did not understand. Dubey laid his hand on the other's paunch, returned firm but calm words. I felt the hostility leak away. The man stepped back. We passed by and headed to the car.

On the dashboard, the familiar statue of Ganesh, the elephant god, wore a fresh string of jasmine around his neck, but the bobble-head Mickey Mouse Wizard doll beside him looked the same.

Dubey had arrived every morning during David's weeks in Mumbai and waited outside the hotel until the valet summoned the car around to the front. It was an hour's drive out to New Bombay, to the company buildings that echoed the flavor of a Microsoft campus at home.

On the last day of David's consulting job, after the fog of thirteen and a half time zones had begun to lift from my head, Dubey took me around old Mumbai—to the

Gateway of India on the harbor, to Victoria Terminus
with its incongruous gothic gargoyles, to the musty Mani
Bhavan—Ghandi's home during his visits to the city that
was then called Bombay. I stood before that spinning
wheel and rope bed and took history directly into my
veins.

There was one more stop I wanted to make, something that captured me when I read the description in
the guidebook: "At Mumbai's municipal laundry or
dhobi ghat some five thousand men use rows of open-
air troughs to beat the dirt out of the thousands of kilograms of soiled clothes brought from all over the city
each day. The best view is from the bridge across the
railway tracks near Mahalaxmi train station."

"I come back pick you up over there, Madame. Ten
minutes O.K.?" said Dubey.

Through the glare of the sun I sorted through a tangle
of parked cars and tried to memorize the spot he meant.
My scalp prickled with sweat. From the bridge I looked
out over honeycombed acres of cement tubs holding men
whose skin was chocolate slick from the water that rose
up their calves. With lungis pulled between their legs like
pantaloons, they bent to scrub, beat, and twist. On lines
above, flags of jewel-tone saris: sapphire, garnet, citrine,
emerald, lapis. Next to the tubs, sheets of corrugated tin
slanted against the sun: the roofs of the washers' homes.

I felt a tug on my skirt, then the brush of fingers
across my arm. "Five rupees, only five rupees." I coiled
away from the dangle of plastic birds a little boy was
waving in my face. Something pressed against the
sweaty damp at the back of my shirt and I spun into a
girl with matted hair and crusty eyes, palm out. "Water."
I handed her my half-drunk bottle. Then pleading from
a woman with a baby held close in a dirty sling. More

bodies, more dark eyes. I tried to tamp down a strangle of panic. Had it been ten minutes? Where was Dubey? I couldn't remember where he said he'd meet me. Then I saw him, half standing out the driver's side, beckoning me to the car.

I reeled free and curled into the backseat as Dubey waved off my followers and closed the door. The woman with the baby rapped on the window as we pulled away. "Many beggars here, Madame," he said.

I held a fresh bottle of water against my forehead, searched for calm in the cool beads of condensation. I wished his English were better. I wanted to ask him about these beggars. What was the right thing to do? Where did they live? Did they have homes? Were they like the people I'd seen living by the side of the road, only a blue plastic tarp for shelter?

"You have children, Dubey?"

"Yes, two daughters, one fifteen, other is twelve. And one son."

"Are you from Mumbai?"

"No, Madame. Madhya Pradesh. North. Come Mumbai find job."

I asked if there was a store nearby where I could buy roasted cashews. I hadn't had lunch. He handed back a plastic bag of chips, crisp waffle-cut potatoes with the whiff of curry. A snack his wife had made for him.

"You want go shopping, Madame? Look only. No have to buy. O.K. look only. We have time." I wasn't in the mood to shop. It was the same all over Asia: the hard sell, the bargaining, the commission to the driver who brought you there. But I couldn't find the will to say no.

Like fresh meat on a grill, I was soon being roasted over the rustle of cellophane packaging as the shopkeeper pulled out tablecloth after tablecloth and snapped them open for my inspection. "What size you like? What color? Elephants? Flowers? Perhaps Pashmina shawl. Blue? Green? Feel how soft. I give you good price. You like some tea?"

Seeking relief, I gave in. "You take Visa?"

Dubey was telling us how expensive Hotel Samar was, how we'd pay for a full night even though we used the room for only a few hours before our flight home, how one small bottle of water cost 100 rupees. "But we have a reservation," David said. Steering the car through the exit gate of the airport parking lot, Dubey made a call on his cell phone. "No problem, Sir. Reservation no more." I raised my eyebrows and David leaned forward to speak to him. "But we need a hotel."

"Not worry Sir. I find good place for you."

He was on his cell phone again, and then I realized he was talking to us in English, but I couldn't find the border between Dubey's phone conversation and what he was saying to us. I turned to David who was better at understanding, but he just shrugged and shook his head. "Today my day off" I picked out from the haze of words. His voice felt slow and thick and his driving was loose and lacked its usual demonic focus. Was he drunk? No note of alcohol in the car. Ganja? Stoned perhaps. I began to watch him more closely.

"He very bad boss, Australian, scold me if even five minute late. I work for him six months. Never one time ask about my family."

What was that all about? He was so chatty. On the phone again, one hand on the wheel, steering past a Sikh temple netted with twinkling lights. Was he talking to his wife? To a hotel? I scooted across to David. "Where are we? Where is he taking us?"

"I think it's O.K.," he replied.

What choice did we have? Get out of the car with our bags and find a taxi to take us to a hotel? We had little idea where we were. Better to stick with Dubey.

He put down the cell phone. "I take you Reliance guesthouse, near airport." Reliance. The company David had been working for. A huge multinational, with properties all over India. A guesthouse near the airport made sense.

"What time your plane tonight, Sir? 2 A.M.? International flight always very late. How much your ticket cost?"

We were not surprised at his question. In Asia there is no shame in asking how much something costs or how big your salary or how much you paid for your car. "About twelve hundred dollars, 60,000 rupees, roundtrip."

Dinner at the guesthouse began with soup, a broth infused with saffron and shreds of carrots. David and I sat across from each other, by ourselves at a dining room table for eight. The houseboy brought chicken curry, aloo gobi, chappatis, rice, and dal.

We had rested, showered, made love, repacked our bags, prepped for the long hours of travel that lay ahead. In an end-of-trip ritual, we counted out our money on the bed, not wanting to leave the country with a pile of unspent foreign coins and notes. We set aside enough rupees for departure tax, enough for a big tip for Dubey, and some leftover for shopping at the airport. And then we went in to dinner. We saw no other guests. We hadn't seen Dubey since he had dropped us off and helped us carry our luggage to the room.

"Where are we?" I asked. I reached for a warm chappati. David was the one with the sense of direction, the one who could stay oriented to a city, a landscape, like a migrating bird. "I'm not exactly sure," he said.

I was surrounded by mysteries I wanted to solve. I wanted to know if our room, cleaned upon our arrival while we waited in the dining room, belonged to someone else, who was, perhaps, just gone for the night. What had Dubey done to get us in here? Would we, should we pay for this? Dubey had waved away our questions, but I wondered if he understood what we were asking. And aside from the houseboy and Dubey, no one else seemed to be around.

"Do you think Reliance is covering this?" I asked, even as I knew that David wasn't concerned, wasn't burdened by the questions that buzzed in me. But because he loves me he tried to find an answer that would satisfy me.

"They paid for everything else." He had little difficulty accepting this as more corporate largesse. "This is a lot like the guesthouse I stayed in the second week I was here."

In the midnight darkness of the backseat, I couldn't see the exhaust of cars and trucks crowded around us, but I could smell the blue seeping through the rolled-up window.

Dubey checked the rearview mirror to make sure I was listening. "My two daughters, Madame, they are fine. No problem. But my son, teachers say he need special school. School cost 35,000 rupees every year. 35,000! My salary only 10,000. What to do, Madame?"

I changed rupees to dollars in my head: $700 a year for the school on a $200 a year salary. I was unprepared for such small sums. What David had given Dubey for tips during our time in Mumbai probably added up to several months' salary. Good. David reached around and pulled more bills from his wallet to add to the ones he already had in his hand. But we both knew it did not come close to what Dubey needed for his son.

The plane shuddered through turbulence an hour out of Mumbai; eight more to Paris, the first leg of our journey home. The green glow of the seat belt sign kept us strapped in place. David was already asleep. I stuffed in my earplugs against the whine of the engines and leaned back, but I could not find rest.

Outside the chaos of the airport departure hall, David had pressed rupees and dollars into Dubey's hand, but it was my eyes that Dubey sought. His question hovered in the space between us, fragile as tissue paper that would rip if I took a breath to speak. I had no reply for him, only silent doubts. If we gave him $700 would he spend it on his son or on ganja? Was he telling the truth? Did his wife direct him to ask the American lady for money? Could the special school do what was needed for his son? Did the teachers know what they were talking about?

In the darkness of the cabin, I pulled apart the problem of my unearned power, my craving for certainty. I tried to trace the lines, angles, surfaces of his life. A tide of guilt rose in my throat even as the logic of my questions pushed it down.

It was too late to give him an answer. No, that was not true. We had walked away and into the airport. We did not ask for his address, did not give him ours. He had our answer.

~*~ ~*~ ~*~

Nancy Penrose lives in Seattle. She is a lifelong traveler who writes to explore the territories where cultures converge. She was the Grand Prize winner in the Summer 2008 issue of Memoir (and) *for her essay "The Warp of Memory." Her story, "Flamenco Form," won the Grand Prize Silver Award in the first annual Solas Awards.*

ℐℬ ℐℬ ℐℬ

Ylli's Gifts

They found a modern-day Ulysses
on an Albanian beach.

"Your name," I say. "What…is…your…name?"
The goatherd's chocolate-chip eyes register
confusion.

It's high-noon hot on a forsaken beach in Dhermi,
Albania. My friend and I are trying to strike up a conversation with the only other soul around.

I point to myself and bleat *Jaaaannn*. Then to my
friend. *Maaaah-ni-ka*.

His face lights up as if I've thrown a switch. He pokes
a finger at his toast-brown torso and produces something like *Ewlee*, puckering his crusty lips for the "Ew"
and blowing it out hard, French-style. With a flourish,
he scrawls his name in the pebbly sand: *YLLI*.

"Ah, Ulysses!" Monica says. "He looks like the real deal."

That's for damn sure. He's all sinew and bone and muscle, wild and woolly-headed. Hardscrabble.

"How many?" Monica flicks her chin at the herd of jet-black goats, then pantomimes counting on her fingers.

Ylli says something in Albanian, then bends over again and draws in the sand: *260*. He waves a finger at the rocky range rearing up behind us. His village, apparently, roosts up there somewhere. He and his goats have made the long trek down to the beach, where the cool waters of the Adriatic meet the warmth of the Ionian Sea.

Ylli mugs for my camera. He cavorts with the goats, squints at the sun, hoists his baggy pants up at the waist, flexes his biceps.

I capture the stranger against the wide blue water, all foamy at the edges, with Corfu hazy in the distance. I catch him in a sun-halo, feral and fierce. I frame him soldier-stiff in a line of cypresses, backdropped by a cliff as craggy as his looks.

The Cika range rises breathtakingly to over two thousand meters. A milky mist hangs on the peaks like a thick secret. There are no tourists here, or for that matter anywhere we've been in Albania. Though our beach feels like terra incognita, it's soaked in history. The Byzantines, Ottomans, and Venetians have come and gone. Philip V of Macedon was here in 214 B.C., and Julius Caesar during the Roman civil wars. The ghost of former dictator Enver Hoxha lingers, too, around the bunkers near the shore that he built to ward off "the Anglo-American threat."

Ylli motions for us to sit. He draws a penknife from his duffel bag, and two overripe pomegranates. He ceremoniously slices the top off each fruit, makes six surgical incisions, and peels back the leathery skin so the seeds pop out for the plucking. We pry them from the honeycombs one by one, dropping them slowly onto our tongues, where they explode like Pop Rocks.

"This," Monica says, licking her fuchsia fingertips, "very, very good. *Buonissimo.*"

Ylli digs deeper into his bag and scoops out a cache of whole walnuts. He centers each one on a smooth flat stone, then delivers a sharp blow with a rock, cracking the shells wide open. He offers up nut after nut, gentle and generous gifts wrapped in chapped hands.

A hush falls. Time melts. A picnic with starched linens and champagne flutes could be no finer.

Our host stubbornly refuses to eat a thing, following the rules of *mikpriste*—the Albanian code of Homeric hospitality. *Mikpriste* has enveloped us like armor in Albania, deflating the Embassy warnings against independent travel for women.

The herd's headlong dash down the beach interrupts our idyll. Ylli yelps a curse and lobs a few fat stones. The goats whine and skitter in reverse. Then he springs up, bare feet crunching on hot sand. He muscles his way into the herd, tackles a black kid, and plops it, flush with pride, at our toes. We coo like doves. The kid's hair is soft and rank. As Ylli nuzzles his plush toy, it lunges at my hand. Bites the half-eaten pomegranate. Ylli lets out a bark of laughter.

We smell the sun searing our grainy arms. Time to go. Fumbling in our backpacks, we unearth a Tootsie Roll and a grape-colored flashlight, the only booty we've got other than passports, cash, and lipstick. Ylli unwraps the candy and inspects its gummy surface.

"*Droga?*" he grins.

He's more intrigued by the Long-Life flashlight. He turns it on and off, around and around. His brow folds, as if to say *where's the battery?* But it's batteryless, and we're stumped, too. The three of us look at each other, shrug, and laugh.

Ylli drums his chest, an Albanian gesture of heartfelt thanks. We follow suit.

"*Mirupafshim*, Bye!" we shout over our burnt shoulders on the way to inspect a bunker.

It's the dark heart of Albania—chill and *pissoir*-pungent. Through the narrow gun slit, I see a mass of black at the water's edge. Ylli has shed his trousers to reveal hot pink bathing trunks. He's charging past his flock, sea-hungry, arms like madcap windmills. The bunker echoes with his full-throated whoops.

He has nearly vanished into Poseidon's realm as we leave the beach. Only his corkscrew curls bob on the waves.

"Do you ever fantasize about a man like that?" Monica asks, shooting me a glance.

We erupt in giggles. But we know the enchantment is not physical. It's magical. We have escaped the twenty-first century and crossed a long bridge back in time to lotus land—to a place where Helios spread his warmth, Triton romped in the sea, and languages were one.

Jann Huizenga is a writer and photographer from Santa Fe, New Mexico. This story won first prize in the Book Passage Travel Writers and Photographers Conference essay contest, 2007.

LAURIE GOUGH

✿ ✿ ✿

Lost in Jamaica

In Negril, a town founded by hippies, the author
explores its hedonistic ways.

*J*amaica's taxi vans are notorious for being over-
crowded and mine was no exception. Even though
our taxi was packed beyond capacity, the driver kept
stopping for every person who held out a hand along
the road. I soon had on top of me a Jamaican woman of
abundant flesh and enormous breasts who thought it was
the funniest joke in the world that she was squishing me.
Despite losing circulation in one leg, I loved flying along
the bumpy ride to Negril, passing cane fields, fertile
mountains, wooden huts with corrugated roofs, fishing
villages, children waving, and the occasional glimpse of
the turquoise sea. All this was accompanied by the good-
humored passengers who laughed easily and took life
merrily, had a zest and affection for life unparalleled in
northern climates. The sun poured down on a dazzling

103

world of indigo blue and fairytale green, a world brimming with tropical abundance—the cries of birds and
uproar of insects, extravagant blossoms, giant white
lilies, wild red orchids and jasmine drenched in scent.
In all directions, wild beauty was shrieking with life.
The Jamaican wind whipped back my braids, the giant
laughing woman crushed my body, and the glory of the
earth radiated around me.

When we arrived at Negril, the pile of us spilling out
of the van like gushing water, the driver called out to
me, "A hope yu like yu trip a Jamaica," and sped away.

Negril was founded by European and American hippies and by the time I was there it had gained a reputation for hedonism and a swinging night life. Yet, it had a
small village atmosphere with many cheap places to stay
and several campgrounds dotting the beach....

Every evening I'd watch the sun dip into the sea, the
sky bleeding as if it had been stabbed, and listen to palm
fronds rattling in the breeze. Afterwards I'd usually find
a live band at a reggae or calypso bar on the beach where
I'd dance for hours under the stars. It was something
of a dream, my Negril days on the turquoise bay, but I
wanted more. Even though I was relatively new to the
traveler's life, I knew a beach vacation wasn't all I was
looking for. That's why when I met Joan and she invited
me to stay with her, I jumped at the chance.

Joan was a full-size Jamaican woman with generous hips and a curvaceous, assured body which seemed
incongruous with the shy expression on her face. She had
Hershey syrup eyes which warmed when she asked me to
try on one of the straw hats she sold. She also sold t-shirts,
necklaces and colorful shorts at one of the beach stalls of
Negril's market under the trees. I guessed her to be in her

late twenties or early thirties but it was hard to say. After we'd been talking a while and I'd told her how I wanted to see more of Jamaica's countryside, she said, "You come stay with me and my family in my village. You like it there. It's by the river. My kids would love you."

I took the bus with Joan to her village of Little London the next evening. The highway east from Negril crosses several miles of swampland before emerging onto the vast Westmoreland Plain with its cane fields, pastureland and small villages. As we approached Little London, the roads narrowed and curved, becoming thick with voluptuous vegetation. Blossoms swirled off branches, and as night fell quickly upon us, the tropic's stirring scent combination of palm oil and jasmine filled my nostrils with an unfamiliar longing.

From the bus stop, we walked down a dirt road under a sky rhapsodic with stars, then went down a country lane until Joan stopped in front of a wooden shack lit up from within by the dim glow of lanterns. We stood for a moment in the quiet night, looking upwards. "Sometimes moonshine lights it all up instead of the stars," she said, then pointed to the house. "That's where I live. Come."

Within seconds of walking through the door I was surrounded by at least twenty people, half of them children. It was a sudden flurry of commotion in the little house as relatives rushed to shake my hand and kiss me, one girl calling me, "My Lady," giggling. I met Joan's three kids and her brothers: Glen, Graham and someone who I was sure said his name was Shirley. I met cousins, nephews, and nieces, and then, from another room, arched over a cane yet entering like royalty, came Miss Sylvia—Mamma to the rest of them. The others cleared a path for her as she shuffled towards me with her arm outstretched, smiling as if welcoming a long-lost daughter. A toothless vision of timeless beauty, and clearly, the head of the entire household, Miss Sylvia had what can only be described as wisdom in her face, a face that I noticed immediately was fully prepared in its openness to look directly into mine.

Like many in the family, Miss Sylvia didn't speak much English—she spoke the Jamaican patois—but we seemed to communicate nonetheless. "Me run tings here," she told me proudly that evening, and I could see that indeed she did. Everyone revered her. In the days to come I'd learn that not only are the elders of Jamaica deeply respected, but the women of Jamaica hold the real power. I came to believe that Jamaican society, desperately poor, dispossessed, wracked with economic instability and violence, is kept from some terrible and final dissolution by the courage and nobility of its women.

That night I slept in a bed with two of Joan's little children, Tracy and Vinard, and realized for the first time that sleeping in a bed with children gives one fanciful, child-like dreams, something I'd notice again in Fiji a few years later. Just before the sun rose, the shrieking of fifty insane roosters began rousing the world, and Joan entered the room through a curtain, slapping little Tracy awake: "Git-up! Git up!" I found Joan's abrupt wake-up technique alarming but would soon learn that a Jamaican child in the countryside is expected to do chores much of the day: making beds, washing clothes, preparing food, cleaning the house. Not wanting to appear lazy, I jumped up out of bed too, ready to help with the chores. After all, what was I doing there anyway?

The children took me to the river that morning, showed me how they washed clothes with a washboard, and laughed when I did it wrong. Later, we went to visit Miss Sylvia who lived alone in a small shack near the river. She was cooking rice outside over a fire and offered me a bowl. It was difficult to guess her age. She carried herself with such noble grace, it seemed she must have been living since the last century. Her bones were just barely hiding beneath the surface of her translucent skin and cataracts filmed over her green eyes. She wore a big straw hat and smiled the entire day as if she found the world perpetually amusing. I looked into her deeply etched face and thought of how as our bodies shrivel, we become our faces. Our bodies shrink, crumple, lose their robustness, while the face gains distinction and beauty. How sad that we don't see enough old faces in the youth-crazed West, I thought. Surely some ethical damage occurs when the faces of old people aren't on view, or their faces have been tucked, pulled, and made-over, preventing wisdom from seeping through the cracks. It seems dishonest to keep hidden what becomes of our true faces. Our souls must notice what we do with them. We live these long and magnificent lives to develop lines on our faces, much like the world itself lives to develop lines on its face, and we should never be afraid of how that face looks.

I wondered what Miss Sylvia's life had been like. I wondered what became of her husband. Was he dead or had he just left one day? Already I'd noticed the odd lack of men in the countryside. It wasn't as if there were no men, they just disappeared into the background, drinking Red Stripe beer on the curbs and watching women stroll by with baskets of laundry or the day's food on their heads. The women seemed to do all the work, took full responsibility for the children, and managed the entire household. The men seemed adolescent.

Fifty percent of Jamaican households are run by single mothers and each child in the families I saw seemed to be fathered by a different man.

That afternoon I met Shirley again, Joan's oldest brother, who lived by himself in a hut next door to Miss Sylvia. For some reason I found Shirley to be a fascinating figure, not just because of his name, or the way he dressed—yellow and white striped pants that were a foot too short for him, a screaming bright floral shirt, and a headband that looked suspiciously like a J-cloth—but because of his innocence. "Tell me where you live, Miss Laurie," he said, his voice betraying a craving for worldly things. "Tell me which way Canada is from here."

I thought about which direction north would be. "There, Canada is that way." I pointed north.

Shirley knotted his forehead in puzzlement and said, "No, that be where Aunty Charlene live, in Grange Hill town. You don't live by her."

We stood staring at each other for what felt like a full minute.

"Well, way beyond where Aunty Charlene lives. Canada is another country, way beyond the water, in North America, north of the United States, not part of Jamaica. Jamaica is an island."

His eyes widened to alarming proportions, his face filling to the brim with wonder at this news. Perhaps we all do this on some level, I thought, experience ourselves as the primary center of the universe. Shirley was just taking this tendency to extremes.

"Wait here, Miss Laurie." Shirley disappeared into his hut and soon came running back with a tattered world map taken from an old *National Geographic*. We unfolded it. The kids and Miss Sylvia gathered around as did some passers-by from the road. Immediately the map created bewilderment. It took a while to establish the basics of what was continent and ocean, what was Jamaica, the other Caribbean islands, and what was Africa, from where these people's ancestors had come.

Gazing at the map with my new friends, I felt as if I were seeing the multi-colored display of countries for the first time. Suddenly it seemed miraculous that we all exist in this floating blue world on islands big and small, islands spread across this worn map that was causing such wonder and disbelief. The map seemed to communicate its magic to some degree in all of us, as if a foreign vibration were quivering through the air. Finally, Shirley shook his head. "No, Miss Laurie. I think you fooling us." Miss Sylvia looked at me suspiciously, and for a brief moment I thought maybe they were right in their suspicions. Theirs was a geography uncomplicated by facts, lines of latitude and tropics of cancer. I recalled how I'd once memorized all the capital cities in Africa and how this never proved useful in real life. Here, all these people knew was their small turquoise island and still their eyes shone with the things they had seen.

On Sunday nights in the Jamaican countryside, people celebrate and go to "town," which in Little London meant walking up and down the road to watch everyone else walk up and down the road, and maybe, if people were brave enough, they'd look in the window of the ramshackle roadside bar at the crossroads to see what unspeakable events were occurring inside. Some of the men would even enter the bar, giggling, while their girlfriends and children watched from the windows. Everyone, including the children, got dressed up in their finest clothes for the big night out, and the women and girls spent hours doing each other's hair.

As we set out on the road, the children clamored to hold my hands, some of them skipping ahead in excitement, eager to point out to me who everyone was. We walked for miles. The women don't really walk, they meander, they mosey, while the men swagger. We stopped often to admire each other's hair and clothes, to chat and laugh, until the stars came out, and we came to the crossroads bar.

Joan's cousin Melba was a wild card of whimsy, a ham, a trickster, a woman of ecstatic enthusiasm for everything she encountered, and she explained to me on the walk that she was determined to go into the bar that night for the first time in her life. In fact, she'd been planning it for months. Her sisters and cousins didn't believe she'd do it, and either cheered her on or tried to discourage her. "Oh, no, yu cyan go in dat place! Dat place evil. You don't know what happening in der. The women bad in dat place."

We stood outside the little bar gazing through its dusty windows like street urchins. I felt ten years old and wondered why we didn't just go inside, not that it looked very appealing. I would rather have kept walking under the stars. Still, I was curious about the bar. It was dark inside with just a few red light bulbs hanging down to illuminate the faces of the ten or twelve men inside, mostly young men, who sat on stools drinking beer and watching the empty dirt corral of a dance floor with an anticipatory air. Music blared, but evidently, nobody was ready to dance. In a corner of the bar, I noticed three women in miniskirts laughing amongst themselves.

Melba stood outside the door looking resolute, although just as she was about to open the door, I thought I saw a shadow of fear darken her face. Finally, she shouted at us, "Mi gawn!" and walked inside.

The rest of us resumed our positions by the windows. The men inside were clearly surprised by Melba's sudden entry, calling things out to tease her, things I didn't catch. She made her way towards the line of men while the women and the children next to me either laughed uproariously or were shocked into silence. Clearly this was an unprecedented event.

We watched and waited for something to happen and finally, something did. A slow song began to play over the jukebox. The song was "Unchained Melody" by the Righteous Brothers and in my memory I recall that it thankfully was not a reggae version of that old tune. Melba stood up and walked alone towards the dance floor. The men at the bar cheered her, as did those of us outside, but very quickly, we grew quiet. I think at first we all assumed she was trying to impress one of the boys at the bar and we speculated on who he might be. It soon became clear, however, that the boys at the bar had nothing to do with Melba's intentions that night.

Once she reached the middle of the floor, Melba stood still for a moment and I noticed that something miraculous was happening to her face: it was opening up like a flower. Then, gradually, her body began to move, slowly at first, around and around, with her arms outstretched as if reaching for something beyond what she'd find in the bar, on the road, or anywhere in the village. She twirled and swayed perfectly in time to the music, eventually throwing in inspired and unconventional versions of ballet, modern dance and even an occasional head thrust from the tango. She was ethereal, as if she'd had dancing lessons from God, creating another world not only for herself, but for all those who watched her. We stared at her with a sense of awe bordering on the religious. Melba, who people thought was merely a jokester, had become a beacon of light, hope, erotic spirit, and whirling brown arms. Never had I seen anyone with such a storm of beauty.

And then, as soon as it had started, it was over and the jukebox began playing a reggae version of a Phil Collins song. Melba came back outside. She didn't say anything and neither did we. We all walked back along the road, a road that now looked strangely altered. I'm not sure if anyone else felt this way, but to me it felt as if we were walking through a different world, a world that was from some golden age of human happiness, attained sometimes by children, but rarely by adults, as if the world was full of promise and hidden mystery, as if it were just beginning. I suddenly felt as if my own life was just beginning and I'd just learned everything I needed to know.

I had to leave Little London soon after that because I burned my leg. Joan's brother Graham had taken me on his motorbike through Cockpit Country, a succession of wild wooded hills stretching mile after uninhabited mile. On the way back, he let me drive. On a small dirt road, Graham shouted something over my shoulder that I didn't catch, so I slowed down to hear him. Of course, as always there was the question of communication. He spoke both Patois and English, but he didn't speak English in a style normally associated with the language, and even when I stopped the bike entirely, I still couldn't make out what he was saying. Thinking perhaps he wanted to drive again, I got off the bike. As I was doing this, I happened to put my calf directly down on the hot muffler, a muffler not covered by any sort of protective plate, and I burned my leg. Stupidly, I was wearing shorts that day. Graham told me not to worry. He immediately unscrewed the oil cap, pulled out the oil dipstick and proceeded to apply dirty hot engine oil all over my burn. "This good fe yuh," he said proudly. Did he think dirty engine oil had magical curative powers? I yelped in agony. The burning oil felt even worse than the burn itself. It had all happened so fast. If only I'd thought to put on aloe vera which grew all over the place, or even cold water from a nearby stream. Burning myself confirmed in Graham's mind that women shouldn't drive motorized vehicles and the last thing he said before we walked into Joan's house was, "Remember, Miss Laurie, is yu kawz de accident."

He was right that it had been my fault, but regardless, it also meant that the next day I had to leave and go back to Negril to get medical treatment. My leg had gotten much worse overnight. I was sad to leave Little London. I'd miss the family, especially all those sweet kids who continually made their way into the world, and I spent my last morning taking pictures of them, promising to send them copies. I hoped to return to Little London after Negril, perhaps to volunteer teach, but knowing how one place always seems to lead to the next, I couldn't be sure.

I decided to stay at a beach campground in Negril where I rented a tent for a dollar a day. I loved sleeping so close to the ocean, the sea surrounding my sleep, the pounding surf invading my dreams. On the coast, I felt engulfed by tropical rhythms and a pearly orange light. One afternoon as I was walking along the beach, I passed a man who reminded me of a young Robert De Niro: thick brown hair, a shy smirk that either meant mischievousness or intelligence or a combination of the two, and narrow questioning eyes. It occurred to me that it's unwise to compare regular people with movie stars since a regular person can't possibly live up to someone who has clever lines written for him, but I said hi to him anyway and he said hi back. We each kept walking. Then, we each turned around, as if we realized we might be passing by something that looked like fun, or casual distraction, or the question, who are you? which might, later on, lead to a piña colada.

His name was Richard and he was a journalist from Philadelphia. He'd been told about his resemblance to Robert De Niro before. Ten minutes after meeting we were drinking piña coladas at the nearest beach bar and discussing urban travel myths. We also discussed Jamaican politics, Jamaican male chauvinism, and Jamaican food, which made us hungry.

On our long walk down the beach towards Joe's Irie Diner, I learned that Richard had recently broken up with his girlfriend, and this trip was his way of trying to forget her. I kept stealing glances of Richard and the farther we walked and the more he talked about his life as a journalist, the more handsome he became. He seemed so knowledgeable and worldly, while I, only just beginning to discover the world, had much to ask him. Just as he was telling me about his motorcycle trip through South America, however, we ran into Miss Monica, and because of that chance meeting, I never did find out about the rest of his motorcycle trip, or get to know Richard the way I thought I might.

Miss Monica was a very old, hunched smiling woman with a cane and a filigree of crow's feet at her eyes. She stopped us on the beach, asked our names, then went digging into her woven basket, saying she had something that may be of interest to us. I thought she'd show us beaded necklaces, or maybe a seashell shellacked miniature pet with plastic eyes that I'd buy out of sheer guilt. But instead, from her woven basket she produced something that looked like a large piece of banana cake wrapped in wax paper. "It's the ganja cake. I make it every morning. I eat a piece of it myself every afternoon. Only two dollars." She thrust the dark heavy piece of cake in my hand. "Tek it! Tek it!" Miss Monica's eyes burned into mine with a curiously fierce passion.

I wondered if this was how children felt when confronted with drug dealers—the pressure is overwhelming. "I don't know," I said. "I don't like to smoke the stuff myself. How do I know how strong this is? And…"

"This just a nice dessert. It's makes you laugh, feel happy, very mild. Makes the sunset redder."

"Well…"

"Tek it!"

I'm not sure whether it was the cane she kept stomping in the sand or the fire in her old eyes, but Miss Monica was much too good a drug pusher for me to refuse. I bought the cake and must admit the purchase seemed a lot more interesting than any shell souvenir would have been. Richard declined, explaining those days had been over for him since one night years earlier when he'd smoked hashish in a Moroccan bar and woken up the next day, mysteriously, in Algeria.

We continued on to the beachside restaurant where Richard ordered lobster, and I decided that instead of eating dinner, I'd eat my ganja cake.

Only half an hour after eating the innocent-looking dessert, the strangest feeling began to creep over me, literally, as if something were crawling up the back of my head, an electrical surge of power, tingling at first, and then much stronger. The surges persisted as Richard was telling me a story of traveling through a desert in Africa. Suddenly I broke out laughing even though the story wasn't funny. It was his moving mouth that was so hysterical, the fact that words were pouring out of his mouth. I looked down at the sand and noticed a crab scurrying by at a furious pace. The crab seemed to be running sideways yet going forward and I knew then for certainty that these remarkable alien creatures had to have landed here from another planet, just like the spores of mushrooms. Loudly enough for all those at the restaurant to hear, I pointed at the crab and shouted, "Alien! They're all aliens!" I looked at the giant tree beside our table and nearly keeled over when I realized the tree had an actual soul that I was seeing. It wasn't just a tree, but a living, breathing, thinking, feeling creature who was fully aware I'd just discovered this and was trying to tell me something. "What? What?" I asked the tree. I could see its shimmering aura. I looked at Richard's lobster and was appalled that those animals had been swimming just moments before, truly alarmed that they were going into Richard's mouth which was also pouring out words, although by then, Richard wasn't talking so much as gaping at me in horror.

I couldn't stay seated and felt compelled to walk along the shoreline. It seemed to take forever to get there, as if I were on a treadmill, even though the ocean was less than forty feet away. Richard followed closely behind me. Suddenly, patterns began popping out at me: the pattern on the upper edges of my mother's cat eye glasses that she wore when I was a baby, followed by the exact design on what must have been my baby spoon. All those swirls on the spoon and on my mother's glasses I must have studied intently before the age of one. They'd been imprinted on my brain and were now resurfacing with disturbing persistence. I could almost reach out and touch them, and I couldn't make them go away.

Walking on the sand, I was overcome with the feeling that there is no such thing as linear time, that everything is the perpetual present, everything existing at once in a single flash of intensity. My thoughts were jumping from frame to frame, thought to thought, with no memory of how I'd arrived at each moment. The thoughts were flying far too fast to hold on to, to process. Words were wholly inadequate. In fact, I wasn't sure if I was forming sentences at all, although I had a sense I was having a conversation with Richard.

I arrived at the edge of the ocean with its shimmering green surface, the sea lapping gently under the moon. The moonlight sparkling on the water was the most real thing I'd ever seen, fragile and pulsing with life, and I was flabbergasted it had traveled all this distance through the atmosphere to shine on my skin. "I'm not separated from the otherness of things," I realized with elation, although whether I said that out loud or not, I didn't know. All I knew was I was getting a secret peek into another world that had been here all along. I kept thinking that this was like Plato's allegory about the people living in the cave, the people who believed the shadows on the cave walls were the reality because they couldn't see the real life that was making the shadows. In the cave they were chained to their limited view of their world, not realizing there was something beyond outside the cave. On this Jamaican beach, I realized, I'm getting out of the cave, no longer seeing the shadows but what makes the shadows, the reality behind everything.

I also realized Plato must have been on drugs to have thought that up.

Staring at the ocean I felt overwhelmed by ancient memories of a universe forgotten for eons. The moon and stars were bursting out of the sky, thoughts were flaming through the atmosphere, and the wind, alive and amused, was breathing sea salt into my lungs. Everything was familiar, yet everything was new. I felt all the light of the entire galaxy beam down on me, and I reflected that light back until I was glowing like a human-shaped star.

I was as high as a kite.

For a while, I was visiting my childhood, lost after so many years, where the touch of water was as electrifying as it was when I was four. I continued to look out at the sea for what could have been either five minutes or an hour, and then gradually, something truly frightening began to happen: I felt as if I were entering the throbbing heart of the earth itself, deeper and deeper into the soft and flaming core of the planet. The moment seemed to take up my whole life.

I'd now plunged into much too broad a spectrum of reality and I'd had no idea it was that immense. I wanted out. The reality became overwhelming, all powerful, and I longed to get back to everyday life, back to the everyday surface of the earth where so little reality is allowed. Later, I read that Aldous Huxley had the same experience on his famous mescalin trip: "Anything rather than the burning brightness of unmitigated Reality—anything!"

I walked farther along the beach, trying to grasp each thought, but the thoughts were whizzing through me at lightning speed. Did Miss Monica really say she ate this stuff every day? She had to be eighty-three. I passed a reggae show at a beach bar and although normally I would have ventured over there, at that point, the idea seemed absurd. Richard kept asking me questions: Are you disconnected from your body? Do you want some iced tea? Do I still look like Robert De Niro? A woman in her forties, Swedish perhaps, approached and began spraying me with a storm of words. She spoke at some length, the words growing harsher and more guttural. I couldn't comprehend a thing she said. What she was doing or saying was a complete mystery, even with my grossly heightened perceptual advantage. I stared at her for several moments, trying to be normal, but was too high to make it stick.

I walked on. I wanted water. Never had I been so thirsty. I came to an almond tree and threw myself under it while Richard went off to find me a drink. Looking up through the branches of the tree I was absorbed in its inner workings, its shining leaves, twisting limbs, and multitude of textures. Until that night I'd never really *seen* a tree before, probably not since I was one or two, too young to be able to label it a tree. Now, like an amazed baby, I was back in the world of pure perception, where things aren't subordinated to a concept: that's a tree, that's a house, that's a person. I was seeing, as Aldous Huxley described, "the miracle, moment by moment, of naked existence."

All I could manage was to sit very still. Even looking down at the sand for too long was dangerous as I became lost in every extraordinary grain. Then, from behind me, two young Jamaican boys approached, asking if I'd like to buy peanuts. I said no thank you, but after that, more peanut boys appeared, and then more, every few minutes, an occurrence I found deeply unsettling. I kept whipping my head around to look for them and more kept coming. "Peanuts! Peanuts!" they called, their voices alternately clanging in my ears, then fading with the sound of the surf as they continued down the beach. I felt very afraid. I've glimpsed into the abyss, I thought, and it's full of little boys selling peanuts.

Finally, Richard returned with a large bottle of water which I guzzled.

"What's happening to you?" he kept asking.

"Too many thoughts, too many thoughts. Sorry about all this."

He tried to tell a story but I couldn't make sense of it. Finally, when he realized his story wasn't being absorbed, he stopped and said, "There are more planets in the universe than grains of sand on earth." The enormity of this practically shut down my brain.

After a while, I began to run along the beach and eventually found the campground, where I fell into my tent. Staring up towards the sky, I began to drift backward in time, back three years to my twenty-year-old self, then back to my seventeen-year-old self, and farther back, to every year preceding that until I was very young. I recalled with exact precision how I looked, felt, and what I thought about at all those ages, even what my clothes looked like, my various haircuts throughout the years, who all my friends had been. All of our selves remain hidden inside us as we age, I discovered with surprise. And then, I felt as if I were going back even farther, beyond this life, and into the womb itself, which felt very much like the center of the earth where I'd been earlier that night. Suddenly, I came to an explosion of flaming brilliant color and blinding light like the sun itself—the point of conception perhaps? Should I ask my mother about this? Jesus. At that point I thought surely I was dying, never to return, and must have fallen into a deep sleep. I dreamt of my mother reading our hometown newspaper with an article and a picture on the front cover about a girl who'd gone to Jamaica and died of a marijuana overdose administered by an octogenarian with a cane.

The girl in the picture looked happy though, as if she'd had a pleasant vacation.

I was amazed to open my eyes the next day, amazed to be alive. I hadn't died after all, and was incredibly happy about this. I stumbled out of my tent, groggy and elated, and went searching for as much pineapple-coconut juice as I could acquire. At the market I ran into one of the local Rastafarians with one of the old-fashioned English names—Winston or Emerson or Winchester—and he told me he'd heard I'd met Miss Monica and asked me how my night had been. I tried to describe some of my night but didn't know where to begin. He interrupted. "God gave us the sacred plant so we can see more of the world. The sacred plant allows humans, trees and animals to communicate. It's our translator." I understood what he meant. If he'd told me this the day before, I would have thought him the world's biggest flake. The thought occurred to me that perhaps now, after my enlightening night, I'd be considered a little out there myself.

After finding my pineapple-coconut juice and sitting down on the sand, a friendly, middle-aged couple from Ohio came by. The woman stopped and looked down at me. "Oh, we remember you from last night, Dear. You were the girl who spent fifteen minutes telling us about the virtues of the color green."

I had no memory of that discussion, or those people, whatsoever.

I thought I should leave Jamaica as soon as possible after that. My leg was badly infected and I was worried about gangrene, and besides, I'd seen enough of the place, and in fact, enough of the entire universe, to last me the rest of my life. It was time to leave the fabled little island that would from now on, for me, glow with a kind of supercharged emerald and luminous light that might be difficult to diffuse. I needed a paler, winter light, and perhaps, a sudden rush of cold air.

ॐ ॐ ॐ

Laurie Gough is author of Kiss the Sunset Pig, *from which
this story was extracted from a longer story about Jamaica, and*
Kite Strings of the Southern Cross, *shortlisted for the Thomas
Cook Travel Book Award, and silver medal winner of* ForeWord
Magazine's *Travel Book of the Year in the U.S. Her stories have
appeared in travel anthologies such as Salon.com's* Wanderlust;
AWOL: Tales for Travel-Inspired Minds; Sand in My Bra; *and*
Hyenas Laughed at Me and Now I Know Why: The Best of
Travel Humor and Misadventure. *She has written for Salon.com,*
The L.A. Times, The Globe and Mail, The National Post,
The Vancouver Sun, Outpost, Canadian Geographic, The
Daily Express, In London, *and* World Hum. *See her web site*
www.lauriegough.com.

※ ※ ※

The Ringer

An American girl plays the field in Kenya.

t low tide, the white sands of Mombasa's northern beaches stretch nearly half a mile out to sea. The shore is framed by palm trees, run-down hotel buildings, and wooden stalls selling fried cassava chips and cold Coca-Cola; in the distance, the vivid blue of the Indian Ocean is flecked with the faded colors of tiny fishing boats anchored in the shallow water.

In my hometown of San Diego, California, a beach of this size would be crawling with toddlers in floppy hats, skinny girls in skinnier bikinis turning on their towels like meat on a spit, and hairy men dozing in bright trunks.

In Kenya, the girls are fully covered and the men play soccer.

I sit at the periphery of a game of local boys and watch with an eye to join. The field runs about forty yards

124 JENNY D. WILLIAMS

along the beach, sticks standing upright in the sand marking the goal posts at each end. Width is determined by the tide. There are thirteen players, meaning one side is a man short. This could be my ticket in.

There are strategies to joining a pickup game and rules to abide by. You have to size up the teams and the style of play—are there designated positions? Is the action mostly passing or dribbling? How seriously are they taking the game?

Most importantly: am I going to get my ass kicked?

There's an additional factor when you're a girl attempting to join a game of men, especially in a country like Kenya where serious women's sports are still something of a novelty. Being among the conservative constituency of Kenya's predominantly Muslim coast doesn't help either. Context, I conclude, might be working against me.

It's a position I've been in before. In college I played in a regular pickup game with a crew of guys from Iran, Japan, Argentina, Scotland, Ghana, and a dozen other countries—many of whom hadn't realized that girls could play. Although they were skeptical to begin with, my background on a national championship team served me well, and I soon earned a place on the field.

Now, as I sit on the warm sands of the Indian Ocean coastline, I weigh my status. It's been over a year since I touched a soccer ball. My current aerobic capacity, to put it generously, is somewhat lacking, considering my greatest exertion the past month has been running to catch a departing *matatu*. Plus I've never played in deep sand like this.

Even so, I've been watching this game for twenty minutes, and I think I can hold my own. I'm taking mental notes on which players seem to be on the same team, which ones have skills, and which ones have already cast a curious glance in my direction.

Someone takes a shot and it goes wide, sending the ball rolling far behind the goal line; one guy jogs after it. As the other players mill about, I decide to make my move.

"Hey," I offer to a defender idling close by. "Is this an open game?"

He gives me a blank look. "You want to play?"

"Yeah. Can I join?"

He hesitates, then looks at a teammate who shrugs in response.

"Sure," he says, turning back to me with a grin. "You can play on this team, we need one more."

Introductions are made all around, and I promptly forget everyone's name except Mohammed, the guy who let me on. Off to a good start.

I spend a few minutes outside the main action, trying to get my bearings. I'm wearing the only clothes I brought to the beach—a sarong wrapped around my waist, tied up in a dozen knots to keep it out of the way, and a tank top. My feet are bare and burning on the hot sand.

When the first pass comes from Mohammed, I still feel awkward—the ball is slow and unpredictable, and my feet are heavy. The boys are shouting at me from all directions and it's hard to figure who's on my team with the blur of dark bodies and faces running in front of my eyes. I'm not wearing my glasses so I can't recognize features; I try to pick out shirt colors but even that can be deceiving.

Suddenly I feel another body behind me, his feet scraping for the ball. The pressure to get rid of it is high, but no one's open on the receiving end. I look up at my assailant and recognize him as one of my own team-mates.

"Hey, we're on the same team," I say, thinking it a misunderstanding. He tightens his jaw and lunges for the ball again.

"What the fuck, man!" Caught off-balance, I get pushed to the side and he manages to dribble the ball away. I'm disoriented and pissed off.

When the play is over, I turn to Mohammed angrily.

"We're on the same team. What's his problem?" It's not about losing the ball; it's about respect.

Mohammed brushes it off. "I think he didn't know. It's O.K., just play."

Determined to win acceptance, I try to shake it off and concentrate again on the game. Just jogging in the sand for a while has trained my feet to lift a little higher, and I'm feeling comfortable in a sort of center back posi-tion. My strength is in defense—I've never been a flashy player—and I make two solid tackles in the space of a few minutes. I note a couple raised eyebrows and a slight sense of approval.

Another ten minutes, and I feel in tune with the rhythm of the game. The pace goes in spurts—a moment of intense action followed by a leisurely few minutes of casual passing. The boys are mostly smiles and good humor, especially when someone gets nutmegged (an embarrassing defensive lapse when the ball goes between your legs). There are no out-of-bounds, no throw-ins or corner kicks. If the ball goes behind the goal, the defend-ing team brings it back into play with a pass. Sometimes the sport takes us into the water, where the ball gets pulled by the tide and there's more splashing than kicking.

I have a momentary flashback to when I was in high school, playing for the Surf Soccer Club in San Diego.

People who weren't familiar with the club sometimes asked, "Oh, Surf—do you play in the water?" After all these years, I can finally answer "yes."

For a while I notice that people are noticing me— passersby stop to watch a bit of the game that has been joined by this strange white girl. But the oddity wears off quickly and I become just another player, another set of feet on the pitch.

I get the feeling that the boys, too, are forgetting I'm not one of them. I get passes more often and they're not so tentative when going in for a tackle. One of the greatest compliments I can get on the field is when the guys stop treating me like a girl. They don't ask if I'm O.K. every time I get knocked off the ball. They don't shy away from defending my dribbling. They send the ball elsewhere when I put on pressure.

In a moment of action, I intercept an opponent's pass and send it forward. It connects with the teammate who'd earlier been my attacker; he's in a perfect shooting position and the ball slides between the goal posts. The team cheers and my former adversary gives me a nod on his jog back.

"Good pass," he says.

"Nice shot," I reply.

The sun's getting hotter and my shoulders feel baked. After an hour of sand, sweat, and soccer, I decide to call it a day. My legs, I already know, will be punishing me tomorrow. At a break in the play, I start walking off the field and wave goodbye to the other players.

"Thanks for letting me play," I say. The boys wave back and call out their farewells.

"You're leaving already?" asks Mohammed. Maybe it's just the way he's squinting in the bright sun, but his face betrays a bit of disappointment.

"There will be other times," I say, sure that there won't. I'm leaving tomorrow to continue traveling up the coast, and it's not likely I'll be back. But maybe I'll find other pickup games along the way, and maybe this time around I'll be smart enough to wear shorts and bring water.

And maybe the next girl who wants to join *their* game won't have to ask first.

Jenny D. Williams developed wanderlust early on, as the child of travel-junkie parents. She regularly traveled to soccer tournaments across the United States and backpacked for several summers in Europe. A year after college graduation, Jenny traded her job at a book publisher for a one-way ticket to Africa. She spent the next two years traveling and volunteering in Africa, the Middle East, India, and Southeast Asia and writing about her adventures. Now back on American soil, Jenny works as a freelance writer and "book doctor," and is currently News Editor for Ethical Traveler. Her web site is www.jennydwilliams.com.

❦ ❦ ❦

Becoming Coco

She found her inner Chanel at the Paris Ritz.

J have been Maria Von Trapp on many a mountain-
side. Isak Denisen eating on fine china in Kenya by
day. Ernest Hemingway smoking cigars and drinking
warm scotch around the campfire by night. I have yet
to be diagnosed as schizophrenic but have undergone
distinct personality changes while traveling. It begins with
the accent, spreads to the appetite, the look, the lifestyle,
the worldview. I have been Spanish, English, Ecuadorian,
Galapagos Islandian, Australian and just once, a Maasai.

In *Tender is the Night*, F. Scott Fitzgerald describes this
phenomenon while witnessing a group of Americans in
Paris "undergoing a sea-change, a shifting about of
atoms to form the essential molecules of a new people."
It's one of the ways travel literally changes us.

It happened to me recently at the Ritz in Paris.

This was my second visit and I have to admit, being the seasoned Ritz veteran did not ease my front-desk anxiety—that extremely long moment when I clearly expect one of the staff to look at me and say, "Madame, your passport lists your place of birth as Ohio USA, which is, shall we say, déclassé at l'hotel Ritz."

Even though I managed to pass inspection I secretly wished I were someone else.

Someone with jewels and a little pooch in a little-pooch-bag, smelling of Joy and reeking with attitude. But, la-di-dah, la-di-dah, I was Annie Hall at best (must've happened on the flight over) and determined to feel a part of this hotel. I gave the staff a gee-whiz grin hoping that my hearty thanks would make up for every snub they had ever suffered. The clerk looked at me as if I had spoken to someone else and the bellman actually backed away, just a hair, as if something had fallen out of my nose.

Was it too much to ask if I could be Coco Chanel for just five minutes? I suddenly craved oversized glasses with dark frames and cigarettes in cigarette holders. I wanted mannish clothes with white piping. I needed style. Coco had after all lived at the Ritz for over thirty fabulous years, from the thirties into the seventies. In fact, it was she who said, "How many cares one loses when one decides not to be something but to be someone."

Indeed.

I followed the bellman through this bastion of elegance where even the noise is moneyed and fights with cigarette smoke for air space. Inspired by the palaces at Versailles and Fontainebleau I wondered what it would do to one's head to walk through here day after day for thirty years. My walk was wrong, my hair was worse, my clothes stood out like a maraschino cherry in a martini.

The room did not disappoint with its crystal chandeliers and tapestries on the walls amid much molding and gilt. The bathroom was peach, an ingenious touch by Cesar Ritz to make whomever we are at the moment look gorgeous above the golden swan faucets. His was also the first hotel to not only have bathrooms but to install them with bells for assistance after the Prince of Wales, the future Edward VII, became stuck in his bathtub. Or maybe it was just someone pretending to be him.

I changed out of my orange Patagonia trail-hikers and went straight for "the little black dress" which Coco made famous and which I had brought for an evening out. As I slid it on, Coco began to crystallize. The shoulders went back, the chin up. The hair went both back and up.

The Bar Hemingway was waiting. Rumor has it that Mr. Hemingway came to the Ritz during the liberation of Paris, fired his pistol into the air, came to the bar, ordered martinis and said that he personally had liberated the hotel. Okay, not what Proust, another regular, would have done, but then he didn't have Idaho USA stamped on his passport. Proust also dined in a fur coat.

The bar has a British club feel to it with rich paneling and books, newspaper memorabilia and photos of Mr. Hemingway watching the patrons at the tables in front of the bar transforming into Oxford grads or Tony Blairs, perhaps. My champagne cocktail had an orchid floating in the preferred-sized bubbles. According to Ritz lore Scott Fitzgerald, there with Mr. Hemingway, saw a beautiful woman in one of the bars, unfortunately not alone, and sent over a bouquet of orchids. When she returned them promptly, Mr. Fitzgerald began eating them and wouldn't stop until she agreed to meet him.

Apparently, even the rich and famous are occasionally out of character.

My first crystal goblet of champagne cost twenty-three euros or roughly forty American dollars. I would imagine that Coco preferred Dom Perignon but then again she worked at Chanel. I work on a computer next to my clothes dryer.

Leaving the Bar Hemingway is a hallway lined with 120 glass cases of objects that you can actually buy. I developed Coco's eye, tsking at the more opulent items. I don't think I had ever really tsked before in my whole life but it's wonderful when you don't speak the language. It was Coco herself who said, "Elegance is refusal," so I refused every multi-thousand-euro piece of jewelry that caught my eye. She also said that "a woman who refuses perfume has no future." I was at the Chanel case and yes, I was an imposter but I was determined to have a future so I popped for a quarter of an ounce of No. 5.

In my future I would buy faux pearls and a cigarette holder in the Paris flea markets. I would wear red lipstick and leave smears of it on small espresso cups and champagne flutes. I would order thick slabs of pate and garlicky escargot. In my head Fred Astaire would sing "Putting on the Ritz."

I also vowed to one day occupy Coco's suite even if it meant just standing it in with an armed guard and a tour guide. Her apartment at the hotel has been recreated by an art historian and advisor to the great designer Karl Lagerfeld, who once worked at the House of Chanel.

But this was only day one. As I crossed the lobby stuffed with history's furniture, a mouse shot out from underneath a Louis XVI sofa and high-tailed it across the sumptuous carpet. Yes, it was beginning to feel like home.

I walked slowly in my heels, my shoulders back, trying to look bored and aloof. I have never walked so well or on better carpeting. I was an amoeba and my one-cell was brimming with sophistication. I stopped by the front desk and asked for my room key and then, because I thought I, Coco, lived there, I also asked for my mail.

"Is there any mail for me today, monsieur?" I made my voice deep. The desk clerk looked at me like Halloween was over. And then, not because he was truly professional, I think, but because he believed Coco had returned, he actually looked for it. Then he said, "I'm so sorry Madame, the postal service must be on holiday today," he paused and met my Coco eyes, "but I do not think so."

It took everything I had not to apologize and say just kidding. My gaze held his as my body turned toward the elevator and I left him with a whiff of my expensive perfume.

As sleep hovered I wondered: What if every famous guest could be gathered together for just one more evening at the Ritz? Cole Porter. Colette. Jean Cocteau. Arthur Miller. Pablo Picasso. Maria Callas. Princess Di. Winston Churchill. Who knows, I thought. Their transmutations may be checking in right now.

Ginny Horton is an award-winning advertising copywriter. Besides staying at the Ritz she likes being on safari and wading through the Amazon rainforest. Her next adventure will be driving in an international road rally with her husband in a 1940 Buick. She is currently at work on her first novel and hopes to become Doris Lessing. This story won the Bronze Award for Travel and Transformation in the second annual Solas Awards.

☙ ☙ ☙

Perfect Sitting

A meditation retreat in Japan becomes a battle
between mind and body.

"Just eat your cookie and drink your tea," Nika said
calmly when I told her I was anxious about the
retreat and confessed I had not been practicing meditation for several months. Nika, a bright blue-eyed Dutch
monastery resident of four years, was fluent in English,
and was assigned to give me general instructions about
the seven-day meditation retreat. I had done a number of
these retreats before and knew how hard they were even
when I was practicing every day. But although anxious, I
was also excited about doing a *sesshin,* meditation retreat,
at Bukkoku-Ji, Japan.

After tea, Nika took me to the *zendo,* the meditation
hall, and showed me my space with two cushions facing the white wall. The area was clearly marked with
my name written on a rectangular black wood block in

white Japanese characters. The familiar smell from the incense she lit at the altar brought me comfort in the midst of language barriers and unfamiliar faces.

Then Nika showed me my sleeping quarters, a small room with my bed, a futon rolled up on top of a tatami floor, between two other women. The schedule of the daily activities for the *sesshin* was posted by the door:

SESSHIN SCHEDULE

3:50 A.M.	Wake up
4:00 A.M.	Taiso (exercise)
4:30 A.M.	Zazen (sitting meditation)
5:10 A.M.	Chôka (morning chanting)
5:50 A.M.	Zazen, dokusan (meeting with the Master)
6:30 A.M.	Shukuza (oryoki breakfast)
7:00 A.M.	Zuiza (break)
8:00 A.M.	Gyôibaitô (plum tea)
8:15 A.M.	Zazen (sitting meditation)
10:30 A.M.	Teishô (dharma talk)
11:30 A.M.	Saiza (oryoki lunch)
12:00 P.M.	Zuiza (break)
1:20 P.M.	Gyôcha (afternoon tea)
1:30 P.M.	Zazen, dokusan
4:00 P.M.	Banka (evening chanting)
4:30 P.M.	Yakusei (oryoki supper)
5:00 P.M.	Zuiza (break)
6:20 P.M.	Zazen, dokusan
8:50 P.M.	Shiguseiganmon (ending chanting)
9:00 P.M.	Kaichin (bed time)

Sesshin practitioners are asked to limit bodily distractions by refraining from taking showers for the whole week and to wear only black clothes which blend in well with the stark colors of the monastery. Nika gave me a black blanket for the cold mornings and a small white towel to wipe myself clean if I felt too dirty in the muggy June weather.

After luxuriating in a hot shower, my last for the week, and a little unpacking—getting out a few toiletries and all the black clothes I had in my suitcase—it was time for *zazen*, sitting meditation. After that, we were done with talking for the rest of the week. All residents and guests were about to immerse themselves in a fasting of the senses. We were expected to direct our gaze inwardly, follow our breaths and take refuge in the space between thoughts. There were sixty of us: a third ordained priests and the rest lay practitioners. A handful were foreigners like me.

The following morning we woke up with the bell at 3:50 and by 4:00 we were all lined-up in the main hall. *Ichi, ni, san, siyon, go, roku*...one of the monks counted as we did our daily exercise. It was a vigorous series of pushups, moving in position for the blood and energy to circulate, followed by stretching. The routine was efficient and the count in Japanese made it sound even more vigorous and austere.

During my first *dokusan*, a meeting with Roshi Sama to discuss practice, I asked him: "How should I follow my breath?"

"Continuously, from here (pointing to the belly button), natural, like sleep, great emptiness, everything continuous. Count until ten and then repeat, continuously." He replied.

It sounded very simple, very doable, but after almost twenty years of practice, I still felt like a beginner. On the other hand, Zoe, a tall red-haired American woman, seemed advanced in her sitting. I often overheard her as she spoke in Japanese with Roshi Sama during *dokusans,* which made her sound very official. She had studied with him for over two years and I loved to see and hear her discuss practice with the Master, as I waited for my turn in line. Zoe yelled a Japanese word—an austere, firm and ecstatic yell from someone who seemed to be touching truth with her heart. I recognized one word that often reverberated in the room: *Shikantaza!*—Perfect sitting. This must have been a word of self-encouragement, similar to a "Go Yankees!" in an American baseball game. Her dedication was inspiring, her stamina enviable. Some people, including Zoe, meditated during most breaks and often through the night, and there was no movement or shift in position in the *zendo,* just a steady silence.

At the end of the second day, my body started to ache and I could not find a position without my legs going numb. My body was in an utter state of unpreparedness, lazy and indulged with excess sleep, food, and lack of exercise before I arrived at Bukkoku-Ji. I had been traveling for eleven months around the world, and although it was my best intention to practice during this time, it had not happened as planned. I wished I had been better prepared but being true to myself, I dove right in without any consideration for how I would get through the *sesshin.* I had made plans to be at this Japanese Zen monastery when I was still living at the San Francisco Zen Center a year earlier, and did not think of the consequences of diving into it without practice.

One evening I was in so much pain I craved the stick. In Zen practice, during meditation, a specially trained priest walks around with a stick made of light wood, about four feet long. Anyone who asked received a stimulating smack on the muscles of the upper back when one felt tired or sleepy. In my case, I just wanted to distract myself from the pain in my legs and knees. So I bowed when I felt the priest's presence behind me. He touched the stick lightly on my right shoulder to let me know what was coming, and then he gave me a good whack. It hurt a lot, but at the same time, it was good to feel the blood rushing to my upper back and the tingling sensation vibrating long after it. The sensation moved from my upper back to the top of my eyelids and then to my breath. Then I suddenly felt grief surrounding me.

The image of my mother appeared just above my brows, clear and unmistakable. But it was not the excessively energetic and disciplinary mother I grew up with, constantly screaming at us children to get our teeth brushed, eat our vegetables and stop running around the house driving her crazy. Rather, she was serene, content, and looked relaxed, accepting her role as a mother of ten children. This image made me flash back to one of my visits to Brazil, where I had been born and raised. My mother offered me a traditional Portuguese dish of codfish and potatoes she prepared for lunch, which I did not take because I did not eat meat. For twenty-five years I lived more than seven thousand miles away from my immediate family and childhood friends; I acquired habits and followed practices that created not only a physical and cultural distance but also an emotional one. My breath was steady as I sat in the *zendo*, with sadness dripping slowly into my cells until my whole body was saturated and immersed in grief like a heavy blanket. Instead of following my breath and finding relief in the void of no mind, I found myself in a mixture of deep sadness, physical pain and emotional dislocation, seeking solace from the white wall in front of me.

From that day on I was engulfed in a cloud of confusion, in a battle between body and mind. In physical
pain, but also feeling the peace that comes with sitting in
meditation for days without outside stimulation, I started
to doubt a practice I had been following for twenty years. I
considered myself a modern monk, who worked and lived
in the world, outside the monastery, but did not want to
have much to do with it, thus alienating friends and family. That day was pivotal in my reflections about a need for
balance, which ensued from my sadness and broken body.

One day, the bell suddenly sounded loudly and everyone, except me, seemed to know it was a cue to start a
screaming session. For fifteen minutes we screamed as
loud as we could. It was hard for me at first, having not
uttered a single word for several days, but it was quite
liberating to scream from the top of my lungs when I
could finally make a sound in my throat. But I was glad
when the bell rang again and the dead silence returned
to the *zendo*. The screaming session felt expansive at
first, but soon, it jangled my nerves and I felt a desire to
return to my cloudy state of numbness, disturbed only by
bodily pain, sadness and reflection.

The *zazen* was so silent at Bukkoku-Ji that I worried
my two or three very subtle shifts in position during a
sitting session would disturb the entire room. This was
my own censorship and perception, no one said anything or gave me the "eye," but I was self-conscious my
changes in position could have disturbed the focused
attention in the *zendo*. So, instead of moving, I suppli-
cated for Amma, my Hindu guru's help, by chanting my
mantra silently as if my life depended on it, and endured
the pain in my legs and back.

We are here because of the grace of all beings... lumps of
self... drop self cherishing... die now to the ego and attain

true mind—you owe it to yourself...shikantaza—Perfect sitting... Words from Roshi Sama flashed through my mind like fireflies through my mantras. I was hallucinating with discomfort.

The last day of the retreat finally arrived as Roshi Sama began his last dharma talk of the week. We were all ears, sitting crossed-legged at the *zendo*, with dirty hair and the men with seven days' beard growth: *Is the* sesshin *really over?* He started, *No! No matter how many distractions you find, somehow, somewhere, it will pop up again—no matter how much we try to stuff it with distractions, we find our way back to practice.* Roshi Sama spoke for forty-five minutes and ended his talk by answering his own question.

The following day, thinking the *sesshin* was over and that I was free to go, I packed my suitcase and was rolling it out the door when I heard a familiar chant. It was The Heart Sutra—Prajna Paramita. It sounded good: *kan Ji Zai Bo Sa Gyo Jin Nan Nya ha ra mi ta sho ken go on kai ku do is sai ku yaku...Sesshin* participants were going around in circles chanting it repeatedly in a resonating way as we often did at the San Francisco Zen Center. I felt a sudden happiness in my heart and wished I was there with them—*Gone, deep in Prajna Paramita, clear...free of all pain, grief...form's the real void, void's the real form, so in void there's no form, no sense...thus mind's unblocked. No blockage, so have no fear; far past all upside-down, vain hopes, nirvana after all.*

I wanted to say goodbye to Nika, but it was hard to find a moment as the regular practice at Bukkoku-Ji started right after the *sesshin*. At the Zen Center at home, we had the day off and usually gathered in the kitchen and the courtyard with our bagels and cream cheese in self-congratulatory excitement for one more retreat accomplished. At Bukkoku-Ji, everyone continued with *zazen*, work period and chanting. The monastery had returned to "normal" life, which had only a slightly different schedule than the *sesshin*.

After breakfast Nika gave me a hug and asked me how the *sesshin* was for me. I mumbled something to the effect that it was hard and I was in much pain, but I didn't elaborate further as I knew there was not much time to talk because the work period was about to start. My suitcase was already outside the main building and I quietly rolled it out under the gates of the monastery and onto the streets, to the bus station. My mind was quiet but inquisitive and I was ultra-sensitive due to the lack of stimulation for seven days. My body ached everywhere and I could not walk without limping. I found out later that I had injured two vertebrae in my lower back from the long sittings.

It was an hour journey by bus from Obama, where the monastery was located, to Omi-Imazu, and then another hour from there by train to Kyoto. With one foot in the world of the senses and another in the stillness of the void, I heard Roshi Sama's words come back to me: *"All is well... So you say, does it really matter if we attain the way? It does because you won't feel satisfied unless you do."*

The feeling of stillness stayed with me for several days after the *sesshin* and I realized I could no longer continue to ignore life beyond the white wall of the *zendo*. The revelation for me was that my life had been out of balance. Maybe I would find my home to be a monastery again one day, like Nika and Zoe, but I realized then that the white wall of the *zendo* no longer served me. Although I was attached to the views of myself as non-conforming, rejecting a world that everyone was happy

to accept, and discounting secular activities as unneces-
sary, I was on the verge of letting go. I craved partici-
pating in the vast world of consumer culture, a lover's
embrace, and a delicious meal eaten without strict rules.
Maybe I would return to practice someday, but the years
of solitude, voluntary deprivation and austerity became
a heavy weight I no longer wished to carry.

On the way to Kyoto, it felt exquisite to travel on a
bullet train with a static body and mind that was slowly
adjusting to the fast pace of life around me. As I limped
out of the train station into the streets, the moon, high
in the sky, invited me to enjoy the evening in any way
it pleased me, without rules or schedules. The air in the
city was warm and festive and I felt I was thawing back
into life.

After checking into a *ryokan*, a traditional inn in
eastern Kyoto, and calling my mother in Brazil, I craved
sashimi, as if redeeming myself for not eating her lunch
of codfish and potatoes years before. After years of nag-
ging me to go back to Brazil and give her many grandchildren like my other siblings, my mother had long
accepted my lifestyle and was always happy to hear from
me, wherever I was.

I went to an *Izakaya,* a pub, where I met Jumpei, a
Kyoto native and English teacher. Although we were
complete strangers, he realized I didn't speak Japanese
and helped me order different kinds of foods I would
not have been able to do on my own because there was
no menu and no pictures of dishes I could point to. I was
also glad to converse with someone beyond a phrase or
two. Although the rest of the people in the bar did not
speak English, it felt as if I was among friends and family. They passed food for me to try, and someone bought
me a glass of delicious warm sake which I happily drank

in a few gulps. Maybe they could sense I was in desperate need of human contact and tender loving care, or maybe they were just proud to have a foreigner in their midst.

Several sakes later, I was drunk when Jumpei and I left the pub together. He showed me a bathhouse near the pub where I soaked with half a dozen women from the neighborhood until close to midnight. I sat in a large deep tub, filled with warm bubbly water, blissed out and in a state of drunkenness that numbed my body pains and lightened my spirits. Words from Roshi Sama echoed in my mind, as if in a dream: *Shikantaza, shikantaza, shikantaza...Perfect sitting!*

Marisa Pereira worked for the California state government in San Francisco for twenty years before she got itchy feet and quit her job to travel. When she is not in British Columbia working on her book about her travels, she is traveling around the world. Some of her travel stories are available at www.marisatravels.com. She is originally from Brazil.

ℬ ℬ ℬ

Where No Traveler Had Gone Before

The famed Scottish castle paled in comparison.

*I*n the '80s cult-classic film *Highlander*, one of the immortals runs around chopping his competitors' heads off with a broad sword, proclaiming, "There can be only one!"

He's referring to the top-dog immortal, who will live through the movie with head attached. I felt the same way about Eilean Donan, the spectacular waterside castle so enticingly featured in the film.

There are dozens of castles in Scotland, from the Iron Age forts known as *brochs* to medieval fortresses with story-book names: Claypotts, Kildrummy, Old Wick, Kilchurn on Loch Awe. Many were built in the craggy Highlands, evidence of the bellicose clans of old and the kilted feuds they fought before one of the world's most rugged—and most beautiful—backdrops.

That's where I was headed. I had begun my Scottish adventure at Edinburgh's Castle, strolled down the Royal Mile of slate-colored stone to the World's End—and then traversed over heath and heather northwest to Inverness, the "capital of the Highlands." Along the way I had felt the warm sting of peaty single-malt on my tongue at many a dark pub; watched waterfalls carve their way through bare green hills from my bus window; studied the glassy skin of Loch Ness for any sign of the monster; heard the ubiquitous bag pipes drone for an audience of Highland cattle, their handlebar horns at attention, their shaggy russet coats hanging in thick tufts over their docile eyes.

But after everything that I had experienced, that single castle—*Eilean Donan*—still brooded in my imagination.

It is the one of the most photographed sights in all of Scotland: the brawny cover-model for calendars and coffee table books and countless tourist brochures printed on backgrounds of red and blue tartan. Situated near Dornie village not far from the Isle of Skye on a little strand between three deep gray lochs—Long, Alsh and Duich, the castle lends itself to remarkable shots of stone and sky and water reflecting endless undulations of the muscular bare backs of the Highlands. It is no wonder the movie producers chose it for the home of their MacLeod hero (though the real MacLeod chiefs were denizens of Dunvegan Castle in northwest Skye), silhouetting its picturesque shape against a hot orange sky. And it was no wonder it had taken root in my own imagination. I had pictured it again and again, seen it through the Highland mists in my mind's eye ever since I was a wee thing, and become intent on seeing it rise up before me, tangible and majestic, on my journey to Scotland.

But, by all accounts, it was not the time to visit. At the end of my trip, I was not only running out of time, but was feeling a money crunch so desperate I had resorted to rationing a crumbling scone or two a day for sustenance. Meanwhile a bevy of anxious, thick-brogued meteorologists had been warning everyone for days: a massive storm was due to sweep across the Highlands from the Arctic circle, swallowing Skye and its environs, rendering exploration inadvisable, if not downright dangerous.

I studied my map. I was painfully close. What was a little rain, I thought, a little danger? This was *Eilean Donan*, the most photographed castle in Scotland! Sean Connery fought at this castle!

It was official. Somehow I had lost *my* head in the intrigue and romance of it all. I was off to see that castle.

The rain had begun, insistent, falling from the sky like glistening sheets of metal. I took a bus to a barren strip of road completely emptied of tourists, synched up my water-resistant jacket, and walked the bridge to the fortress, a lone, hooded pilgrim.

I bought my ticket, and climbed a narrow, curving stone staircase lined with framed still photos from the movie set, my excitement mounting with every step. I took the time to steep myself in the history of this storied place: built in the thirteenth century and named after a sixth-century hermit, Eilean Donan became the stronghold of the Mackenzie clan in the fourteenth century. It stood proudly for the next four hundred years—until it was destroyed in 1719, its Jacobite defenders defeated nearby at the Battle of Glenshiel, where peaks over a thousand meters high towered over the soldiers falling in their long shadows. Only in the early twentieth century had it been restored to the structure in which I now stood.

I entered a dim, smallish room and studied a sword used at the battle of Culloden. That bloody day spelled the end for Bonnie Prince Charlie and the Jacobite uprising against the British crown—and the suppression of the clans and the Highland culture that still draws visitors to this place. Studying the rest of the room I saw other weaponry, gleaming and brutal, and fading crests; a dining table of ancient wood and its heavy implements; dark stone walls growing more gray as the storm snuffed out the light outside.

There wasn't much else to see. But I lingered, waiting for something. I don't know what I was expecting; what lavish scenes my imagination had forged over the years. But here in person Eilean Donan seemed a rather cramped, dreary affair: the kind of place that reminds you that if life as a peasant had been bad, life inside the castle was only shades better; the kind of place that chastens you to recall that there wasn't anything romantic about life in this place, those times, at all.

Back outside, the rain had really begun to roar. The wind lashed strips of hair against my face like whips; my eyes stung; my "rain-resistant" jacket completely surrendered. But there I was in the midst of the storm, walking around the gloomy grounds trying to capture the sort of snapshot I had seen in all those glossy brochures. Instead I only found myself sinking deeper into the mud, the rain pelting the lens of my camera with furious beads. Even today my photos are unimpressive tokens of my venture: the mighty fortress reduced to slabs of wet stone, to grays upon grays, streaks of water marring the film.

Waiting by the roadside, I shifted from foot to foot in the familiar in-place dance of futility to try to keep warm. I had seen the castle. And now all I could think about was when the bus, already late, was going to show up, when I could get out of the rain and find someplace warm. Where was the bus? A half-hour, hour, more it seemed, passed with no transportation. I had tried to keep sane by writing in my journal, but my hand was frozen and the pages warped in the rain. A few teen-agers were the only other souls I saw there that day, laughing as they sped past—at me, I was convinced. Apparently, there could be only one American tourist stubborn or foolish enough to visit the *Highlander* castle in an arctic storm.

Finally a charter bus driver took pity on me and pulled his purple juggernaut to the side of the road. I climbed on board, soaked, dripping, and spitting out breath in wet, angry huffs. Somehow the tourists on board, in shirt-sleeves exposing self-satisfied tans, looked like they had just left Club Med. They met my eyes with a mix of horror and fascination and stared at me as I trudged down the aisle, as if Nessie herself had just slunk aboard.

The bus's destination was tiny Kyle of Lochalsh, directly across the water from the Isle of Skye. In the days before the Skye Bridge, Kyle was the ferry port, and with nowhere to stay on the mainland, I would have to take my chances on the rusted boat, which bucked all the way to the Isle on angry waves. I would then have to find a room somewhere—anywhere—on the island for the night. Sickened, waterlogged, and colder than I had ever been in my life, I trudged to every hostel I could find, to every B&B that hung a placard, growing increas-ingly more pathetic and my lips more blue. But at each doorstep I was told with the same sympathetic shake of the head that the establishment was full for the night.

The disappointment of the day was turning into desperation, when finally I saw it: the Backpacker's Guest House in Kyleakin, its cheerful white clapboard gleaming like a beacon. It was really my last hope, so when the curly-haired man at the desk told me again with his deep burr that the hostel was full, I almost began to weep.

"But I do haf a caravan in the beck, if you'd like," he offered.

I had no idea what that meant. All I knew was that he was offering some sort of bed, somewhere, out of the rain. "Fine," I said. "That's great! Thank you *so* much!"

"Ya understand that there's no loo. You'll a haf to make yar wae beck to the main house to use the facilities."

"That's O.K., that's fan-tas-ticccc." My words were like ticker-tape through the clatter of chattering teeth.

"Alright then, lass," he said. "You're a gonna be Uhura for the night."

I thought a minute. Was this some strange Scottish dialect, or did he just call me *Uhura*? I was familiar enough with the name, from my father's penchant for watching old sci-fi episodes and a particularly nerdy stage of my own in middle school. And yet, here in the Highlands of Scotland, on the day I had seen Eilean Donan castle and almost drowned doing it, I didn't process what he was saying.

"I'm sorry?" I asked, tripping along behind him as he led me outside, behind the hostel. He pointed through the sweeping rain to a warped metal trailer, a sad, hunched heap of a thing, perched a foot off the flooded yard on a few crumbling cinder blocks.

"Ya know *Star Trek*," he bellowed over the storm, "Yar American show?"

And with that he threw open the door.

Inside the narrow trailer was an almost religious tribute to all things Trek. Posters and paraphernalia plastered the walls: Spock splaying his fingers in the "live long and prosper" sign; young William Shatner, in his most rakish Captain Kirk pose; buttons and bumper stickers and boomerang-shaped insignia. It was the freaking bridge of the USS Enterprise smack-dab in the middle of Brigadoon.

Slack-jawed, I gazed around in disbelief. Cots were pushed together, shoulder to shoulder. Each was labeled with the name of a character—Dr. "Bones" McCoy and Sulu and, yes, Uhura—in the same off-kilter handwriting that was scrawled on the soggy scrap of paper the owner slipped to me before he disappeared, shutting me into the metal bubble like an astronaut in a capsule.

The few drowsy people inside, flung together, I would learn, from as far afield as Quebec and Australia, looked up at me from their cots with raised eyebrows worthy of Spock himself. "I know, I know," they seemed to say. "Can you even *believe* this?"

With apologies I began the climb over my crewmates' bunks to find Uhura's place on the bridge. I inched closer to the ancient space heater buzzing on the floor to try to get warm. Tugging at my clothes I realized that even my underwear was waterlogged, sticking at odd, uncomfortable angles to my body. My boots made a slurping sound as I tugged them from my feet, pale and shriveled as alien skin under my water-stained socks.

Collapsing on my cot I just tried to breathe. It wasn't more than a few moments before I felt someone tap me on the shoulder.

"Um, excuse me," a French Canadian waif asked shyly, "Would you mind trading Uhura for Dr. McCoy?"

I indulged her, and she crawled across to my bunk and nuzzled against her friend, "Mr. Chekhov." I never learned anyone's real name. The good-looking blond Australian would forever be "Scottie;" the sniffling Austrian in the corner was a doomed red-shirted "security officer."

Exhausted, curling up at last, I wondered how I would ever get dry. There was nothing to change into, as everything in my bag had suffered the same drowned fate. I clenched my eyes tightly shut and tried to will myself to sleep. At first I thought I was hallucinating even more water, but when I looked up I saw the skylight above me was leaking—drip, drip, dripping onto Bones' bunk. It's the last thing I remember before falling into the deepest sleep of my life.

Sometime in the middle of the night I was awakened. I felt dizzy. I grabbed the sides of my cot and tried to determine what was going on. And then I realized the vertigo wasn't in my head. The room was *spinning*, slowly swinging one way, then the other.

During the raging storm the water in the yard had risen so high that our little Star Trek caravan was lifted off of its blocks completely. It was floating like an unseaworthy vessel, keeling on the floodwaters.

The bridge was aflutter with chattering and nervous laughter and, from the new Uhura, an occasional high-pitched squeal. From out of the darkness the Australian Scottie shouted in his best, most hysterical brogue: "*Captain, I canna hold it!*"

There were some heroic efforts aboard our brig that night. Wrestling the space heater so we could all avoid electrocution. Banding together to bail the water out. I gazed around me at my motley crew, built from strangers from all over the planet, all joined together here in an improbable plot.

When I awoke the next day, the storm had all but cleared, and hints of the beatific beauty for which Skye is known were whispering on the horizon. I wrung my clothes dry and stood beside the Star Trek caravan, warped and dented and leaning akimbo in the new light, a few feet off of its cinder blocks. My shipmates and I parted company, saluting each other with our Star Trek names.

"So long, Sulu."

"So long, Spock."

"Dr…" Scottie extended his hand to me, and I shook it with a broad, appreciative smile.

And then I stood alone beside my Scottish Star Trek caravan and laughed. My hardheaded trip to Eilean Donan had been something of a disaster. And yet it *hadn't*. Not because I had seen the castle of film fame, but because I had been reminded that real travel isn't about the famous sights. It's about the unexpected destinations, the moments you never could have predicted, never could have found in any guide—a Star Trek caravan in the Scottish Highlands; a makeshift crew on your own floating brig. As I left that day I knew. I really had gone where few travelers have gone before, a final frontier indeed.

♪♪ ♪♪ ♪♪

Jennifer Carol Cook earned her Ph.D. at Brandeis University and teaches writing and American literature at Bentley College. She is the author of Machine and Metaphor, The Ethics of Language in American Realism. *Her creative work includes poetry, fiction, and creative nonfiction, and her essays have appeared in the last two editions of* The Best Women's Travel Writing. *Her current book project—for which she traveled to eight countries, fourteen cities last summer—is a work of narrative nonfiction about the life and work of the painter Johannes Vermeer.*

Y.J. ZHU

SO SO SO

Taklamakan Desert
Moon Ride

The only woman in her group, this forty-something
motorbike rider braves a 1,550-mile course
through China.

We have descended Tian Shan and entered the
Taklamakan Desert, a barren landscape painted
in ecru—no shrubs, no grass, only waves upon waves of
naked ridges the color of buff, the highest few spotted
with white specks of snow. The chill of high altitude still
in my bones, the lonely road ahead has no end in sight.
I speed up, feeling the skinny tires of the Green Knight
motorbike skipping on the surface of the gravel, hearing
the crispy sputters of rocks spewing out from under them.
Long stretches before gentle sweeping curves, the open
panorama, the absence of other vehicles, the roughness
of the road, the thrill of being in Taklamakan—this is

riding at its purest. With every mile I grow more confident on the bike. I concentrate on the road, on being one with the elements, the reward of riding, of taking the risk, of conquering fear. Standing up on the foot pegs like a downhill skier, I bend my legs at the knee, absorbing all the bumps; my hands tremble on the handlebar, shockwaves traveling through my arms. I feel the movements of the bike. I open the throttle a bit more.

We are a group of ten riders, all male except me. Mostly young men afforded by youth, energetic and vibrant, unable to conceive danger, incapable of imagining pain and loss, they are as sweet as they are wild. We are making a mad dash to catch Stage Two of the Second Annual Around Taklamakan Desert Car and Motorcycle Enduro Race, a race that is both enduro and rally—a distinction completely lost on us. It is held in three disparate stages over ten days, spanning a distance of 1,550 miles, without maps, without prior knowledge of the racecourses or destinations. Our group, mostly foreign nationals, is denied the privilege to race in Stage One which is taking place in the Chinese nuclear testing ground of Lop Nor area inside the Taklamakan Desert. We are forced to ride a long loop around without any support vehicles or means of communication with the race committee. Neither our bikes nor we have license to be on the road we are on. Stage Two begins at Ruo Qiang (Chaqiliq), which is about three or four days of riding away from Ürümqi, the capital of the Xinjiang Uyghur Autonomous Region in northwestern China.

I did not mean to go in to the Taklamakan Desert; the desert of my dream is the Sahara; but when I learned of an enduro rally organized by a local motorbike club that would take me riding around the Taklamakan Desert, my heart jumped. It seemed a fun thing to do for vacation. Most people, once they learned of my plan, asked if I had a death wish. A fair enough question, but the answer was I didn't. In fact, I very much enjoy being alive. Then why must I go? I couldn't answer. Perhaps it's the chance to experience the desert, to ride where few have; perhaps it's an opportunity to meditate with a spaciousness and quietude of mind, away from the noises and mundane demands of an affluent society, the dullness of safe modern living; perhaps it's an occasion to reflect on the masculine virtues away from the conformity of feminine expectations in our culture.

Growing up on the coattails of Mao's Cultural Revolution in Beijing, I was schooled in the gender-neutral outlook of an empowered modern Chinese woman; coming of age in America, I was surprised to learn the figments of an effeminate vision I contradict in my adopted homeland; the juxtaposition was disconcerting.

The road narrows, the sun is slanting, we continue to descend; the earth changes from rocky to sandy, still barren without vegetation, still a desert of high altitude. I look down between my hands at the odometer; we have ridden a little more than 125 miles since leaving Ürümqi, the starting point. We have yet to see a town of any size, or meet another vehicle. Our destination for the day is Krola, the second largest city in the region; it is some distance away. Max, the de facto group leader, is not sure of the actual distance between Ürümqi and Krola. In the Taklamakan, distance is of a different proportion; everything is approximation.

A little-known desert in China, the Taklamakan sits between two famous mountain ranges, Tian Shan to the north (from where we have descended) and Kun Lun Shan to the south. The desert borders all the "stan" countries (Afghanistan, Kazakhstan, Kyrgyzstan, Tajikistan, Turkmenistan and Uzbekistan) to the west, Mongolia to the north, and Tibet to the south. On the map it's a large blank space about the size of Texas. It's known as one of the most inaccessible and dangerous places on earth; it is terra incognito. Taklamakan is often translated as "Place of No Return." Peter Hopkirk wrote in *The Great Game: On Secret Service in High Asia*: "The Taklamakan desert...had always enjoyed an ill reputation among travelers, and over the years a sad procession of men—merchants, soldiers and Buddhist pilgrims—had left their bones there after losing their way between the widely scattered oases. Sometimes entire caravans had been known to vanish into it without a trace. It is no surprise to learn that Taklamakan, in the local Uighur tongue, means 'Go in—and you won't come out.'"

At a rare sharp bend in the road, Jona and Kyle, the two fastest riders of the group, are standing by their bikes, helmets off. I stop too. But they wave me on.

"Go! Don't stop! Wait for us at the next town."

"How far is it?" I yell through my helmet.

Jona hollers back, "Don't know. But there's a village coming up soon. Should be the midpoint between Ürümqi and Krola. Wait there."

We left Ürümqi at noon; the sun is about to set now. I do a quick calculation in my head: If the odometer is correct, then we have ridden 125 miles in about five or six hours; we will be lucky to make Krola by midnight. With that thought, I fly off, wanting to arrive at the next town before darkness falls. The road is deserted, the sun fading fast. I hear a bike coming up behind me. It is

Jona. He overtakes me, kicking up sand dust in my face.
I sense his smile inside his helmet. He disappears from
my sight quickly.

Riding is a lonesome sport, even when one rides as part
of a group. The rider alone battles the elements of sun,
wind, noise and the condition of the road. It's a sport that
demands mental agility. To survive, the rider must be
aggressive to be defensive; must be in constant fear of sudden death, or worse, half death; must be thinking ahead
and constantly calculating distance and timing, searching
for the escape routes if one spills; must be an amateur
psychic, anticipating the moves of others on the road and
doing everything in her power to avoid collision. Then
there are the most unpredictable of all, children and dogs
attracted to a bike like little magnets to steel.

The wind is picking up. The road takes me lower and
deeper into the desert. Ground-hugging shrubs the color
of dead leaves begin to dot the landscape. I have entered
the warm desert of lower altitude. Suddenly I see the
formation of a small tornado on the sandy road in front
of me. The late afternoon sandstorm has arrived. The
road narrows, another sharp bend. I feel the rear tire
skidding sideways while I lean into the turn. Mentally I
note to slow down before the next turn. I wonder how
far ahead Jona is and how far behind is everyone else. I
wonder what the chances are of getting lost. There are
no road signs or anyone to ask for directions. I push the
bike to go where the road leads me, trusting there's road
beyond the next turn, trusting the road will lead me into
the town, hoping the sandstorm stays small.

   I hear dogs barking in the far distance. I must be getting close to the town. More sandstorms are forming on the

open desert, swirling like mini tornados, gliding hurriedly across the road one after another. The visibility is reduced to less than 100 meters, sometimes rendering me blind. My little Green Knight feels light and nimble. Without knobby tires and no pavement to grab, there is very little traction control on the loose sandy gravel terrain. I place my full trust in this little machine, made in China, powered with a copy of an old Suzuki 250 cc engine.

The barking of the dogs is getting louder, before fading away to a distance. I assess the situation: Jona must be close in front of me. He must be O.K. if the dogs are running away. But I know they will come back once they hear the sound of my engine. What should I do?

They hear me coming; their barking furious, their fury chills me to the bone. I open to full throttle, putting my faith in the Green Knight, in the road. I see the dogs in my peripheral vision, a pack of three or maybe four, running towards me across the wide-open space. If they bite me, it will be my right leg. I calculate the time I have before they reach me, ten or fifteen seconds maybe. Can I outrun them? Do I have time? I am already at full throttle; this is as fast as I can go! Hunching down, I keep my eyes on the road, concentrating, willing the Green Knight to go faster, praying the tires track the gravel and the road stays straight.

They are so close I can see it's a pack of three; I pass before they reach the road. I breathe. My head is clear, my heart is pumping; I slow the Green Knight down.

In the distance comes the barking of more dogs; they are going after Jona. How far ahead is he? Should I extend that distance to give the dogs a chance to return to their home base, to increase the space they must cover to reach the road, but risk losing momentum for myself? Can the Green Knight accelerate fast enough?

I decide to keep pace and take my chances. Sooner than I expected, I'm upon them. The second pack seems bigger and fiercer than the first, perhaps because they are closer to the road. Their dark muscular bodies rushing towards me, I open to full throttle once again, giving the Green Knight all the gas there is, and barely escape. I breathe in deeply to calm the trembling of my heart.

How many more packs are there? I hope the town is close. Like a crescendo rising, the dogs' barking is now insistent, urgent. They are eager for an attack. The next pack, the most vicious, the most massive, as big as the Hounds of the Baskervilles are almost at my heel. I hold my breath; I lift my body off the bike. Time slows; my vision sharpens. I can see the fury in their eyes, their yellow teeth. In a flash the dogs disappear from view, I skim past them.

Suddenly, in front of me on the road, a figure appears among the settling sand dust. It's Jona, standing in the middle of the road beside his bike, helmet in hand. I squeeze the brake, coming to a skipping stop. I almost hit him. Covered in dust and sand, a big grin on his face, he calls to me, "Ha ha, ha! I just want to see these dogs attacking the next person behind me!" With that, he pulls on his helmet, flips onto his Green Knight, and flies off into the distance. My heart in my throat, I curse inside my helmet.

Slowly, the dust settles. I breathe and regain my composure, and open the throttle gently. In less than three miles, the road surface begins to change, less sandy, more gravel, it narrows. Low buildings appear here and there along the road, dull brown shrubs covered in dust next to them. I slow down. The road forks, another figure stands in the middle of the road, waving his arms high above his head. I brake and come to a complete stop slowly. I take off my visor, but keep my helmet on.

The man in the middle of the road wears a uniform; he is a policeman. He speaks to me in Mandarin.

"What are you doing here?" He walks around to my rear. "Your bike has no license plate. Do you have a license?"

"We are in a race," I reply in Mandarin.

"Which race? There are many races!"

I explain.

He murmurs, "No one told me."

"We have a letter. It will be here in a while." I do my best. Max has the paper.

"Go over there, I need to call Ürümqi." The policeman points to where Jona stands against a mud wall, next to his parked Green Knight, a big grin still on his face.

"Is there a restaurant in town?" I ask.

The policeman considers the question for a moment, and then gestures for us to follow him. He leads us—he on foot, we on the bikes—to a small courtyard with one low rickety table and a few stools. A young girl watches as we approach. The policeman disappears. It's dusk by now. Light is fading. I find a faucet in the courtyard, when opened ice-cold water trickles out. I wash fine grains of sand from my face. My skin feels soft and supple, fully exfoliated by the blasting sand. I walk across the yard into the dark room, its ceiling low, a stove by the door. I ask the young girl if she can cook us some food. She says she has only five instant noodles left. I realize the restaurant also serves as her family's home. I order a bowl for Jona and me.

Minutes later, Kiwi John and Chris arrive. The sun has set. I watch as they wash and rest and talk about the dogs. One by one the rest ride in. The policeman never returns. I sit at a stool making a tally of day one's riding events:

Chris, an American, a resident of Beijing, lost the gear-shifter of his yellow Yamaha on the col of Tian Shan. Now permanently stuck in second gear, he is nearly out of fuel. Li Lu, his Chinese girlfriend, rides with him without any protective gear, in sneakers and capris!

I broke my eyeglasses at a rest stop, and am now blind in the darkness without them.

Kurt, my buddy from San Francisco, has broken the face shield on his helmet, and his Green Knight's head-light is no longer shining.

Max, a Harvard post-graduate student who speaks fluent Mandarin and Uyghur, and lives part-time in Ürümqi, the organizer of this motley group, runs a tire flat, and has a broken chain. He rides two-up with Jenny, his Canadian girlfriend of two weeks, who skipped a trip to Paris to be here.

One of our support vehicles, an SUV, has a leaky radiator, now duct-taped. "A dog did it," Kurt explained to me. I did not need to know more.

Happily, the rest are in good shape, except the usual gamut of traveling problems—hunger, thirst and fatigue.

Kiwi John, a New Zealander living and working in Shanghai, is my age. We two are the over-forties. The rest are under thirty.

Jona, another Kiwi living in Ürümqi, owner of FuBar, the place to be seen for the in-crowd of Ürümqi's expatriate community of missionaries, oil explorers and whatnots, is a certified mountaineer.

Kyle, of New York, is the man to bet on to win the race.

Ari is the team journalist, also from New York, a sensitive sort who just graduated from Columbia.

Fireman John proudly displays the NYC Fire Department banner on his Green Knight.

Tian Jian, a Han Chinese from Ürümqi, who placed second in his class in last year's race, assists Max in the organization.

Du Tao is our esteemed mechanic, a quiet, determined young man from Lanzhou, Gansu Province, and a close friend of Max's.

Two support vehicles carry our bags, tents and some spare parts: an SUV driven by an apathetic but spruce young man from Tian Jian's work unit, and a van driven by the enthusiastic Manager Wang, general manager of the dealership that sold us the Green Knights.

We reach Korla in the small hours the next morning. It is a big oasis town booming in the middle of the desert with grand plazas, shopping malls, cinemas, concrete high-rises, and paved roads! We repair our vehicles and ourselves; we provision, buying gallons and gallons of bottled water and two trash bags full of homemade trail mix. I find two pairs of new eyeglasses for less than $5, including eye exam, in a modern shopping mall, in the middle of the Taklamakan Desert! Knowing the scarcity of resources ahead, I fully enjoy all the amenities the city offers.

Refreshed, rested, and replenished with lamb *kawap*, the Uyghur kabab, and *ban mian*, a kind of spaghetti meatball noodle dish the taste of which diminishes with each meal, we hit the road, paved this time, in mid-afternoon. Soon the restless young men decide to go off road to ride in the soft sand for fun. For the first time, I try riding up a small sand dune; too quickly I realize I lack the strength to do it for very long. I watch enviously as six-foot-five Kyle maneuvers his Green Knight like a little toy around the sand. I think about my goal for the race—to complete or to participate.

We pitch tents in the sand dunes that night.

In the morning, I awake to find a layer of sand as fine as powder covering me. Outside the tent, everyone is in some stage of shaking out gear and getting dressed.

"Did you shake your boots?" Kyle asks me.

"No."

"Lucky there wasn't a scorpion in them!"

"Scorpion! I didn't see any!"

Kyle shows me a plastic water bottle. Sprawling inside are little sandy colored, almost translucent scorpions he and others have been collecting since last night.

"They are everywhere. See." He points to one crawling near me. I jump. He laughs. I thank my myopia.

Later, Du Tao tells me he found a scorpion under his sleeping bag that morning. I ask him why did he not say something. He says, it's after the fact, there's no point. We share a tent.

Breaking camp, we are on the road again. Max is in the lead, the van taking up the rear. We head for Ruo Qiang riding leisurely on a new road, following the calm, poplar-lined Tarim River. It is the longest inland river in China, at places narrow and deep creating interconnected ponds that are wide and shallow, serene and peaceful. Moistening air opens the suffering nostril passages, inviting the sweet smell of fresh water to flush into my open lungs. Sky is reflected in the pools, creating a moving mirage. The Tarim River is full of hope of life in this desert of death; I want the river to last forever. Home seems a distant past; I slip into a nomadic life.

Max veers off and leads us to ride a yellow brick road, built in a herringbone pattern between 1966 and 1971, and in use until 2002. Its original length was 152 miles, following the bank of the Tarim River. Now a small section is saved where a simple marble memorial stands to extol in exhausting detail the superficial statistics— over 600,000 bricks per one thousand meters, using over 612,000,000 bricks, built by over two thousand workers. It fails to mention these workers were mostly young men and a few women in their late teens to early twenties from Beijing who went west during the Cultural Revolution. Max looks to me before explaining to others that the road was built by forced labor. It's all a matter of perspective. I know these patriotic youth volunteered to come here, not knowing what fate awaited them.

That night, we make camp in sun-baked, dry-cracked, seashell-like desert, decorated with parched shrubs, low and thorny. Under that thin layer of hard surface is soft, sinking, liquefied powdery sand. In the fading twilight, Du Tao teaches me how to ride in this hard and soft contrasting nature with careful control of the throttle, brake and clutch. Time and again I fall off the bike. Getting back on I sink my wheels deep into the sand; the Green Knight stands without help from the kickstand or me. I push and push, running beside it at full throttle, but I am too short and too weak to jump onto the bike. I fall over again and again. How I wish to grow a few more inches. Kiwi John comes over; we discuss how to pivot the Green Knight for me to pick it up. It's certain I must learn how to fall without injury and pick up my bike without help. Exhausted and bruised, I become anxious about the upcoming race.

The racers from Stage One are near, we can hear them on the radio Tian Jiang brought with him. He tunes in. I sit in the dark with him that night while others have gone to sleep, listening to the communications between the racers and the race committee.

"Where is the sweeper? I last called two hours ago!"
Silence.

"Race committee, race committee, please reply. We are still lost. Which direction is the road? Is it due north? We have no GPS, we are running out of gas, please give direction!"
Silence.

"When are the sweepers coming? We have not moved since this afternoon. We are still waiting. When are they coming? Did they miss us?"

The increased desperation in the voices alternates with the silence of the desert accompanying me as I fall asleep inside the tent.

Arriving early at Ruo Qiang the next day, we cannot find lodging. The small town is overrun with racers, race organizers, support personnel and media. Every room in town is occupied. Max and I ride around searching for a suitable guesthouse. We find one cheap, in poor condition at 10 RMB ($1.25) per person. It has a very hot and powerful shower. The owners are happy to house us and agree to let us use the shower. Water is at a premium in this desert town. It's not Motel 6, but it's better than I could hope. We settle down and shower one by one. I walk into the shower fully clothed in riding gear, without the helmet. Standing beneath the shower head, I watch the water run until it's clear without sand before peeling the riding suit off piece by piece. I find sand creeps into every conceivable part of my body and clothes. Sand is invasive.

Refreshed, I go out in search of other racers, finding them congregated in the only hotel in town where race organizers stay. I hear about the progress of the race. I learn more than half of the racers have been eliminated crossing Lop Nor, and hear rumors of a team still lost deep in the desert. I meet other racers; one from Beijing, tall, dark and full of optimism, crisscrossed on his chest are two army issue water canteens from WWII era. "One is for water, one is for fuel." He pats them proudly, "I'm glad you are here. I'm the only racer from Beijing. It's such a comfort to hear one's native tongue. Want to see my bike?" It's a 125cc, smaller than mine. He is a giant straddling it. "It's the best for this desert," he tells me. I notice another young man watching us. A very handsome face, a deep scar runs from his left eyebrow, down his cheek, crosses his upper lip, stops at his right lower chin; a beautiful smile, his eyes longingly caress our bikes. I ask if he is racing, he shakes his head, and walks away.

A crowd forms in the front yard of the hotel as a Unimog moves in slowly like a war machine on a mission. A Unimog is an awesome sight, the toughest of the toughest, a beast that is a lifesaver. In the front of the hotel, one is mounded high with motorbikes; the towering jaw of the heavy equipment lift fishes out bikes one by one from the pile—all twisted, bent, missing critical parts. Many racers stand watching, waiting for their bikes to emerge. The sight sends chills to the spine and races blood to the heart. I consider the objective of my vacation.

We are ignoramuses when it comes to the rally. None of us, except Tian Jian, has ever participated in one. We are not racers at home. The average length of motorcycling experience for the group is less than three years, with some only a few months. We know nothing about the differences between time-keeping enduro and hare scramble, rally and motocross. The race committee knows this. They send a seasoned referee to explain the details of the race, and to teach us how to use the route chart-book of rules, check points, navigational guides, and timing regulations. It's a lot of information to absorb the evening before the race. Nerves are taut. The words of the head referee come back to me. "It's not a race for amateurs." Standing high on the podium at the pre-race racers briefing in Ürümqi four days ago, he spoke eloquently, solemnly, "It is tough, it is dangerous, it is not child play, it is not only physically challenging, it's mentally challenging as well. I have seen grown men cry and crumble. Think hard, search in yourself; if you are not up to it, *do not* participate. Leave right now."

But we are here, all lined up next morning, race day, anxiously waiting to be led to the starting point for Race One of Stage Two. There are fifty motorbike racers and 180 off-road 4x4s. Many vehicles are bandaged with tape, some missing windows, others doors; Lop Nor has not been kind. A police vehicle in the lead, we follow like a battle-worn army marching through the city, into the desert.

Soon, the sky disappears, then the riders before me, finally the road. I see nothing but sand. A heavy sandstorm has engulfed us. I am reminded that Taklamakan is one living, organic desert. Constant, severe sandstorms move earth ground to powder across this vast arid wasteland, shifting landscapes, giving and destroying life. New dunes can appear overnight. This desert has been raining sand dust in Beijing for years. As a child, I remember waking up to find the whole city a color of yellow—the roofs, the streets, the trees, the sky. Running my hand over my writing desk, I could gather a handful of dust. I now know how far the sand traveled to finally settle on my childhood desk.

Sand sweeps across the road like gentle ocean waves, giving me sea legs on the bike, my head unsteady. Between sand waves I see the road, and momentary glimpses of bikes in front of me. With no horizon to focus on, I concentrate on the nothingness in front of me, imagining the road in my mind to ensure I do not fall off the bike. I hope the road is straight. I have little reaction time if it's not. I worry about the bikes behind me as much as the bikes in front of me. I maintain constant speed. We ride and ride for more than a sixty miles. At a rare break in the sandstorm, a 4x4 comes up from the rear of the line, motioning us to slow down. A few minutes later, another 4x4 comes up from the rear, motioning us to stop. The procession halts. We wait for the sandstorm to pass. I take off my helmet; everyone laughs at the sight of me—covered in sand so thick, hardened to a cake, chunks and chunks of sand fall off my face and body. I chat with other riders nonchalantly, working hard to keep my vanity.

Before there was a road, travelers used the few seasonally dried riverbeds to cross this living desert. Ancient travelers on the Silk Road crossed it in caravans, leaving mounds and mounds of small graves dotting the desert as reminders of a once vibrant trade. Well-preserved mummies appear when these graves are disturbed, revealing a glimpse of this terra incognito. The mummies are a sight highly prized. In local dusty museums they lie as they always did, shrunken dry wrapped in cloth, some still colorful. The fascination with them is cultural, political and a matter of national pride; they appear foreign, inexplicable to today's inhabitants of the Taklamakan. Many who have crossed this land have left their remains; today's travelers are no exception.

Word comes that today's race has been canceled. My heart sinks. I know this race, a time-trial, an almost straight course on gravel that must be completed in a pre-set time frame, is my best chance to complete one race in this rally. With a heavy heart, I ride the rest of way, another 108 miles, to the small town of Qie Mo (Cherchen).

Qie Mo is located on the southern border of the Taklamakan Desert. We have traced the border of the desert more than half way around from Ürümqi.

Sitting in the most modern restaurant in town, we dream.

"Ice cream," Max says.

"Pie. A pie. A freshly baked pie," Jenny says. "Belgian waffles too."

"Oh, oh, Pannenkoeken!" Max has lived in Holland.

Outside in the open pit, a whole goat is roasting. On our table are lamb *kawap* and *ban mian*, barely touched.

That evening, we learn that two people, one young man and one young woman, died during the sandstorm the day before; hence the reason for the cancellation of Race One in Stage Two. Max says he used to ride with them. I brace for the upcoming Race Two of Stage Two, the most challenging of the entire rally.

I lie in the soft sand. Noxious fumes of gasoline invade my nostrils. I watch as fuel drips out of the gas tank of the Green Knight. My chest feels heavy, compressed. I have fallen hard, the bike sits motionless on top of me. The front wheel is at a weird angle. I was the last to start, no more racers behind me. Everyone is in front of me, long gone. This is the hardest course, I was told by the referees. Before my start, one by one, all five stopped by, each asked, almost begged me not to compete. Before the flag came down, the referee asked me one last time, "You are already here, isn't that enough. You don't have to compete." I looked at the tracks made by those who went before me, knowing it would be difficult for me as the last person to follow. Virgin sand is easier to ride on than the deeply treaded tracks. It required a different technique, one I had not acquired. I knew the course was only forty-two miles, but we were given six hours to complete it. I now know why. I still have forty-one miles to go.

I begin to dig myself out of sand, picking up my bike. A man comes out of nowhere to help me, I hear the referee screaming at him, "No! No one can help her pick up the bike. She will be disqualified!" I wave him off. The bike is not too heavy yet at about 125 kilograms, or 275 lb, but I know I won't be able to pick it up again and again. I straddle it and open the throttle, so deeply stuck in sand the Green Knight won't move. I clutch in, making sure it is in first gear, give it all the gas I can, and then release the clutch abruptly. The Green Knight lunges forward, but goes sideways, I lose balance. My front tire is no longer a perfect circle. Once again, the Green Knight lies on top of me, and the sickly smell of gasoline fills my compressed lung. I am now polluting the environment.

Behind me, all the support vehicles are leaving. The referees jump into their jeep, and drive on to the course to where I lie. "Don't go any farther. You will not come out. The sweepers won't be here until dark. Come with us."

I look at my Green Knight, streaked with oil and sand, smelling foul; how miraculous, my rearview mirrors are not even cracked. I look up at the referees sitting in the jeep. My chest hurts and so does my back. As a child, I often wondered if I was a hologram in a dream, hollow in a void, the body just a vapor, a mirage, the world a chimera, all an illusion; pinching my arm always reas-sured me of my own physical existence. The pain comes

back, stabs my back and chest; every breath reminds me
I have bones and muscles, there is a heart beating under
my rib. It's wonderful to feel alive, lying there, absorbed
into the sand, a simple fusion of senses.

The referees watch me, waiting.

"Time to go," the head referee says to me.

I dig myself out of the sand from underneath the bike,
picking it up, inspecting the front wheel, all the spokes
are still there, the handlebar is still aligned; it starts like
a dream, strong without hesitation. I nod.

"Can you ride on your own?"

"Yes."

The referee leads me, they in the jeep, I on the Green
Knight, to the paved road that parallels the racecourse. I
watch as the jeep takes off, leaving me trailing behind. I
ride to the finish line on the road slowly counter-steering
all the way, fighting to keep a straight line. The slightly
oblong front wheel is unwieldy. The Green Knight zigs,
then zags. The desert once again looks calm and serene.
A sense of tranquility, satisfaction, and contentment fills
me, a smile inside the helmet.

At the finish line, I keep company with the referees.
The fastest riders come out in less than two hours. They
ride out effortlessly, lyrically, dancing on the sand. I
watch in awe as they take their bikes apart, cleaning the
filters, greasing the gears, fueling up, blowing the sand
off, riding away leisurely like a Sunday afternoon ride
in the park.

I wait for our group to come out. I watch as Kyle and
Jona race each other to cross the finish line in merely three
hours. I watch as Kiwi John comes out in four hours, triumphantly, laughing all the way, collapsing immediately.
I watch Tian Jian coming out dehydrated, barely making
the time of six hours, insisting the only reason that pro-

pelled him to continue was that he "just wanted to come out for a drink of water." He bursts into laughter, laughing, laughing, uncontrollably, deliriously.

I hear their stories of getting lost in the desert, going round and round in circles until meeting others, begging a drink of water from another racer, flipping over the handlebars, falling again, again and again. I see my hometown Beijing racer riding out on a bike not his own. He recounts to me of tumbling down a tall sand dune, crashing his bike, catching fire from the fuel in his canteen, he shows me his singed eyebrows in good humor. He tells me of helping other racers picking up their bikes—"it's all about comradeship"—riding another's bike out because his own is trashed, and the other racer is too exhausted to continue, and has simply given up. More than seven hours after the race began, Max comes out screaming at the top of his lungs, "This is a fucking professional course! What are they thinking?!" He is the last of our group to ride his bike across the finish line.

Dusk turns the desert ocher, pale, almost opaque. All is quiet, nature is composed—no wind, no storm, no more drama. One by one others leave, except our little group. Referees also prepare to leave, talking on the radio with the sweepers, as these powerful, strong, tough Unimogs begin the final task of combing the racecourse meter by meter, picking up broken vehicles and racers. As the night falls the longest ride awaits us. We must begin the march to the next village some 155 miles away. Kiwi John and I partner up. We agree to stop every thirty miles to refresh and rest.

The desert a black hole, the moon is hiding, and so are the stars. I lead. There is no light except our headlights, drunk in by the darkness hungrily, swallowed whole. There is no heaven, no earth, no spectrum of colors. I

ride carefully, slowly, conscious of not out-running the
short beam of light in front of me. I fight to keep my eyes
open while battling the oblong front wheel. Soon I stop
every thirty miles, then twenty, then fifteen. We arrive at
the village at 3 A.M., waking up the night watchman of
the only hotel in the village. A bed never felt so restful.
I sleep in full riding gear. Morning comes; we continue
our march forward to Stage Three.

At the city of He Tian (Hotan), the starting point for
Stage Three, I decide to fly out to Ürümqi, while others
continue up the He Tian riverbed to Aksu, then back to
Ürümqi, making the full circle. Du Tao agrees to ride my
Green Knight back for me. As I watch, the group rides
off one by one, waving me good-bye. My heart settles to
quietude and serenity. Having lived life to the fullest for
a short moment, having rocked insipid senses out of their
complacency, I find life vibrant, inviting and fulfilling.

A sudden yearning for a touch of delicate femininity
seizes me. I long to feel the freedom of movement in a
dress, the sensual touch of silk against my bare skin, the
sweet smell of freshly shampooed hair. Ten days I inhabited the allure-killing riding suit, armored head to toe,
riding a machine, hard and tough; rolling in sand, living
a nomad life, austere and spartan.

I roam the ancient bazaar of He Tian in search of
a red dress among the dissonance of merchant hollers,
bicycle bells, motorbike motors, and car horns. I pass
the spice sellers, drinking in the aroma of bags and
bags of pale cumin seeds, black cloves, red peppercorns,
saffron-colored paprika, green marjoram, and a hundred others whose names are not in my vocabulary;
I pause in front of a machete-wielding fruit seller slicing
watermelons to relieve my thirst; I walk by an old man
selling lamb *kawap* and *nan*; I watch a man ladling milk

from a small tin bathtub; I chat with a man hammering intricate patterns on tin-covered trunks using nails; but I do not find the dress I seek. In the end, I find a simple skirt, the color of the desert, and a headscarf, the purest white. Putting them on, I find joy within, suddenly full, complete and happy, finding femininity while brushing against masculinity.

I head to the airport, arriving thirty minutes before departure. The check-in counter is still closed; there's no one about in this two-room airport. I sit, lounging in a long row of empty chairs facing the street. My mind clear, my body relaxed in my new skirt, free from the restraints of the rigid armor suit, I am at ease, events of past days now a memory.

A taxi arrives, its door opens, and a young man rolls out. I gasp. A figure clad in dirt-covered full-leather armor of yellow and black, blue and dull white, with endorsements stitched on all available real estate; his shoulders padded high hiding the neck, legs bowed at kneepads; he wobbles towards me, in his hand is a decal-covered helmet. I remember the suit and the face. I am astounded to see him here, in this same airport. He can't stand straight, he can barely walk; he recognizes me too. He rides a Yellow Hornet and is from Hu Nan province. We have chatted about our bikes in the sandstorm.

"Where's your bike?" I ask.

"Somewhere in the desert, maybe on the Unimog."

"Your luggage?"

"Same. The Unimog. I'm going home. I can't take it anymore."

He slouches next to me, sighs heavily. His lips are dry, hair a mess, his face looks as if it has not seen water for days.

"Do you want a cup of water?"

"Yes."

I bring a cup of water to him. We sit together silently after. He forces my thoughts back.

The check-in counter opens, fifteen minutes before our flight. "I'm going to check in," I say to him.

"I can't move. I'm broken. Broken."

I check in for both of us, help him onto the plane. There are fewer than ten passengers. I sit by the window, looking at the Taklamakan Desert below, a sea of benign, monotonous oatmeal almost moonlike, the rolling mounds, the simple forms of nature unchanged for millions of years. The plane hums as it gains altitude, I can barely make out the Tarim River sneaking below soundlessly, motionlessly, the fluidity of nature, free from human intrusions. The plane climbs over the snowcapped peaks of Tian Shan towards Ürümqi. I feel levitation.

ॐ ॐ ॐ

Born and raised in Beijing, Y.J. Zhu came to the United States at age fifteen. She's an avid rider of two-wheel vehicles. She lives in San Francisco and is working on two books, a short story collection about inhabitants of today's Beijing, and an account of her overland travel from China to Burma.

ஐ ஐ ஐ

Homecoming Istanbul

An expatriate in Turkey reflects on her life and choices.

The Bosphorus is filled with jellyfish, fish spines and sea foam. This water, in my experience, is a real body—wide and calibrated, supporting transport from side to side, Asia to Europe, a home for dolphin, sea bass, mussels, some garbage and gook and seaweed. It is my mother, I egocentrically think. Although my sister, Mira, and I spread her ashes off the coast of Cape Cod in Spring 2000, a spontaneous choice of the Wareham public beach since she left no clear indication which beach she preferred, I still picture Bilge traveling the Bosphorus. In our underwear and Kmart t-shirts, we swam in shallow water, tore the bag of ashes open, and let her go.

Although Massachusetts was her adopted land, I cannot imagine that she stayed in those waters. The ferryboat call must have been excessively strong—the route

from Kadiköy to Beşiktaş was her glory ride. Holding
a Turkish tea in one hand, and mine or Mira's in the
other, she might have said that there was nothing more
beautiful than that ride, the cumbersome ferries built
before her childhood, and the historical spread from
the Topkapi Palace to the castle in Rumali Hisari. We
always sat on the side of the boat that faced the sun and
never minded the spray on our feet or faces of salt and
breeze and sesame seeds that fell from seagull-feeders on
the upper deck. Mira, Mom, and I—specifically when
and how often we traveled by ferry during our infrequent summer visits, I cannot remember. But how it felt,
viscerally and literally, and qualitatively, I re-experience
every day.

Now, I take the boat from Kandilli to Arnavutköy,
or from Üsküdar to Beşiktaş, or from Kandilli to
Eminönü. I sit outside. I rarely drink tea. Sometimes I
smoke, always reminded that this is a temporary solution
to replace deep breathing. I ride with my own thoughts,
those of my mother, sister, neighbors, the man or woman
across or beside me. It is a ride between shores, between
places, from here to there, destination-interrupted by a
moment to sit and watch and be weathered. It is wind
and salt—it is Istanbul, the place of my mother's and
daughter's births. It is the link between them that waters
two continents, or between my being and becoming, or
between my mother and myself—truly for everyone
in this massive city, the continents speak differently.
Indeed, for me, Istanbul is my motherhood, a city that
witnesses my mothering, and the place that was once my
mother's, and is now my, home.

Istanbul is also the sound of halting traffic, men bel-
lowing their sales of sesame bread or water or phone
chargers, women covered and uncovered, skirted or

sleek, brown and blue and green-eyed, blond, red, brown-trussed, sitting on buses, selling flowers, holding a child's hand, business-suited and high-heeled, cool and low-jeaned and sexy. It is the *sahil*—the coast, it is the square, it is the village after village of fish restaurants and tea houses and now Starbucks, or the Houston-style tower, twins and triplets, mixed with dust from the buses and a barren skyline and variety shops for a quick water, soda, sweet or phone card. Istanbul is Sultan Ahmet— the Old City, the Grand Bazaar, the Spice Bazaar, the Blue Mosque, Aya Sophia, Palaces, Ottoman relics, pre-Ottoman stones and crumblings, and much more.

But this is not, truly, where I feel Istanbul in its entirety. I feel this city as a vibration, genetic and expatriate, as an insider/outsider/besider. I am not a stranger here. I know this city from my mother's school days stories, of climbing the tall stone wall that surrounded her educational privilege to kiss boys, or whispering at night to her best friend in the dorm, or being an average student at the best school in the country at a time when the population was less than a million (now over 10 million). I know this city from my own feet, as they transpire, perspire, sorely and surely cross streets and passages and cobblestones, gravel and asphalt. I know the bumps with a stroller from Nişantaşı to Maçka Park, or even Fulya to Akmerkez, the roads without sidewalks, the sidewalks without roads, the uneven and even landscape, the hills, the tulips, yellow-pink-purple wild flowers that ensconce the side of every highway at once beautiful and surprising, not lush, just patches or spots or dots.

There is no "my" Istanbul as I think many expats wish there could be, there is just this reality that I live here, that I exist in this vibrant uncompromising city, that I am Turkish, and American-born and grown, and wist-

fully French, and that yes, I believe my place is somewhere between here and there—here being Istanbul, for
the moment, there being elsewhere—an unknown.

I write most evenings from where I have been living for
the past two months, a cottage on an estate in Kandilli,
Istanbul, a village on the Bosphorus that leads upwards
toward overbuilt and awkward hills. How could I even
begin to describe this place that unlike anywhere else in
the world embodies Europe and Asia. My mother, born
in this city in 1934, later spent forty years of her life in
Boston and Philadelphia, returned here four years before
her death in 2000. She wrote a few months before she
died that living again in Istanbul was "truly recovery in
an archeological sense. I ran away to America. But there
was no place, no possibility to run away. Deceptions
followed me in all other facets and places of my life.
I became disoriented from fear and abandonment—
ultimately, I abandoned myself. Lucky that I have come
back in a way that I never have been here before."
   My husband and I moved here in 2001, a year after
my mother's death. Istanbul, memory, motherhood.
Mine, my mother's, my daughter's. Recently separated,
I live alone and with my daughter, Gabriella, our four-
year-old who also shares her father's—once our—home.
And finally, for the first time that I can remember since
I was twenty-six, living in a similarly small apartment
in an old Victorian house in Old Town Alexandria,
Virginia, I am writing.

Now answer this, who does not get that we are alone,
virtually and literally, spiritually and metaphysically
no matter where we are? Who really does not have
heart palpitations at some moment at the realization,

or remembrance, that death is a solo activity? Who has not known being in bed with a lover and feeling utterly separated by some invisible division, myside/yourside, or hey, we made love, but was that it?! It seems rather late in my life to consider that until now, I have functioned with the belief that friends and lovers, somehow, or another, should take place of that alone space with unconditional love—that which we also expect, perhaps more reasonably, from our parents and family. This, of course, is not how it really is. I no longer rely on such imaginative cultural expectations—not, however, because I lack experience with unconditional love. It is just that for some reason, I have wanted more than is truly reasonable—to be adored and coddled, to have free range of conversation, to process the process of processing on my terms, endlessly, when I have needed it, which has been far more often than I think is desired by most.

In the barest terms, I have wanted to be home everywhere and anywhere, and it has been within relationships that I have sought that homecoming. It is no surprise that I never quite find it, or when I do, that it is transient or elusive. This year, as I worked toward the separation from my husband, whom I can easily remember coming toward me at about 7 P.M. on a rainy evening thirteen years ago, I have learned how unreasonable this is.

God came through the phone line and through the window. God came, like an egg yolk sinks down the side of the bowl after the egg is cracked, and dribbled onto the rest of the mix—my flour, milk, sugar, and baking powder. God was in my pancakes, my hot bath this morning, my laundry. God walked with me from a friend's house in the pitch black night, a brisk walk down the unexpectedly curved and rounded back streets of Istiniye,

from the top of the hill, past the fruit and vegetable stand
and corner store, past abandoned construction and private villas, past a *gece* condo (a home illegitimately built
on someone else's land) with a fig tree in front and wood
piled by the side of the door for unregulated and illegal
burning during this chilly May evening.

God accompanied me in the taxi, from the seaside,
over the second bridge, brilliantly lit, as it is every night,
a flexible link between the two sides of this city, between
my wanting—my wish for relationships, of all kinds, to
fill my void and emptiness—and my home. God said,
call your old friend Matthew. And I did. And Matthew
said, be with God. And he chuckled that hearty and
familiar hoot—that I knew some twenty-five years ago
when he was my first lover of choice—at the irony that
he, the intellectually satiated and complete, whose rep-
ertoire was full and verbose and arrogant, could tell me,
simply, to assume that the existence of spirit, and my
acceptance of that, is all that matters. I know he is right.
And I called him because I knew he would tell me what
I needed to hear. In the middle of his busy day attending
to building his new home for himself, his wife, and children, in the sunlight of a smooth Colorado day, he called
me back, listened to my story, my childhood story that
is, the very condensed version, and said what he would
have said had he known none of it. To just be. To believe
that what I am looking for is nowhere else to be found
except right here.

My life these days has been this: I fill myself daily with
chatter; I tell myself stories of now and the past that reit-
erate my culpability and collaboration with and toward
my own self-diagnosed insanity. And yet, I sanely, yes,
very sanely, go into the therapeutic context, whether in

the office, or in my client's home, and stand wise and listen passionately and guide and help those who believe I can help them move from one stuck place to somewhere unstuck.

And I wander, afterwards, with a few bills in my pocket, from this friend to that coffee to this encounter to that verbal discourse about some irrelevant worry that only guides me deeper into my own personal collateral, and from there, hold the hand of an elderly woman on the bus as the driver takes us all on what seems like his last joy ride, at sixty kilometers an hour along the two lane and squiggly sea road, as we rock abruptly back and forth hanging on for what could be the last moments of our lives before we crash.

But we do not crash, and I help my lady out the bus door and toward the boat, perhaps paying her way, as she says, "*canım, sağol...merci...Allah korsun.*" (Sweetie, thanks. Thank God.) I listen to my friends, sometimes fully, sometimes halfly, and offer chips of wisdom and insight, and then I take myself home and bury myself in some smoked and clouded ruminations about what I did or did not do, and a little self-berating or a lot of head-banging denial about who I am not and who I cannot be and why I am lost beyond lost beyond lost—beyond lost.

So, who am I in all this contradiction and compliance? Does that really matter at this point when I am just here, on earth, for some mili-moment until I am not here anymore? Am I choosing, to the horror, I am sure, of many friends and family, for whom God is an offense and a religious term that is a human-reflection and for the most ignorant of our kind, to believe that God could be with me in all of this mundane and repetitive living?

Well, yes, folks, I think I am. I am choosing to believe that God was with me today instead of just some intellectual reflection of my own desire for immortality and potency, that God, for lack of any other word such as spirit or energy or transcendence, is all that matters. Am I nuts? What blasphemy for a non-religious Muslim-Jew who grew up celebrating Christmas, Passover, and Halloween. What stupidity for a Phi Beta Kappa graduate whose intellectual fortitude and abilities were sung by one graduate professor after another. What sin for a non-believer, who does believe in the big bang, in science, fact and quantitative study, and not in creation or the Bible or the Koran or any scripture from any place written at any time. That is all literature, for God's sake! Yes, what insanity for a psychotherapist, trained in a psychodynamic and satanically Freudian/Kleinian tradition, later to discover the wonders of the post-modern and post-post-modern, narrative non-tradition and boundary crossings. What devilish and shocking revelation, such as this, could not prove, beyond any reasonable doubt, that I have gone mad?

Right now, I couldn't care less. I am not empty tonight despite my efforts, my very willful efforts to fill the hole that I so carefully cultivate inside me. Nor am I oozing some uncontainable sewage from my loud and stylish articulate tongue that usually verbalizes every feeling, thought and burp that passes through this far too active mind and body. No, tonight I believe this—that with a certain amount of faith, however defined, in whatever terms, God-Spirit-Goddess-Vita-oh you know what I mean, I will be able to mend. And that, right now, is all I want to think about. As my father said, in 1958, at the end of one of his and my Aunt Ruth's collaborative folk-singing-cassette-recorded, playful and funny commentaries, "and for now, my friends, good night." A muffle from what must have been him placing the microphone beside the recorder, leaning forward toward the off switch, and then…silence.

And so where do I go from here? Rilke, in *Love and Other Difficulties*, remarked that "we must assume our existence as broadly as we in anyway can; everything, even the unheard-of must be possible in it." I capsize into a meal of strawberries and cheese and sesame crackers, below the dim light in my living room, within the twang of guitar and the glide of piano on the radio, inside the quiet that separates me from my neighbors, and beside the complete innocence of my sleeping daughter. I fall into this moment as it is, this moment, a moment, a minute, a second, a snatch of time. I am in a sort of cosmic, uncalculating oneness for which I have no words to describe. This evening is mine. It is all about what I want, being with myself, with my child, then with myself again. It is I, in all my profundity, surety, and triteness, sprinkled with some flecks of spirit and free-speak.

I know not from where my next rent will emerge, nor what lies ahead. Sure, however, that I, a stranger and a familiar in Istanbul, my home, my place for now, will find my way to and from and forward. Clear, at least for this night that I am with God in all the meanings of God and not God. I am homecoming—to this body that was born from my mother and bore my daughter, without hesitation or fear. I live three hundred meters from the other body—the Bosphorus. I speak from the edge of this moment, about the world that I have created outside of my home country, and how I live within/without/beside. That is the point, right? No matter where we reside, abide, and sleep.

જ્રે જ્રે જ્રે

Banu Françoise Hummel, American-born of Turkish and Russian descent, is a clinical social worker, writer, and mother who has lived in Istanbul, Turkey since 2001. She grew up in Boston and Philadelphia, and later lived in the Washington, D.C. area for ten years. Since arriving in Istanbul, she has provided psychotherapy and counseling to asylum-seekers and refugees in both English and French, began and continues to learn and speak Turkish, and maintains a small private practice as a child, adolescent, and family therapist. This is her first publication since she was sixteen years old, when she and her mother collaborated and published a collection of Banu's poems and her mother's etchings.

❧ ❧ ❧

Pain and Pleasure in Liguria

When traveling off-season in Italian mushroom country,
don't forget your parka.

The coldest night I ever spent was in the porcini mushroom country in the hills above the Italian Riviera.
Of course I've survived other cold nights. Just to think of
one frosty Thanksgiving eve, cramped in a drafty tent in
Yosemite Valley, makes me shudder still. And even several
elapsed decades haven't diminished the icy memory of
that snowy New Jersey night when my parents and all
four of us children, left without heat by a blizzard, slept
piled on the floor in front of the living room fireplace. But
this particular cold night was incomparable.

Driving up the Ligurian coast, my husband, Carlo, and
I decide to stop in Portofino, fabled playground of the jet
set since the 1920s. We know that in summer the road

that funnels cars along the Portofino Peninsula and into Portofino is often clogged with traffic. But this is a weekday in May, and we plan to treat ourselves to lunch at a restaurant we've read about in an American food magazine.

We find Portofino a gorgeous, empty stage set. Its compact piazza slopes down to steps leading right into the water; green-shuttered pink and yellow houses round the bay in that serene, impossible convex curve I've seen in so many photographs. Only a couple of yachts are visible, reminders of their many missing fellows, which will be jostling for anchorage come summer. A fisherman has tugged his boat out of the water and carefully layers on the traditional cream paint edged with red and blue—a touch of reality that will probably disappear in June with the onslaught of tourists.

No traveler can discover Portofino; one can only revel in its myriad glories. We follow more than a thousand years of visitors, drawn by the mild year-round climate, lush vegetation, and an ideal natural harbor. In the early Middle Ages, when Genoa was one of four great sea republics, her sailors had sheltered here. Richard Lionheart stopped on his way to the Third Crusade. Even further back, Pliny the Elder wrote, Portofino was called Portus Delphini, Port of Dolphins, by the Romans, because so many dolphins frolicked here in the Gulf of Rapallo.

At a café in the piazza, a couple of syrupy espressos fortify us for the hike to the lighthouse at the peninsula's western tip. The hike really is only an easy amble, a mere hour's round trip, but time seems to stretch the path like a well-made pizza dough in expert hands, and it feels as though we walk for hours. Perhaps it's the richness and variety of things to discover as the terrain shifts constantly, first the view of the town from above, then creeks running through the dense undergrowth, flowers, and pine, olive, and yew trees; glimpses along the way of peach and ochre villas secreted behind ornate twisted wrought-iron gates; slashes of views of towns and coves looking back south along the coast. Pausing, we can't resist stumbling down a side path to one of dozens of tiny, rocky coves, happy to splash our feet in the cool water. When we reach the whitewashed lighthouse, the view extends back the whole seventy miles to La Spezia.

It's no accident that this peninsula, though inhabited and visited since antiquity, is still a paradise of rare plants and animals. The people of Portofino have stood firmly against modern buildings and housing. And the Italian government, often shamefully lax in protecting its astounding inheritance, has safeguarded this area since 1935, when it established the Parco Naturale Regionale di Portofino to protect Monte Portofino and the entire peninsula.

Refreshed by our hike, we are ravenous. The odor of garlic-scented oil drifting out of our chosen restaurant is enough to make me reel. There are only a few other diners sitting outside facing the piazza. The owner himself—slight, friendly—leads us to a table. We order a bottle of Cinque Terre white, house-made pasta *ai funghi*, salads of bitter greens with the local delicately perfumed, sweet olive oil. The food comes quickly and, whether because of our appetites, the balmy air, the sun on the water, its own excellence, or some of all of these, it is *perfetto*. Perfect like deep, dark chocolate, like new babies, like kisses on the lips. I decide then and there that if I ever have only six months to live, I would be happy to spend most of my time right here at this table in the sun. I'd just have to get someone to arrange to keep the other tourists away.

While we drain our espressos, we watch idly as a good-looking boy of about twelve, neatly dressed and wearing a backpack, comes through the piazza directly to the owner and kisses him tenderly on both cheeks. The owner's face as he returns the double kiss is so fond, so gratified, it seems as though the two have been separated for years instead of what we can assume has been the length of a school day. I think that this is probably one of Italy's now-ubiquitous, treasured only children. Our host's expression reminds me of the look I sometimes glimpse on my own parents' faces when they greet my own only twelve-year-old boy, a look made even more fervid by long separations and their more acute awareness of time. Perhaps I am reminded of my parents partly because of the oversized sign that stretches the whole elongated length of a restaurant on the far side of the piazza. *Ristorante Stella,* it proclaims in big blue letters; Stella is my mother's name.

Somnolent after our late lunch, we talk about whether we should search out a room for the night, but decide to press on. I love the sea even more than the mountains; Carlo loves the mountains even more than the sea. We both have delighted in the shifts, sudden as a storm, that have happened to our Italian journeys when we've simply headed up into the mountains. They're never far away, not in this country that is 39 percent mountainous, with another 40 percent hills. On other trips, we'd followed a mountain road up to Carrara, with its snowy cliffs of stone; coming from Parma to the coast, we'd traced the kinks of a mountain road through ancient hamlets where we never saw a car other than our own; in Umbria, we'd seen precipitous villages that appeared to be reachable only on foot. The revelation of these trips into the hills has been how close these remote-feeling places are to popular resorts and art towns.

We decide to continue west past Genoa, where the Riviera de Ponente turns into the Riviera de Levante, so we can end up closer to St.-Remy-de-Provence, across the French border, where we're meeting friends the following night. Randomly, we choose one of three squiggles on the map, leading up and away from the coast. We find our turnoff at Finale Ligure. The road curves gradually uphill and then folds into a series of switchbacks. We'd left Portofino in what felt like early summer; as the road climbs, we find ourselves in late spring, looking down on carpets of fledgling grass and wildflowers, and scattered woods, trees rich with lime-green leaves. Rounding one corner, we squeak to a stop. A half-dozen handsome alpine goats, with their great curved horns, stand casually blocking the road. I wave to their young shepherd, and he waves back, leisurely, as he herds them to the other side.

A rouge-streaked sunset finds us in the most severe set of switchbacks. We have a plan of sorts: look for a hotel before dark; if there's nothing obvious, continue on to the town of Calizzano, the next town on the map. After the goats, we see no more animals nor any signs of humanity. Which is why the sign for Calizzano is greeted with whoops; we aren't looking forward to more switchbacks—no guardrails, of course!—in the dark. Driving through town, the street is just wide enough for our car; there are no lights and nothing that resembles a hotel. We're debating the relative merits of going back to investigate more of Calizzano, or driving on to see what might be up ahead, when we spot a lit room in a big building off the road. Drawing near, we can see the sign, that international word so beloved by the traveler: *HOTEL.*

"*Buona sera, una camera per la notte, per favore.* Good evening, a room for the night, please," I say to the dark-haired, middle-aged woman at the reception desk.

"*Si, va bene, Signora,*" she replies, grabbing an enormous set of jingling keys from a hook. She takes our passports, and we follow her down a long, tunnel-like hallway, so dimly lit I can't see the room numbers on the doors, only the glint of metal in the gloom. She opens a door and switches on the overhead light, exposing a room of utili-tarian ugliness. It is noticeably cold.

"May I please see another room?" I ask. We three continue along the cold tunnel in the eerie light, and she opens another door. The room is an exact copy of the first one. We perform this exercise several more times, at one point climbing the stairs to a second floor with a matching icy tunnel of rooms. Clearly, this hotel has dozens of rooms, exactly the same; equally clearly, they are all empty; and even more apparent, she is bored enough to parade around with us all night if we wish.

"No people?" I inquire.

"Oh, no, no, Signora," she replies, apparently happy to explain, "This isn't the season. They come for the mushrooms."

"When is that?" I ask.

She looks surprised that we don't know. "In the fall," she tells us with a smile, opening another door.

"*Va bene.* This room, please," I say. After all, there's no reason to retrace our steps to the first, identical room.

She hands us the key and, as we stand together in the center of the room, I notice that the ugly room, like the corridor outside, like the other rooms we've looked at, is cold—the musty insidious cold of a room that hasn't been used, or heated, for some time. In fact, it is much colder in this building than it is outside.

"Can you tell me where the heater is, please?" I ask her, rubbing my arms.

"There is no heat, Signora, not after April." I know there is no use arguing with this logic. In many Italian hotels, heat, or the lack of it, is controlled by the calendar, not the climate. If it is not the season, there will be no heat—even if it snows in the room.

My husband and I lock gazes in the way of married couples who are also practiced travel companions. Neither of us is willing to contemplate getting back in that car. "*Sì, grazie, signora,*" I say, grudging but compelled by her good manners to be equally polite.

After she leaves, I explore the room, which takes less than one minute, and find one of those deep small bathtubs, the kind with a built-in seat. There may not be heat, but there is hot water, and the water pressure is torrential.

"Do you want to go back to town to find something to eat?" my husband asks, as I throw off my clothes and practically dive in. I raise my eyebrows at him from my perch, sunken to my ears in hot water. A practiced reader of eyebrow-Braille, he grabs his wallet. "O.K.," he continues, "I'm going to go look for something."

"What a good idea," I say, because we had, not that long ago, an enormous lunch, and I'd rather starve than leave this tub.

The hot water holds out well. Every time I begin to feel chilly, I run some more. Only my nose is cold. When he returns, my husband carefully balances a large white package. "What's that?" I ask.

"Dinner," he replies, the self-satisfied hunter returning with the kill. I consider staying right where I am, but I think it would be difficult to eat without removing my arms from the water. So I get out and gather up nearly every piece of clothing in my suitcase and layer them on top of each other, finally pulling on the jacket I thought I'd never wear. While not *alla moda,* I am quite warm now and optimistic about the evening ahead.

Carlo, meanwhile, is unwrapping his package, which turns out to be a pile of thick white plates, big white cloth napkins tucked neatly on top, the whole swaddled in a heavy, ironed white linen tablecloth. The food is simple: tortellini with pesto and salad. The hot food is sending up clouds of oil and basil-scented fog into the cold air. Gratified at the success of his conjuring trick, my husband pulls cutlery from his pockets and sets a bottle of water and one of wine on the bedside table.

"Wow," I ask, "how did you pull this off?"

"Well, I ordered the food, and I told the waitress *a casa,* and she looked confused, like she wasn't sure what to do. I don't think she'd ever sent food home with anyone. And then we chatted for a while—she'd never heard of San Francisco, and she wanted to know all about it, so we handed the dictionary back and forth. And then, when the food was ready, she just got out this big tablecloth and wrapped it up. I made a sign to say I'd come back and said, *'Domani,'* and she acted like that was fine."

We make our picnic on the bed, the only flat surface in the room other than the tiled floor. We are warmed by the waitress's trust in us, *stranieri* after all, and, very quickly, by the food, not to mention the wine. I am still warm from my long immersion. In a little while, I spread every blanket in the room—including the ones in the closet—on the bed before settling in.

A couple of hours later, the cold wakes me. I am so cold I would wonder if I were dead except for the solid evidence of my breath. The part of my body that is crushed against my husband, who is always less dramatically cold or hot than I, is less cold, but only a little less. Several times, I consider getting out of bed to run another bath, or to search for my book and little book light, but then I'd have to expose myself to the air in the room, which is inconceivable.

I tell myself to think of Portofino, hoping to trick my skin temperature into rising a couple of degrees. Unfortunately, my Portofino reverie does not make the night pass swiftly. It feels like the sun-warmed afternoon has been a scene from a novel or a movie; it is impossible to believe in it. The cold is like some terrible entity in the room, sucking all warmth and life.

The Frigid *Funghi* Hotel, as I came to think of it, turns out to be the rare hotel in Italy that offers no breakfast. This is fine with me; I can't wait to flee the place. My breath is still a solid shape and when I pull the drapes, bright light fills the room, offering hope of a better, warmer world outside. Muttering, *"Arrivederci, grazie, un momento,"* we skulk past the reception desk, my husband carrying the bags, me balancing the tower of plates robed with the folded tablecloth. For once, we have no desire to revel in the usual courtesies. I wait in the car while my husband hurries back in to sign the bill and grab our passports.

It *is* a different, warmer green world outside. Approaching the car, Carlo beckons to me. We may never come back to this *funghi* country—why not take an early-morning walk before breakfast?

Just a stroll up the road we are surrounded by beautiful, white-limbed trees, graceful as dancers. Here, too, it is still spring, and their curvaceous limbs are clothed with small chartreuse leaves. Ahead of us are rolls and jam and *cappuccini,* and a chat with my husband's new friend, the young woman at the restaurant. Later, I will read that Calizzano contains the loveliest beech forest in the province of Liguria. I will discover, too, that Calizzano and the surrounding towns are famous not only for the *funghi*, specifically porcini mushrooms, but also for chestnuts, and even the occasional white truffle. But all that comes later. It is enough, this fine morning, to walk, enchanted, and in my case, thrilled to be warm, in the dappled light of those beautiful trees.

Francesca De Stefano, who lives in San Francisco with her husband and their son, is writing a book about traveling and eating in Italy. Her story "Living on Venetian Time" was included in The Best Women's Travel Writing 2007, *and "Paradiso" appeared in* 30 Days in Italy. *She credits her love of travel to one of her first childhood memories—standing at the dock in New York, holding one end of some streamers, her grandparents holding the other, as their boat moved off on its journey to Italy.*

_β_ _β_ _β_

Rite of Passage

Was she the kind of person who could
jump from an airplane?

Nestled against violet mountains on the South
Island of New Zealand lies the self-proclaimed
"Adventure Capital of the World": Queenstown. This
alpine resort town has it all—a pristine recreational lake,
nearby ski slopes and the gateway to some of the most
scenic hiking trails on the earth. On almost every street,
advertising brochures beckon from doorways like prostitutes in a red light district. Jet boating, heli-skiing, and
luging lure hordes of thrill-seekers who converge on the
town each season.

The first bungee jump from the Kawarau Bridge in
the 1980s became Queenstown's claim to fame, but it was
the marketing from a skydiving operation that enticed
us the most:

"It takes a certain kind of person to step out of an air-craft at 12,000 feet into thin air. You can expect sensory overload as your mind, soul and body fight against every natural, self-preservatory urge."

Was *I* the kind of person who could jump from an airplane? I wondered. I had just survived a rigorous ten-day trek through the South Island's rugged wilderness. I'd bouldered up cliff faces to tops of waterfalls, crossed rickety swing bridges suspended over rivers, and pick-axed my way atop an ice-blue glacier. You might mistake me for just another adrenaline junkie, but don't be fooled. I was that girl who, in second grade, sat on a bench in a velvet dress and patent leather shoes, refusing to play ball because "my mom told me not to get my dress dirty."

Before traveling to New Zealand I had made a list of things I longed to experience in my lifetime but was too afraid to try. Skydiving was at the top. To put it plainly, I was afraid of falling. Speedily. From treacher-ous heights. In New Zealand's backcountry, trudging under the weight of a forty-pound pack up to a moun-tain cave, my legs had wobbled like a newborn calf. My fingers constantly gripped the slippery hillsides like an old woman clutching her walker. Terror taunted me with images of my body crashing down, bones crack-ing onto sharp rocks below. By the trek's end, I may not have overcome my fears, but I had edged one step closer. Plunging from a plane, my friend Stuart and I decided, would be another rite of passage.

Still convinced that contemplating skydiving must be listed in the diagnostic manual of mental disorders, I asked the sales representative, "Do you really *plummet* toward the ground at 120 miles per hour?"

"Oh no," crooned a sweet young couple picking up their photos from that morning's descent. Though their close-up pictures revealed grotesque facial features stretched like silly putty, they assured us that free falling 7,000 feet in fifty seconds felt more like "floating." Dropping the last 5,000 feet in five minutes, *with* a parachute, would be an afterthought. The saleswoman patiently explained how we would each be safely strapped to a qualified tandem instructor who had performed this feat without incident numerous times before.

I considered the alternative offerings for the extreme sports devotee: I could rappel into a cave to raft its underground rapids, soar across a canyon by a connected cable, or "zorb" down a hill inside a huge plastic ball. Clearly, the decades-old tradition of dropping from the sky, my body attached to another by a few mountaineering clips, was the conventional choice. The risk that the parachute wouldn't open seemed small compared to the likelihood of breaking my neck by dangling from a bridge with a rubber cord tied to my ankles. So Stuart and I signed on the dotted line and waived our rights to hold anyone responsible in the event of injury, dismemberment, or death.

The following afternoon the bright sky was a cloudless canvas, refreshing after a New Zealand summer plagued by the most rainfall in recorded history. While Stuart prayed to the powers that be, my eyes searched the heavens for the distant plane and caught it flickering like a tiny mirror reflecting the sun. One by one, four colored dots emerged as if they descended through an invisible portal in the sky. In minutes they were magnified into rainbow parachutes, each growing exponentially larger before landing in the adjacent field. There, a six-year-old boy in a space suit smiled and waved to his parents as if he'd just dismounted from the Dumbo ride at Disneyland.

Inside the hangar, we donned florescent-colored jump suits with soft, pointed helmets and over-sized, plastic pink goggles. A harness was cinched so tightly around my thighs that I was forced to walk like a bowlegged chimpanzee. My tandem guide was a handsome young man whose face had not yet been weathered by his profession. With a Kiwi accent and a characteristically casual Kiwi attitude regarding anything death-defying, he quickly led us through basic training with only three essential instructions:

1. When you're about to jump from the open doorway, do not hold onto the plane!

2. As you free-fall toward the ground, extend your arms, breathe, and try to relax.

3. To land safely, pull your knees to your chest...unless you hear, "Run!"

"Scared yet?" he added, with a mischievous grin.

Ironically, during the past twenty-four hours, while Stuart's whole body broke out in hives, I had remained completely calm. I should have been alarmed by the brevity of our preparations. I should have closely watched and questioned the man who was packing the parachutes. I should have gathered statistics. Instead, I walked like a zombie to the airstrip, passive as an anesthetized patient being wheeled into the operating room.

Stuart and I crouched across from one another on the floor of a plane so narrow it barely squeezed six passengers inside. Other than two tiny windows, the only indication of our ascent was an elevation watch, the needle hiking steadily like a blood pressure gauge: 8,000 feet and it seemed we could touch the purple peaks of the Remarkables Mountain Range; 9,000 feet and my tandem guide yawned as he fastened my back to his belly. At 12,000 feet the metal door slid open with an ominous screech.

Stuart looked at me with a final, foreboding plea as he scooted toward the exit. The next moment he was gone.

Awkward as conjoined twins, my guide and I crawled, legs first, to the open doorway. While he sat on the plane's narrow ledge, I dangled just outside, attached to him like a baby in a front pack. For a fleeting moment I realized this God's eye view could be my last. Short of death itself, skydiving seemed the ultimate surrender. There was no turning back.

"Ready? Let's go!"

We somersaulted into the boundless sky, catapulting through space with alarming speed. Like a swimmer tossed violently under the sea, all sense of order and form vanished as the earth, and my certain place in it, fell away. There was absolutely nothing to hold onto but my shoulder straps and faith. Instinctively I screamed and arched back against the soft body behind me. We were plummeting!

Within seconds, arms extended, we stabilized into "flying" position. Reaching a rate of 140 feet per second, we continued to free-fall for almost one minute. The furious wind made balloons of my flapping cheeks as my mouth sucked desperately at the freezing air. With my belly toward the ground and my guide weightless on my back, my mind struggled to organize the physical sensations of falling at terminal velocity while taking in the visual panorama before us.

Miles below, Lake Wakatipu was a lazy sunbather stretching her limbs, the deep cobalt waters meandering between mountains. I drank in the liquid blue of the lake's shallow edges that glimmered in the sunlight like aqua jewels. After the parachute ejected, briefly thrusting us upwards almost as suddenly as we had dropped, we drifted down. Queenstown's configurations slowly crept closer. Craggy peaks hugged the lakeshore on one side and sprawled into hill-strewn meadows on the other.

Now hundreds of feet below, Stuart rolled in the grass like an ecstatic dog returning home. Hovering a final moment above the grassy field, we executed the landing of a small bird alighting gracefully upon a branch. I was a proud astronaut returning from space, delirious with relief and the exhilaration of success, for I had broken through the canopy of my fear by falling through the atmosphere without bursting on impact!

The challenges I face these days don't require jumping from airplanes to overcome. New Zealand may have confirmed that I am no longer the girl who won't get her dress dirty, but trying on anything new can still feel risky. When changing one's orientation to the world requires a leap of faith into the unknown, I remember skydiving. Careening through the universe, maybe all you can do in the midst of falling is scream into the abyss. Then surrender your grasp and trust the ground to rise up to greet your safe landing.

Brazilian-born writer Nicole Zimmerman accomplished her first solo backpacking trek in New Zealand, where there are no predatory mammals. Subsequent adventures include swimming through crocodile-inhabited waters in outback Australia, battling food poisoning at a Buddhist temple stay in South Korea and parading in the sambadrome during Rio de Janeiro's Carnival. Her story "One Little Kiss" won the Silver Award for Love & Romance in the second annual Solas Awards. More can be found on her blog Beijos do Brasil (Kisses from Brazil) at selkietravel.wordpress.com.

ॐ ॐ ॐ

Out of India

The lesson she learned about India became
clear only in London.

My alarm went off and I shot out of the hard bed
in my dingy Delhi hotel room, every cell in my
body charged and eager. I was going to fly to London that
day. I was going to pack up my bags, go to the airport, and
fly to London. I was leaving! In a few short hours, I was
going to be *out of India!*

I quickly packed my bags one last time. "Once I'm at
the airport," I told myself, "for all intents and purposes,
I'll be out of India." Airports are non-places, I figured,
the same everywhere you go.

Then, however, I got to Indira Gandhi International.
This particular airport wasn't, I discovered, the same as
everywhere else. I had to deal with multiple redundant
security checks, a surprise "passenger service fee" of 200
rupees, and a scavenger hunt for mandatory baggage

tags. By the time the frisking came along, I had decided that the airport wasn't really "out of India," after all.

So then I told myself that, as soon as I got to the gate, I'd really be out of India. Surely I would have passed every major obstacle by that time.

But then I got to the gate and saw a crowd of a few hundred passengers (it was a 747, after all,) packed in a great mob around the door to the skyway.

Not out of India yet.

After about forty-five minutes, I finally made it past the crowd and the (multiple, redundant) ticket takers. Surely it was over now!

But no! In the skyway were approximately five Indian men in military uniforms, demanding to inspect each passenger's passport. This was, of course, a redundant procedure. The passports had already been checked many times.

Finally, though, I was allowed to board the plane. I settled into my seat with an audible sigh of relief. *Out of India!*

It was a nice first-world airplane—clean and modern and reliable. For the length of the flight, I cackled in glee, drinking soda with ice and eating fresh salad with no fear of becoming ill. There was a real Western toilet, with—my god—its own supply of toilet paper. The pilot spoke with a nifty British accent. Oh, yes.

But there were also things about the flight that struck me as odd. I watched the in-flight entertainment and found myself cringing at images of Western women wearing tank tops and swimsuits. I found myself marveling at the decadence portrayed in Western films—the glorification of sex, money, and drugs. I found myself shocked and scandalized by Western music videos, which dripped with gold jewelry and bare legs. Do these people have no shame?

I was sitting next to a middle-aged Indian couple—I imagined what they thought about the images that were flashing on the television screens. I cringed even more.

Then, when I got off the airplane at Heathrow and took the Tube to my hotel in Bloomsbury, something felt even more gravely wrong. London seemed very different than it had two months previously, when I had passed through on the way to Delhi. That time, I had been blasé. London had appeared much as I had remembered it from previous trips, and much like every other large European capital that I had visited. I had spent that day at the British Museum, looking sadly at the Elgin marbles—gray and lifeless in those humorless galleries—and wishing they were still attached to the Parthenon in Greece, bathed in the gold light of the Mediterranean.

Having just spent two months in India, however, London seemed utterly strange, quite different from how I had remembered it. This time, I did not go to the British Museum. I did not go to the Tower of London. I did not go to Big Ben. Instead, I walked the streets of London. I walked without a destination in mind, feeling my feet hit the pavement, staring at the world that was rotating slowly before me.

I walked for hours, which turned into days. I gradually realized that physically leaving India might not be enough to qualify as being "out."

I was in London, but I was not out of India.

It wasn't just the way people dressed, in immaculate gray wool and pressed slacks, not a single rip or missing button. It wasn't just the obvious wealth implied by clean streets, gleaming storefronts, and electric street lighting. It wasn't just the restaurants, where astronomical prices went to support a clever décor and where the tablecloths are tossed in the laundry after every customer. It wasn't just the cars, which usually had only one passenger. It wasn't just the buildings, which were beautifully painted, with clean glass windows. It wasn't just the air, which was clear and breathable.

More than the obvious wealth of the city itself, it was the people who astonished me. It was the people, and the way that they walked around on these streets, ate in these restaurants, and breathed this air. They did these things as if they weren't remarkable, without thinking, without realizing the extent and breadth of their wealth.

Two months previously, I had been one of them.

If anything, two months previously, I would have said that Europe seems a bit dingy to my American eyes, since the buildings are so old.

They say that India will change your life. I didn't believe them, until I stepped off that 747 in London.

I may never manage to get out of India. And I no longer want to.

Elizabeth Galewski is an independent scholar and freelance writer. Her essays have appeared in many prestigious academic journals, including the Quarterly Journal of Speech, Rhetoric & Public Affairs, *and* Women's Studies in Communication. *This story won the Silver Award for Travel and Transformation in the second annual Solas Awards.*

NICHOLE MARTINSON

ॐ ॐ ॐ

Ich Spreche Kein Deutsch

An American tiptoes through German
grammar and culture.

"You're not stupid; you just don't speak German,"
I had to sternly remind myself as I picked up
a pamphlet from a street-side kiosk in Berlin and was
frustrated—mortified even—that I couldn't decipher a
single word, let alone the general message conveyed via
leaflet to the masses.

Sure, I know I'm in a foreign country, but even after
having lived in New York City—where English isn't
necessarily a priority—I had forgotten what it's like to
not be able to communicate. Can anyone remember the
days of early childhood when letters, words, and sentences were nothing more than an indecipherable, collective noise? Can any of us recall what it felt like before
we could understand the groupings of letters that make
up written language?

Street signs and billboards are collections of incomprehensible scribbling; the pre-recorded voice announcing each U-Bahn stop, a whirl of sound signifying nothing. Conversations fly at breakneck speed as happy and important chatter is exchanged among co-workers, friends, and significant others. Food vendors and grocery stores take me back to times when I used pictures and touch to decide what I wanted, not words.

"You're not a moron, you just don't understand German," I caution myself again.

Somehow, through what is best described as a random series of events, I've landed in Germany; not for school, not for work—and please, I know you're thinking it, not for a man. The questions "Why?" and "For how long?" remain to be answered, but in Deutschland I am, so in Deutschland I will try to survive, excel or at the very least, blend in.

People stop me on the street, at landmarks and monuments and in train stations to ask me for directions—and my face glazes over with that blank, not-fooling-anyone stare. I undertake an extensive mental search, going through language and communication filing cabinets, and still I come up blank. No sentence, no word, not even a tiny squeak escapes my mouth. After a few seconds of no response, people's looks toward me change from inquisitiveness to disdain or maybe pity, eventually followed by the reflective expression of the realization that I don't speak German: "*Ach so,*" a term I later learned is the equivalent of "I see."

Days pass and my hunger becomes obsessive; the pangs of starvation are demanding: "You must eat!" Food procurement and any possible interactions, verbal and non-, that might come with the territory, can be put off no longer. Preparing for my mission, I memorize a phrase with which to order some food. I step up to the white counter and address a seemingly pleasant worker adorned in some kind of unflattering uniform and deliver my sentence.

"*Ich möchte ein Sandwich, bitte.*" "I'd like a sandwich, please."

I feel good, confident; I've made my request properly and seemingly understandably. Then, just as quickly as my ego rises a notch, maybe two, it's swiftly dashed when the unthinkable happens; the vendor asks me a question. No, not a question; you seemed so nice! How could you do this to me? Please, anything but an actual exchange of dialogue! I concentrate as hard as I can trying to dissect any fragment of the question I might possibly have learned somewhere, somehow, but sadly, nothing comes to mind. I frown and shake my head in sorrow: "*Ich spreche kein Deutsch.*"

"I'm really not a bad person, I just don't speak German," I plead internally to the external masses.

Leaving the capital city, my travels to get to know my new country take me to the south, near Stuttgart. I settle into my little town and find a job but I cannot survive in Germany, at least not for long, asking if people speak English, finger-pointing at goods desired and forever hoping that no one will ask me a question. I had tried in the States to enroll in German classes, but people don't seem to be eager and anxious to tackle a difficult language that is not exactly pleasing to the ear, so the one course I had found was canceled. But now the time has come to learn German, through immersion, through submersion, sinking or swimming through three genders of articles, four grammatical cases and more possible plural endings and prepositions than anyone could ever want to digest; hopefully being victorious, coming out on top, becoming a communicator.

Like the millions who have immigrated to the United States, I signed up for the equivalent of an ESL course: "*IntensivKurs Deutsch, Grundstufe A1.*" Back to the beginning, to infancy, to dependency, back to A-B-C and 1-2-3, only in German, simple counting seems to involve more than just simple arithmetic.

Normally, language learning is an exciting and rewarding undertaking for me, but finding myself already in Deutschland, having arrived in the country without previously acquiring the tools to survive and excel on German soil, I feel the pressure to learn, to know, to *sprechen* Deutsch. I walk into the first class session already feeling defeated. Why couldn't I learn the language, secretly, silently, hidden among the natives, as it wafts through the air carrying meaning and messages from one German to another?

"I'm sorry. I'm trying, but I still don't speak Deutsch," I appeal within to the German population without.

Anxieties held at bay, I take my seat in the class. A small feeling of comfort starts to take hold as I see I am not alone, surrounded by eleven other *Anfänger*, beginners, representing nine other countries. This is no ordinary language class. This is a full-blown global exchange with people from all over the world in the same position as I am, wanting, needing to learn, *lernen die deutsche Sprache.*

Camaraderie builds and learning is evident as this motley bunch bonds through classroom explanations given via a telephone chain of languages from one student to another to yet another. Don't tell anyone, but we might be having fun here in our little oasis away from the rigors and demands of daily interactions with the German state. While possibly not intended to be so, the textbook, with its more "open and realistic" drawings, late '80s pictures and campy storylines, is hysterical, and the classroom banter derived from them, comical. The stark white walls and dull gray flipcharts come alive with vocabulary lists and situational examples that only an international group of adults could devise.

We students come to class as perky and motivated as we can so early in the morning, ready, willing—and on occasion, able—to tackle another day, another topic, another tense in which to conjugate verbs. Little by little, the cacophony of noise becomes distinct and decipherable words, even if we don't quite know what the words mean yet. Letters and phrases on a page start to string together into written patterns signifying something.

I giggle with glee when I understand a word on television or can peck my way through a flyer posted on the street. I dance around my apartment like a five-year-old filled with the pure joy and excitement of just learning how to read and write her own name. My German roommates feed off my enthusiasm, taking up my German-language cause, helping me with my homework, sitting patiently as I struggle to piece together a coherent sentence auf Deutsch, and beaming with enthusiasm and pride in their own language as they guide me through its many, many, many peaks and valleys. *"Dein Deutsch wird wirklich jedes Mal besser, ich bin immer wieder überrascht."* ("Your German gets better every time. I'm always surprised.")

It's been over a year now since Germany has become my home. I can't debate the modern irony of Kafka auf Deutsch while sipping a beer at the Marktplatz with friends, but I did negotiate the price and purchase of an antique prayer book on behalf of a visiting friend. The salesman was patient, my friend impressed—and I was just happy to be understood during an actual exchange with a stranger.

Jeden Tag, the polite questions from the ladies behind the counter of the *Bäckerei* become less frightening. "*Sonst einen Wunsch?*"

"*Nein danke. Das ist alles.*"

The people at the cheese store are less intimidating, and the local grocery store gradually becomes simply a place where food and household items are purchased and not the language landmine it had once seemed to be. Learning a language is a huge undertaking, and Deutsch, like my other more established but yet-to-fully-be-mastered languages, will take many more hours of dedication and practice. As with any challenge, I look forward to reaping the rewards, in this case, being able to freely move about the German countryside, able to *lesen, schreiben, verstehen, und sprechen* the German language.

Remember, I'm not a bumbling fool. I just don't speak German—well, not just yet.

Nichole Martinson lives in Germany, where she uses her current position as an English instructor to warp international minds with useful phrases not otherwise taught in classrooms. Originally from San Francisco and Manhattan, her varied employment history includes experiences in local and national television, independent film, and assorted corporate environments. She writes short stories and travelogues and has recently completed a feature-length script with two more scripts and novels in the planning/research stages. When not dreaming about a Mediterranean relocation, Nichole loves travel, fine beverages, languages, cooking, and dancing.

A Woman Alone, A Woman Alone

As a foreign teacher in Laos, she might well lose her privacy—but she'd gain something equally valuable.

A fter two months in the village of Ban That Khao, in Vientiene, Laos, I'd learned the nighttime noises of my house: mosquitoes hitting the mesh net, fans cooling the bamboo floors, motorbikes leaving the beer shop next door. I fell asleep to the roar of frogs from the rice paddy nearby, and woke to the low steady chant of the monks' morning prayers. Across the road from the Mekong River, my house flanked a temple, a beer shop, and a family of nine. My *soi*, the narrow dirt lane, had a rhythm as constant as the variety of smells: incense in the morning, fire-smoke at dusk, scents of salty river and sun-baked dust all day long.

Asia seemed safe to me, and Laos in particular. In 1998, the country of five million people and fifty-seven languages boasted the world's lowest rate of violent crime. I had read somewhere that the Lao "had always preferred festivals to war." Peaceful Buddhism and tropical torpor had drawn me. In Laos I might die of illnesses like malaria, meningitis, or even bubonic plague, but I wouldn't be shot in a Walmart, in an aisle of beanbag chairs, in stale, fluorescent-stained air. I had escaped American ills, the malls and murderers and madness. At twenty-six, I was teaching English for the United Nations Development Program. I felt proud of my work, my Lao language skills, and how far I had come. The fears that marked my twenties could finally recede.

So one night, when I woke to the sound of shattering glass, I bolted upright in bed, lathered in sweat. My heart galloped like a horse wild in its stall. A window had been smashed.

"Fuck!" I whispered, as an adrenalized calm sluiced through my veins, cool and slippery as loose mercury.

I grabbed the phone, realized I couldn't dial 911. The clock ticked too loudly, its short arm angled toward 4:00 A.M. I had a fleeting thought of my Intermediate English class, five hours away, as if preparing my lesson on prepositions and fending off a burglar were equally vital tasks. I floated through the front room, scanned the shadowy dark. Empty. As I swung open the front door, I wanted to scream, not in fear but frustration. I wanted my safety, or at least my sense of it, which like my Lao language skills, lacked complexity but created daily a self-sufficient ease.

I didn't make a sound. Outside, the dense silence yielded only to the whoosh of the Mekong River nearby. The river road, in the day a buzzing cloud of dust from the motorbike traffic, had settled back to a static line of dirt, lit by stars above. Across the lane, the open windows of the monks' dorm were black. I could almost hear their sleeping breath.

I looked down. Smashed green glass covered the porch, right up to my bare toes. It was a bottle, thrown hard from the road. Not a window. I stared at the broken pile as if to see some augury in the shards. My yard, a square of pavement and a tiled porch, had walls on three sides, and a six-foot gate in front. Just inside its bars, a fresh pile of litter darkened the asphalt: several wooden planks, and a black plastic bag. I padded toward them, in a surging tide of panic.

The gate had a padlock, provided by my landlady, Madam Phantiloth. At least weekly, neighborhood children jammed it with fuzzy red flowers, but nothing more menacing than stems and petals had ever been flung at my house. I kicked the plastic bag, expecting to contact a body of a person or animal. But it clung to my bare foot, light. A few fluffy wood chips trickled out. I turned over the three planks, each of them about two feet long and an inch thick, searched them for a threat etched by knife, *go home Yankee bitch*, or *die, imperialist slut*, but they were blank. The meaninglessness sealed my fear in a questioning loop: Was this random, or personal? No way to know.

The night was the shade of a dreary day, like murky sunshine through cheap sunglasses. I still gripped the portable phone in one hand. The white plastic headset with a stubby antenna seemed oddly out of place, like a symbol from someone else's dream had leaked into mine. I dialed five of the six digits for Madame Phantiloth, but couldn't press the sixth. She lived 100 yards away, up the *soi*, and had fretted about my solo living. "A woman alone, a woman alone," she would shake her head and cluck. I hung up. I sat down. A hurled bottle was hardly a crisis, though I felt afraid and alone, as if pinned in an undertow. I rested my head on my knees, waiting for the next thing, which turned out to be sunrise.

The gong sounded in the temple, and the neighbor's rooster cooed at the fading sky from its perch on the fence between our yards. The monks filed out with their cylindrical baskets in hand, barefoot in the chill. They didn't see me sitting on the porch. Their orange robes against the dust-colored dawn made my throat ache. When the sun was fully up, I dialed all six numbers for the Phantiloth's.

"We come right now," Madame Phantiloth gushed.

Inside, I put on jeans and a long-sleeved shirt. Two minutes later, Madame Phantiloth's motorbike puttered up the *soi*, her husband and two teenage sons trailing at a trot. They hung back as she parked, opened the padlock, and surveyed the rubbish, her lips pressed flat. With one fist to prop her arm on her hip, Madame Phantiloth seemed puffed up with air, stiff, as she circled first the planks and the plastic bag, then the glass. The Lao supposedly don't have tempers—clearly not true, though they hid it better than the average *falang*, foreigner. The boys poked the dirt with their flip-flops.

"Say hello," Madame Phantiloth admonished them.

"Hello," they said.

Mr. Phantiloth nodded and smiled, familiar and friendly in the only clothes I'd ever seen him wear: baggy turquoise shorts with a large pineapple print, surf shorts in landlocked Laos. Like my portable phone, the odd item had been grafted to belong.

"What time did this happen?" Madame Phantiloth asked. She had already dressed for her work at the post office, in a uniform of a lavender ankle-length skirt, and a matching lavender blouse. She wore her hair in a tight, low ponytail, and seemed to gaze sternly downward at her sons, at her husband, and at me, though we all towered over her by at least a head.

"Four A.M.?" I said.

"Why don't you call?"

"I don't know."

"You call," she said. "We will run here. We will run."

With a tremendous sigh she deflated a little, then strutted in three tight circles through the mess. In daylight the glass looked a brighter shade of green, the black trash bag smaller. Without leaving the porch, she corralled five monks from across the *soi,* those just returned from their collection of alms. I recognized two of them, one who'd just begun a fully robed bath, with rivulets of water slick on his arms, and one with buckteeth who wanted to study English.

After a rapid exchange, the semi-soaked monk paced away, orange robe flapping.

"They go to get the Nai Ban," Madame Phantiloth said. The village chief.

The other monks squinted in the sunlight. They swayed slightly, as if in a breeze. For a monk, waiting must be the texture of a day. They seemed excited by this deviation in routine. Suddenly I was too, though in a tired and detached way, as if watching a documentary about Laos in which I had only a minor role. My greatest fear as a single woman and the sole *falang* in my Vientiene village was that I would never have a moment's solitude. When I first moved to Ban That Khao, I had wanted to observe the people around me from a distance, as if invisible, hovering between their world and mine. Instead, my presence altered everything. Rather than continue the sacred business of monkhood, the teen novices clustered in the lane to ask me about the lyrics of a Stevie Wonder song, or to borrow my *Lonely Planet Laos*. At worst, I experienced myself as a public TV—a source of interest, an inevitable pull on the collective gaze. After a day of teaching, I often needed to hide. Sometimes, I would duck to pass my front window, to fend off visitors, invitations to the lane.

The Nai Ban looked a youthful forty, with a head of thick black hair, fine posture, and the wiry muscles of a man who had labored physically all his life. He was shirtless and wore a *pah bian,* or prayer scarf, draped over one shoulder and tied around his hip. I'm not sure how a face conveys intelligence, but his did. There's a dam inside the mind, before thoughts pool to words, and the face holds what that reservoir cannot. The Nai Ban studied the scene piece by piece, then picked up a fragment of green glass.

"Green Mirinda," the English-speaking monk said, spotting a forensic shard with the drink's label.

Still holding the glass, the Nai Ban turned the planks over, as I had, and without speaking, emptied the bag of wood chips. He didn't ask me any questions, but conferred with Madame Phantiloth, who dispatched her sons to gather all the neighbors: the Siphays next door, the Pheths who owned the beer shop, the Ku Baa or head monk, and a handful of novice monks.

A sulk loomed inside me like monsoon clouds. All at once, I felt left out. While Madame Phantiloth recounted my story in Lao, the Nai Ban stared straight ahead. She spoke rapidly, using her hands to embellish the explosion of glass, with noises that would be different by an English speaker.

The neighbors formed a loose arc around the Nai Ban, and he invited them to report. The Ku Baa, wrinkled

and serious in his saffron robe, stood next to Madame
Siphay, whose black hair unfurled to her waist. Next to
them, Mr. Pheth, in knee-high rubber boots and a plaid
button-up shirt, furrowed his brow in concern.

"I didn't see anyone," he said in Lao.

Madame Siphay shook her head, lower jaw jutted.

The Nai Ban examined the boards again, now at the
center of a circle more than a dozen neighbors wide.
Three more novice monks had arrived, led by the
Phantiloth boys. These monks, heads shorn, draped
in orange, performed a vivid, vigorous pantomime of
snorting from the backs of their hands.

"*Ya*," they said.

"*Ya*," Madame Phantiloth repeated, "drugs." "*Ya*" is
the word for medicine, heroin, and opium.

"Teenagers," the monks said.

"Teenagers with *ya*," said Madame Siphay, in a low,
solemn voice.

"There were many Thai people at the beer shop yesterday," Mr. Pheth added.

"Thai people." This murmur rumbled through the
yard. The crowd exhaled.

The Nai Ban folded his arms over his chest, his gaze
pinned to a point in space. Suddenly I wanted to give tes-
timony. I sniffled, a hot weepy urge twitched my sinuses.
The lack of sleep and the crash of adrenalin kicked in.
Soon, I would have to face the sloppy class I would now
undoubtedly teach. In the blur of fatigue, this upset me
anew. Eyes bleary, breath fast, I opened my mouth to
speak. Perhaps reading my mind, Madame Phantiloth
glared at me briefly, warning restraint.

The Nai Ban adjusted his *pah bian* and refolded his
hands behind his back as if to stroll, and turned to face
everyone. There was a pause, then he lifted a hand in my

direction. "This foreign woman lives by herself in our village," he said finally, "and we will look after her."

No one moved. The Nai Ban didn't speak again, wielded silence instead.

After a while Mr. Pheth cleared his throat. "I give you my phone number," he said to me, and added, "I will put a light outside my beer shop."

Madame Siphay wrote her number next to Mr. Pheth's and said, "We watch you, we watch you all the time. Maybe my daughters come stay with you, nah?"

"At night, you keep the front light on," Madame Phantiloth suggested. "If the light is off, we come check for you."

The monks nodded. "We watch too."

The orange sun blazed fully into the sky, burned the morning coolness to a final shimmer, before relentless heat tore open the day. A trickle of traffic droned in the distance. The meeting dispersed.

One of the Siphay daughters fetched a straw broom and whisked the glass to a pile, while Madame Phantiloth, a few steps away, barked orders at the girl to get every scrap.

I stood mesmerized, as if I'd just arrived in the country where I'd lived for months. On one hand, this marked the funeral of privacy. But maybe that had never been mine to begin with, just a hold out from the way I'd always lived. In exchange for the shattering of my detachment, I'd just witnessed something essentially Lao: community as the human unit, rather than the person alone, and the grafting of the foreign thing into the fold, me.

"A woman alone, a woman alone," Madame Phantiloth muttered, to the pulse of the broom, each clean sweep. But she stopped when the Nai Ban approached us. He spoke to me directly, for the first time that day. "You," he said, in his quiet and formal voice, "are welcome here."

෯෨ ෯෨ ෯෨

Kathryn Kefauver's stories have been published in The Gettysburg Review, The Chicago Quarterly Review, The Christian Science Monitor, The Best Travel Writing 2005, The Best Women's Travel Writing 2005, A Woman's Asia, *and* Going Alone: Women's Adventures in the Wild. *She won an Associated Writing Programs award for nonfiction in 2003, and was awarded a MacDowell Fellowship in 2004. She recently completed a memoir, and excerpts are included in the Fall 2008 issues of the* Alaska Quarterly Review *and in* The Sun.

❦ ❦ ❦

Orange Who?

She navigated between two desires: to be both
free and at home.

*W*e'd been in Spain for more than four months
before we discovered Prexigeiro: a spot in the
river where the bank emits scalding sulfur-rich water.
There is a *balneario* close by, where you can pay a few
euros and have a bathtub to yourself, but you can rough
it for free: people have arranged stones around where the
hot water comes in, forming small stony egg-smelling
baths full of white sulfur that sticks to the rocks in slimy
stalagmites. We were on our way there in El Salmon.
(We'd bought the car before we arrived, and the color had
been described to us as "salmon." I had imagined pinkish
with delicate ribs of white; it turned out to be red. It had,
however, earned its nickname.)

"Knock knock." Aidan is eight.

"Who's there?" I intoned from the driver's seat.

"Boo."

"Boo who?"

"Don't cry it's only a joke."

Next was Emmet's turn. He's five: "Knock knock."

"Who's there?"

"Um. Ba a."

"Ba a who?"

"Um. Ba-utt."

The two boys collapsed into each other across the back seat in heaps of laughter. Aidan yelled for Neil Young. The car is old and has no CD player and we only had three cassettes: Neil Young, James Brown, and Otis Redding. They sang along in the back seat, *"Tell me whyyy. Tell me why-ayyy. Is it hard to make arrangements with yourseeelf...."*

We were often the only ones in the river, especially since we liked going even if the weather was cold—enjoyed shivering as we pulled our clothes off and the comfortable relief of slipping into one of the hot pools. But lately, there were hippies, camping in vans with clotheslines strung from the roof rack to a tree, their colorful clothes tossed over them. The Ribeiro had been littered with hippies in tents, in cafés, in pop-up vans, because it was *vendimia*—grape harvest season. Helping our neighbors pick their grapes, we'd met plenty of them. Between tulips in Holland, asparagus in the south, and chestnuts across the North, they followed the various European harvests, which landed them here in our adoptive region for a number of weeks in late September.

Colin had been here when we'd come for a dip in the pools the week previous, and we'd had a tongue-in-cheek debate about whether or not the hippies should be allowed to camp along this beautiful and pristine river. I took the right wing, just for the fun of it, and argued that they were "pissing and shitting" in the woods and ruining the beautiful spot for other people. Colin pointed out that the earth is free, et cetera. Neither of us had any stake in our positions—which, I find, is the best situation for an enjoyable argument.

I didn't realize that Aidan had been listening until he said as we walked down the hill, towels over our shoulders, "I hope those people won't be there. Pissing and shitting." With kids you get used to them as babies, not understanding what you're talking about. As a parent, you get a few shocking moments before you train yourself to keep your voice down.

"Aidan, we were only joking," I said, shushing him. There were two vans, and it was pretty certain that both belonged to hippies. We've taken to pronouncing "hippies" the way the Spanish do: with the same sound as in the Hebrew *le'chaim*. *Los chipis*. One of the vans I recognized as belonging to the couple we'd seen the week before— both he and she sported dreadlock tails and striped shirts and had left a roach on a rock by one of the pools.

I didn't see them, and figured that they must be sleeping inside their van, but here were two skinny naked young men laying out their laundry on the rocks. One had a shaggy head of blond hair and the other was a bearded Jesus look-alike—the classic light-skinned Jesus with the brown hair and the beard, the young face, the eyes plaintive and blameless. We pushed past their naked bums and put our bathing suits on. An older woman in a *mandilon*, a housedress, was there with her husband, who was in one of the pools. The water is said to be medicinal, and he was in there with his pant legs rolled up his calves, soaking his bunions.

"*¿Está caliente?*" I asked and he said yes and lifted his leg to show me the bright pink of his calf. The woman approached me looking somewhat conspiratorial, and I thought she was going to say something derisive about the naked hippies. But instead she told me about a traffic jam that she had heard was blocking the road back to Vigo. Had I heard anything? Or had I just come from there? "No," I told her. "*Vivimos cerca.*"

Aidan whispered, "I hope those people leave," and I told him again that I was only joking, that they were probably very nice people. And that we should all be able to go around naked, without being stared at.

Aidan and Emmet played in the pool by snapping the waistbands of their bathing suits to allow in air and then sitting into the pool and letting the air come out in farting bubbles. "*Hize un pedo,*" they laughed. The Jesus look-alike was squatting above us on a rock, everything just hanging there, rolling a cigarette. He picked up his underwear, decided it wasn't dry enough yet, and wandered away, smoking.

I remembered my Grateful Dead days. Well, remember is a relative term, but I thought about that age when life was all about how much you could be free and how much you could have fun. And I remembered the scornful, or maybe envious, glances we'd get as we floated through some middle-American truck stop on our way to another gigantic party. And the times in between the parties, when we'd meet and fall in love with people like us, and interact superficially with plenty of people who weren't like us—the waitress at the truck stop, the man pumping the gas—and then forget about them. I watched Jesus recede into the woods, and realized that I was as relevant to him as the man pumping gas was to me way back when.

I had one of those paradoxical moments that have become more frequent with age. A moment of acceptance and dismay: I relaxed in my invisibility, but I mourned my younger self.

I was still adventurous: I was here, living with my family in Galicia, and we intended to stay for at least the school year. But of course, the planning and execution weren't nearly as painless as they'd been when I traveled in my *chipi* days. Packing away all our stuff, renting out our house, informing the principal at Aidan's school that he'd be gone for a year, figuring out how to fit spring, summer, fall, and winter clothes for all four of us into a few suitcases. Which shoes would keep me for a whole year? These were the demands of leaving. But then there were the challenges of arriving: enrolling the boys in school, getting a phone (this took Telefonica from September, when we ordered service, until February, when they finally arrived—three workmen, one to sullenly dig a hole for the new post, the other two to stand on the road smoking), and of course, procuring El Salmon.

In contrast, as a *chipi* I used to take off with a few skirts and tie-dyes in my old secondhand external-frame backpack, tying onto the frame whatever wouldn't fit in the pack.

Aidan and I plunged into the cold water and then slid back into the hot while Emmet looked for gold beneath the surface.

The older woman got restless because of the traffic jam and her husband lumbered onto a stone to pull his socks and shoes on.

As we were getting dressed, Aidan asked me, "Well, so why don't you go naked, Mommy?"

"People would look at me funny," I explained. I didn't go into it, but the fact is I was trying to fit in. Vaguely proud of myself every time a Spanish woman in a housedress talked to me. I'd shrug and giggle quasi-embarrassed when I forgot to put on my shoes and went to the market in my slippers. Just like a native. Being accepted by the old woman in the *mandilon* felt like a triumph: as though I were back in high school and I was the nerd and she was the popular girl, accepting me. When the woman chats with me and I chat back, and we understand each other, I feel at home somehow. Speaking Spanish!

The hippies seem so out of place, and I'm starting to feel accepted here in Spain, but I see that that's all I've ever wanted all along—to feel like an insider. It occurs to me that it may not be that I've grown older and so changed my allegiance—from the young and the free to the old and the staid. But that I've always been trying to fit in with whoever was the most foreign. And this is the curse of the traveler, I think—the desire to be both free and at home. To enter foreign worlds and become a part of them.

Yet I realize too there is something different here. When I was a hippie, there was a feeling of antagonism. I was rebelling and people who weren't rebelling were, on some level, a part of what I was rebelling against. And I felt it from them too—maybe a low-level disdain that I'm convinced was mixed with a portion of envy. But here, something feels different in the relationship between the *chipis* and the older couple. It's not that they get along. The shaggy blond doesn't lend one of his panpipes to the housewife to play; Jesus doesn't ask the husband for a light for his rollie. But there's something in everybody's demeanor that's more accepting of each other. Irrelevant to each other, but not divisive. (I just hope they're pissing and shitting in a toilet somewhere, and using biodegradable laundry soap in the river.)

"Knock knock." Emmet started as we climbed into El Salmon.

"Oh God. Here we go. Who's there?"

"Orange."

"Orange who?"

"Um. Orange. Banana."

I waved to Jesus as we pulled away. He'd put on his underwear.

Sara Fraser has lived with her family in a village in Galicia on and off for a number of years. She has had stories and essays published in Carve, The Best Women's Travel Writing 2006, 365 Days, *and* Women in the Wild. *She taught freshman composition at the University of Massachusetts for almost ten years and is currently working on her second novel.*

CHRISTY QUINTO

ɻ𝄢 ɻ𝄢 ɻ𝄢

In the Shadow of Potocchi

In Peru, the author shares a bittersweet
homecoming with her husband.

otocchi towered stoically above the town of
Huancavelica, Peru, on the opposite side of the
narrow valley from Tía Domi's house. I had imagined the
mountain since Moisés first told me about it years earlier,
but now I was seeing its vertical slopes and eucalyptus
stands with my own eyes. In the shadow of the mountain, Moisés's *tías*, his mother's sisters, scurried about the
patio in their wide skirts and petticoats arranging a circle
of chairs, long braids swinging from underneath their
gambler hats. Tía Justina's braids were jet-black ropes; Tía
Domi's plaits had thinned and lost their youthful sheen.
Gap-toothed grins revealed the *tías* delight that their
sister's eldest son had finally returned.

And with a gringa wife! They never imagined that
a gringa might visit the house—the town with its thin

air and frosty nights received few foreign visitors. Tía Domi handed me her thickest sheepskin to cushion the wooden chair, while her son scrambled to find some '80s music to blast in honor of the decade in which Moisés had left. As I sat on my chair, Tía Justina stood beside me petting my light brown hair in slow, firm strokes with the flat of her hand.

But the joy of the reunion was tinged with sadness that Moisés's mother was gone—she had passed away not long after he left Peru. Moisés asked to see their photographs of his mother. Tía Domi brought a framed photograph down from the wall of her living room to the patio, and passed it to her sister. Tía Justina reached into the pocket of her apron and drew out a flimsy plastic bag full of coca, a mild stimulant used throughout the Andes to overcome hunger and fatigue. She emptied the leaves onto Tía Domi's apron, then crumpled the bag into a ball, wiping the frame and every inch of the glass with it. She gazed longingly at her sister's image before passing the photograph around the circle. When it came to him, Moisés perched the portrait reverently on his lap. I could recognize him in his mother's face—her brown eyes were sad and kind, like his.

As more family photos circulated and Moisés recounted episodes from his life abroad, Tía Justina made her way around the circle giving out coca to the adults to chew. When she reached Moisés, she tossed a handful of leaves onto his lap and studied them. With her index finger, she pointed to three whole leaves that had landed upright. "Positive, positive, positive, but…" she touched half of a leaf that had settled upside-down, "…that one means *tristeza*." And seeing that sadness in his bowed head and averted eyes, Tía Justina rested a compassionate hand on her nephew's shoulder. Then she turned to me and said,

"Boys who love their mothers grow into men who love their wives, and Moisés loved his mother deeply." That morning with his wonderful *tías*, I felt how profound a loss it is that I will never know her.

When the brilliant Andean sun burned down from high overhead, we bumped along the road to the cemetery in a taxi with Moisés's youngest sister. Celia remembered that when their mother died, the mourners had walked to the cemetery—there were few cars in Huancavelica then. Celia had been eight years old, and was instructed to stay at home with the other young children during the burial. But the adults had misjudged how much Celia understood. She donned the only suitable dress she could find, a green one that was enormous on her, and stumbled along the potholed road to the cemetery at the far end of town, tripping over the hem of the gown every few steps. When she neared the somber crowd at the cemetery, she strained on her tiptoes, but the taller bodies of the adults blocked her view. Then the sky started to spit fat droplets of moisture. The adults scattered for cover under the overhangs and trees, and as the rain flecked dark blotches onto her dress, Celia saw the deep hole in the earth and the forlorn wooden box at the bottom of it. And for the first time since she lost her mother, she began to cry.

The taxi dropped us outside the cemetery gates. Women vendors waited behind buckets of lilies and gladiolus and baby's breath. "What color should I buy?" Moisés's voice quavered. I could only shake my head that I didn't know. It took all my energy to hold back tears as I watched him deliberate over the flowers, delaying the final moment a little longer, because once we reached the grave, his mother's death would become real. He seemed to feel that if he kept going only half the distance toward her grave, toward his grief, he would never have to fully feel the pain. But soon he had pressed the coins into the women's weathered hands, and with the spears of red and yellow gladiolus cradled in our arms, candles and matches in our pockets, we walked through the cemetery gates.

Celia's black ponytail swished back and forth across the nylon of her jacket as we followed her past the imposing tombs inside the entrance. An archway led us to an open area of modest graves. Tears obscured my vision, and I stepped through a blur of iron crosses, concrete slabs, and flower bouquets that had dried out in plastic vases fashioned from Inca Kola bottles. "There it is," Celia said, and we closed the final distance to the simple concrete slab—smooth round stones had been pressed into the mortar and painted the color of brick. Moisés squeezed my hand and tears spilled hot onto my cheeks. "I'll go find water for the flowers," Celia murmured, giving us a few moments of privacy. We lay the flowers gently on the grave and held each other. Even there, Moisés followed the custom of the men in his town, containing most of his tears. The mountain stood silent witness. Legend says that Potocchi is full of water and will explode one day and inundate the town. In my mind, the mountain is brimming with a pool of the men's unshed tears.

Celia returned with two containers of water. We snapped off the long stems of the gladiolus, arranged them to evenly distribute the yellow and the red, and slid the honey-scented flowers inside the iron cage at the head of the grave. We knelt on the ground next to it, and with our bare hands, brushed off the dirt and decaying leaves and pulled away the weeds. Celia and I piled rocks to form a shelter from the wind, heating the base of the candles before setting them inside, holding them in place until the wax had solidified.

We sat and contemplated the flickering flames. I gazed up at the mountain, scanning its impervious face for any hint of internal disquiet. I took a deep breath of Andean air and smelled the hot wax, the smoke of the candles, and the scent of eucalyptus on the breeze. The red and yellow flowers seemed to glow in the iron cage above the grave. A kind of peacefulness had descended over Moisés's face. I let the breath go.

Tía Justina had arrived to join us in our vigil, more candles and a bag of coca bulging from her apron pockets. I chewed the bitter leaves into a wad and pushed the ball into my cheek. When the candles had burned down, our tongues were numb, and the aching in my heart had begun to ebb. We stood up to leave. Tía Justina stooped and slapped the side of the cement slab that covered her sister's grave, like she might have patted her shoulder.

"Moisés is here," she said to her. "Your son has come home."

Christy Quinto holds a Ph.D. in anthropology from the University of Otago in New Zealand and a masters in Pacific Islands Studies from the University of Hawai'i. She juggles parenting a three-year-old, working in book publishing, and writing a novel through the low-residency MFA Program for Writers at Warren Wilson College. Originally from Long Island, she lives in the San Francisco Bay Area.

꧁ ꧁ ꧁

Requiem for a Little Red Ship

She never understood why people referred to ships as female—and then she met the *Explorer*.

A t first I thought I'd woken up with post-Thanks-giving dementia—some sort of morning-after corollary to the traditional food coma. But no. By my fifth or sixth re-reading of Richard's e-mail, I concluded that I was perfectly, lamentably lucid.

"News"—the too-terse subject line—foretold the following message:

November 23, 2007

Hi. If you have not already heard…you will soon…a cruise ship hit ice and was abandoned, will most likely sink…on the Antarctic Peninsula this morning. The

ship was the *Explorer*...I am safe and well...we were
on scene with a larger vessel for the evacuation of all
passengers and crew safe and well to the larger vessel.
A sad day down here...but all are well.

R x

A biologist-guide whom I had befriended in Antarctica
four years earlier—when I was on assignment aboard
Lindblad's *National Geographic Endeavour*—Richard
knew I'd be a head case when I saw the first sketchy
reports from the Bransfield Strait that morning. Not
just because my knowledge that he was working in the
area guaranteed I'd presume him dead (I descend from
two carriers of the assume-the-absolute-worst gene), but
because he knew I loved the sinking ship at the center of
the looming media storm. God, did I love that ship.

She was, after all, my first.

Until the MS *Explorer* took me from one end of the
Amazon River to the other in May of 2003, I was an
expedition cruise virgin. In fact, the closest I'd come was
the Pirates of the Caribbean ride at Disneyland, circa
1979. And with all due respect to Captain Jack Sparrow,
I defy anyone to top a two-week float through the jun-
gles of Brazil, Colombia, and Peru.

The truth is, you can't. Not without copious quanti-
ties of scarlet macaws, pink dolphins, and silver piranhas. And Werner Herzog-issue mists every morning.
And tiny stilt-borne villages on the edges of flooded
forests. And dugout canoe armadas populated entirely
by the K-12 set.

A typical day aboard *Explorer* on the Amazon went
as follows: After waking up to the dulcet tones of the
expedition leader's piped-in voice, you would immediately look out the window to verify that yesterday's

crazy jungle-scape hadn't been some sort of halluci-
nation. Sure enough, the solid-green imbroglio—all
fronds, vines, and leaves—was still there, accessorized
with the aforementioned vaporous ribbons. With Team
Photosynthesis present and accounted for, you would
proceed to breakfast in peace, then onto the day's first
landing: perhaps a village visit, forest hike, or piranha-
avoidance swim. Next came lunch, siesta, and landing
number two (see options above). Finally, there were
cocktails and dinner, followed by hours of lounge liz-
ardry for anyone so inclined.

No, this was not your average trip. Or at least not
mine. And while the transport itself may seem second-
ary to the proceedings, the Little Red Ship (as she was
known to her countless loyalists) was, in fact, a central
character.

Yes, I used the word "she," though the whole boat-as-
woman thing used to bug the hell out of me.

Hypocritically, I was always a car anthropomor-
phizer—egregiously ascribing all sorts of personality
traits to, say, the rhapsody in pleather I drove in high
school. But using "she" in reference to anything you
could dock struck me as painfully J. Petermanesque—
unless, of course, you had just pulled in from the North
Sea with a wild beard, a Connery-grade accent, and a
mental jukebox of a thousand sea chanteys.

But then I met the *Explorer*—a ship that out-girlied
me by far—and I instantly understood why only feminine pronouns would do.

Painted a shamelessly cheery red ("Candy Apple,"
in nail salon parlance), she was a diminutive thing,
favoring intimacy above all else. Sliding easily into the
remote, narrow waterways that her big sisters could only
dream of, she lived to put you face to face with wilder-

ness, and any inhabitants thereof. If other ships were like general admission tickets, the *Explorer* was the all-access pass, one that—in Amazonian terms—meant entry into tributaries, forests, and villages that most cruise passengers never saw.

But she fostered just as much intimacy onboard. When 100 strangers are thrust into close quarters in the middle of an endless jungle (or ice field, for that matter), a funny thing happens: warp-speed bonding (or God forbid, the opposite). And while I admittedly bristled at the occasional passenger—not least, the woman who demanded to know why the Amazonian villagers "looked so clean," as though they were violating the terms of some implicit Savagery Package—I also made dear friends on that trip.

Principally staffers (the exception being the captain's daughter, who happened to be onboard at the time), these were the people I drank, blabbed, sang, and danced with every night in the *Explorer's* tiny lounge. And while I like to think that we would have befriended one another in "the real world" had we met there instead, you can't beat tight space and prolonged isolation for breeding solidarity.

Since saying goodbye at a Peruvian dock almost five years ago, my *Explorer* friends and I have traveled together, met all attendant significant others, stayed in one another's homes—and now, gaped collectively at the demise of our original bond.

The day the *Explorer* hit fatal ice, my inbox flooded with lamentations. But the most haunting was one I'd had around much longer: It was an elegy written five years prematurely, when everyone thought the *Explorer* was going to retire soon after our Amazon trip. Though G.A.P. Adventures wound up buying and refurbishing her, a resident naturalist wrote a song before that news had broken.

He concluded with these lines:

> She was a Grand Old Lady when she went into
>   retirement
> And her sailing days were done,
> More modern ships remain, with TV and
>   videogame,
> But they never will be so much fun.

Of course, I don't love that a ship exactly my age was deemed a "Grand Old Lady" and—at least temporarily—put out to pasture. Still, I take odd comfort in knowing that she lived a full life. And though she wouldn't have wanted this to be the final chapter—who would?—may she nonetheless rest in peace.

Abbie Kozolchyk is a New York-based writer who contributes to National Geographic Traveler, Forbes Traveler, Allure *and other publications. This is the third year her work has appeared in* The Best Women's Travel Writing.

STEPHANIE CHABAN

✍ ✍ ✍

Al-Ajnabiya
(the Foreigner)

A solo traveler to Jordan finds solace in
the company of women and children.

*I*t was happening again.

Tears streamed down my face as I ran down the
stairs that led to the Citadel. How many times had this
happened before? How many times had I been followed? Flashed? Grabbed? Eyed? Solicited? Three
months on my own, traveling through Eastern Europe
and now the Middle East, had earned me more male
attention than I could handle. Jordan, the current site of
my travels, proved to be no different.

Not five minutes earlier, I was surveying the view
over Amman, Jordan's capital. Climbing up one of the
many labyrinthine staircases cutting through the city in
order to reach the Citadel, its highest point, I noticed a

young man staring at me. It happened everywhere, especially in Jordan with my ever-lightening hair, cut short in a bob, and my fair skin. It also didn't help that I found it difficult to keep my arms and shoulders covered in the searing summer heat.

I headed back down the stairs not wanting to draw any more attention to myself. It didn't matter, because all I could hear were uneven, sandy footsteps behind me. I couldn't seem to move fast enough. In a matter of seconds the young man from the Citadel was in front of me, cutting me off, and cornering me. He was dressed in a long white *thob*, or robe, like many of the Bedouin I had seen in the south. His face was a blur as I tried not to make eye contact, believing that if I appeared "shy" he would eventually give up. Afraid of looking him in the eye, I decided to keep my head down, choosing to focus on the worn out, threadbare sandals unraveling from his filthy feet.

The stares, the comments, the occasional touch, were normal, but actual confrontation was new. The young man reached for me, and I pushed him away. He regained position. I turned left and then right, but he was faster than I and blocked each of my turns. In a gesture of defeat I stopped and pulled back, and he offered me his hand, communicating that all he wanted was a handshake. While I didn't believe this, it seemed to be my only option. I offered my hand and he pulled me close, closer than I would have liked. His face came towards mine, his lips barely brushing my own mouth. I pushed him away, shouting at him, at the empty alley, and at the city of Amman.

I ran down the steps. That's when the tears began.

I had spent the past three months traveling on my own, having previously dropped out of college for the third time. I left behind a job in a café that paid minimum wage, a string of uneventful relationships, and an array of unknowns. I didn't really have a plan and I wasn't sure what I was looking for. All I knew was that traveling on my own left me feeling empowered.

After the encounter, I tried to find a way back to one of Amman's main thoroughfares. I couldn't breathe. I couldn't see. Memories of the previous male encounters raced through my mind: the man in the Czech garden who looked me up and down before lifting his shorts to masturbate; the Romanian police officer who proposed marriage to me over a glass of blueberry liqueur and then tried to shove his tongue down my throat; the drunk man on the train from Romania to Bulgaria who refused to leave my compartment and managed to ungracefully lunge at me before I summoned the conductor to evict him; the man who stalked me through the spice bazaar and the streets in Istanbul until I got the attention of some police officers; the Cypriot crew member who invited me to sleep in his cabin on the boat from Limassol to Haifa; the young shepherd who shouted sexual obscenities my way and then threw rocks at me as I approached Petra. Where were all the women and children in this world and why didn't they want to talk with me?

Sura! Sura! Sura!

I looked down. A group of young children, walking home from school, blocked my way. "*Sura, sura,*" they shouted at me, taking snapshots with phantom cameras in their hands. They looked up at me, beaming expectantly. I patted my bag and realized that I had no camera on me, just my water bottle and guidebook. We stood, unable to properly communicate. Each one shouted something to me in Arabic and all I could do was shrug my shoulders and shake my head. I smiled, apologized, and smiled some more. Finally, I simply waved to them and moved on, relieved to be free of the awkwardness of the moment.

I continued on, a bit depressed that I had missed my chance to interact with children that genuinely seemed eager to meet me. The young man in the alley had upset me, now I was upset with myself for walking away from these children. Not knowing my way, I continued along the path in front of me.

Allo! Allo! Allo!

I turned around. The group of children caught up with me from a different street. One girl, about eight, was eager to show me something. She ran up to me with her open backpack and pulled out a workbook. Showing me the cover, she flipped through the pages until she reached a diagram of two people facing each other on a street. Looking at it for a second, she decided on the appropriate figure and then pointed to the bubble just above his head. "Nice to meet you," it read in English. Quickly, her small finger pointed to another phrase, "How are you?" Her eyes, as well as the eyes of those around her, met mine for a response. She turned the workbook towards me; it was now my turn to select a greeting for her.

I could see her handwriting in the margins, confirming the greetings in her own language, Arabic. The opposite page had a small vocabulary lesson on adjectives. After pointing to "Nice to meet you, I am fine," I pointed to her and the word for beautiful, *jamila*. Everyone giggled, and tugged at my clothing so that I could have a "conversation" with them, me labeling each of them as *jamila*, *latif*, *sa'ida*, or *shaatir*. "My name is…Fatima," she said, pointing to the workbook once again, and then to herself. After exhausting the printed dialogue in the workbook, she managed to convey to me that I should follow her.

Ta'aali la beitee! Come to my house!

I politely refused. How could I, a foreigner and a complete stranger, possibly go home with an eight-year-old I met on the streets of Amman? I certainly wouldn't have followed an eight-year-old girl home in the United States. I can't even begin to imagine the reaction of my mother if I had done the same when I was Fatima's age. It didn't seem right, but Fatima was having none of it. She was adamant, and I was intrigued. Was this my second chance?

I had just been lamenting the dearth of contact with women and children during my travels. This opportunity seemed serendipitous, but I never figured it would manifest in the form of me as a shiny object found hidden in the street gutter ready to be taken home as show-and-tell to a young girl's family...least of all in Amman. I hesitated, and then gave Fatima my hand.

In a matter of moments I was in Fatima's home and, at her urging, this is where I spent my remaining days in Amman. Between the television located on the other side of the room, and myself, sat an assortment of people Fatima would introduce to me as her family. She seemed to have a large family, though it was unclear to me who was who. Men came and went, but women and children were constants.

A silver platter with a bottle of warm Pepsi and an assortment of store-bought cookies had been presented to me. Each person eagerly took turns urging me to eat and drink. Fatima's mother, with a three-year-old on her lap, beamed at me. Her two brothers kicked a soccer ball around the room, each with an eye on me and another on the Italian soccer game playing on the television. Two older sisters, close to my age, sat nearby; one was Hiba, the other, Wesam. In the far corner of the room sat a shrouded figure gesturing emphatically at the air and talking more to herself than anyone in particular. Strands of henna-ed hair shot out from her all encompassing black *abaya,* filmy cataracts covered her eyes, and wrinkles and Bedouin tattoos graced her aged face. This was grandma.

The older woman had clearly lost her mind, and sat talking to herself about the past, present, and future. One moment, I looked over to see her rocking an invisible baby in her arms, her face like a proud mother, her clouded eyes bright and her voice soft and cooing. A few minutes later she began sobbing; apparently the baby had died. Other times she tried to get up and walk about the room, bumping into the furniture. Fatima's mother and sisters paid no attention to the outbursts; they were simply part of the background just like the soccer game on the television or the traffic from the street below. But this wasn't negligence. They certainly did not ignore the grandmother, rather, they included her in their space, and during my time in the household, they held her hands, brushed her hair, calmed her down if her emotions got the best of her. As someone who hails from a part of the world where the elderly often are institutionalized or given their own space so as not to be a "burden," it was fascinating to see how the grandmother's condition was not only integrated into the family, but treated with humanity.

Ahlan wa sahlan, habeebtee! You are welcomed, my dear!

Fatima's mother welcomed me, choosing to call me her beloved, a term of endearment normally used for close friends or relatives. I could not imagine my own mother doing the same to a near-stranger.

I sat in the middle of the living room, like the shiny object that I had come to believe I was, smiling awkwardly at my new caretakers. They did not speak English. I did not speak Arabic. All I had to offer for conversation was my guidebook, full of pictures and maps. I traced out my three-month trip as best I could for them, trying to convince them that it was perfectly acceptable for an unmarried twenty-three-year-old woman to be traveling around the world by herself.

They didn't seem convinced, but played along, asking me through gestures and pictures what I had seen and what I had done. Had I been to Kuwait, to Saudi Arabia, to the Emirates, to Iraq? I found it odd to be asked about these specific countries. The questions were not necessarily about me, but an introduction into their lives. It turned out that not only did they have family in these countries, but that they were originally from Iraq.

Large albums were pulled out of storage, and I was soon introduced to the extended family. There was a wedding in Kuwait, a picnic in Saudi, a richly decorated apartment in Dubai, a newborn in Baghdad. I had no pictures on me, just a random assortment of postcards from various countries. I had no family or friends to show off. No husband or boyfriend. I was alone, just how Fatima had found me on the street. Had I actually been with someone that afternoon, I am sure that I would have never taken the chance and walked home with her.

As Hiba scooted close to me, her smile was unrestrained and infectious. She held my hand, patted my short, straight hair and told me that I was *helwe*, beautiful. I sat with her and Wesam, and they quizzed me about things that women should care about.

How much do meat and eggs cost where you come from?

Hmm, not quite sure since I don't eat either, but I'll just guess.

How much do a pair of women's underwear go for?

Well, that depends, what is the style? Are they cotton, silk, lace? Which store are they from?

How do you shave your legs?

Excuse me? I pulled my skirt down a bit further, conscious of the abundance of hair that had worked its way out of my follicles over my three-month trip.

Immediately, Hiba set about drawing me a pictograph recipe for the sticky solution they used to remove hair from their arms, legs, and face. It was a combination of lemon juice, sugar, and water. At the time, I had never heard of such a thing, nor did I know anything about threading. Hiba leaned in to examine my eyebrows and again I became self-conscious, as I had never concerned myself with any hair removal. She slipped away for a moment and returned with a cat's cradle of string. With Wesam as the model, she showed me how to shape eyebrows as well as remove errant hairs from my legs and arms.

My female hosts continued to school me in the womanly arts. After the lesson in body hair removal, we continued on to dancing. Wesam took this topic seriously, as she had been performing impromptu moves since I first arrived. I was neither a serious, nor a talented student but it didn't seem to matter, as the entire household, including myself, took delight in my awkward *ajnabiya* rhythm.

My final night in Amman fell on the same day as Jordan's Day of the Child. Fatima was to have some of her friends over and we were all to gather on the veranda to watch the fireworks. A handful of young girls came over, most of whom I remembered from my first encounter with Fatima on the street. They gathered around me in a semi-circle, staring at me, speechless. Occasionally one would lean over, cup her hands around her mouth and whisper in my ear, "Love you," quickly pulling back and giggling at what she had dared to say. This went on for about fifteen minutes, much to the amusement of the girls' mothers. I didn't anticipate the evening to change much, aside from the fireworks, until I smelled smoke.

I looked over, and from beneath her long coat, one of the mothers had pulled out a box of cigarettes. Each woman eagerly snatched one from the box and took long, slow drags, as if they had been waiting all day for this moment. Then, a boom box appeared and without notice, music began to play and the women, the mothers, rose up and began to dance. As if on cue, the fireworks began and the women swayed to the beat of the explosions and the music, clapping as best they could while making sure their cigarettes were still smoldering.

The women ululated as the fireworks reached their apex. The little girls jumped up and down, clapping elatedly, exhaling a *helwe* for every excited breath they took in. Fatima eventually grabbed my hand and pressed it against her flushed and beaming face. The dancing continued well beyond the fireworks, and I was eventually coerced into joining. Wesam's lessons did not go to waste.

Afterwards, after the mothers and children left, we ate roasted eggplant with fresh bread and salad under the Amman moon. We had fruit for dessert and drank over-sugared black tea. We lay on mats on the veranda and stared at the stars until we fell asleep. I left for Jerusalem early the next day.

Predictably, I lost Fatima's address. I never sent the letter I promised to write or visited Amman again. It's unfortunate because the few days that I spent with Fatima and her womenfolk changed the course of my life. It wasn't immediate, but gradual. I eventually went on to graduate from college. I traveled elsewhere in the world and began to study the lives of women outside the United States. My experience in Jordan drew me back to other parts of the Middle East, first as a tourist, then as a graduate student, and finally as someone committed to working in the region on behalf of women. Before my trip to Jordan, I had viewed the region as difficult to access, both geographically and intellectually. I had felt like an *ajnabiya*. Now, I had an eight-year-old Iraqi girl to thank for opening the door to what would eventually become my life's calling and my new home.

Stephanie Chaban works with a women's organization in the Palestinian city of Ramallah. Since meeting Fatima and her family in Amman, she has had similar encounters with women in her travels. Someday, she hopes to be as generous with a fellow woman traveler as other women have been with her.

ટ્ટ ટ્ટ ટ્ટ

Fish Out of Water

In a Bahamian resort, three sisters experience the
"hyperreal"—and remember the art of play.

I was starting to panic. Not the sudden, debilitat-
ing type of panic, but the kind that starts far away
and gets closer, like hooves in the distance, a cavalry of
fear approaching. I climbed the stairs behind my sisters
(who were blazing a trail to the top of the tower without
hesitation) pausing every once in a while to re-read the
warning signs. As a healthy thirty-four-year-old woman
of average height, there was no real reason I couldn't be
there (and trust me, I checked). I wasn't pregnant, no
discernible heart problems, no recent back injuries. I was
out of excuses.

This was the first family vacation we'd been on in
about twenty years, and about as many years since I'd
put myself in the uncompromising and unflattering
position of being frightened at the top of some foolish

amusement. We were in the Power Tower, one of the newest attractions at Atlantis in the Bahamas. This "exhilarating new waterscape" promised to "deliver a sensory journey unlike any other." The subtext being, "guaranteed to scare the shit out of you and your whole family." If you call hurling yourself from fifty-eight feet in the air down a wet surface a "sensory journey," then a root canal could be described as a bone-chilling thrill, and my last Pap smear, a probing, inward exploration.

And if you've never been to Atlantis, let me sum it up for you in four words: Club Med on crack. With its larger-than-life scale and Disney-esque artifice, it's what Italian novelist and scholar Umberto Eco would call an example of hyperreality: a superior fake that not only seeks to imitate reality, but to improve upon it, to exaggerate the edges of experience in order to make them bigger, better—more real than real. It's sort of the driving principle behind Disney World, Las Vegas, and for that matter, Chuck E. Cheese. And it's why we flock to these places to begin with: We've had it to here with real. We want something more.

The conceit, in this case, is obvious: The resort is modeled on the lost city of Atlantis, that mythic place first described in Plato's dialogues as a highly evolved civilization destroyed by an earthquake around 9500 B.C. and swallowed whole by the sea without a trace. Many argue that Atlantis was never an actual place, but a metaphor for utopia—a perfect ideal which the material world is doomed to forever fall short of. And yet, the legend persists, and the debate of Atlantis's rise and fall rages on, no doubt feeding the appetites of an obsessed few, while providing fodder for the occasional special on A&E.

But here, of course, the idea of Atlantis remains very much alive. Families by the thousand pay top dollar every year to rediscover, in a sense, their own lost cities, the ones where their imagination and sense of play once thrived, and which, like Atlantis itself, were swallowed up somewhere along the way, submerged under years of sediment.

Meanwhile, my own, long-buried memory of being an unadventurous kid at a water park had come screaming back to life. "Oh God. Ahh crap," I muttered as I lowered myself into the plastic raft. I looked around: slack-chested men, teenage girls in impossibly tiny bikinis, mothers waggling their pedicured toes. "It can't be that bad," said my sister Lori, hitching uncomfortably at her flowered bathing suit top. "Seriously. Any ride in a tube can't be too intense." I nodded, though the logic escaped me. "I mean, look at that kid," she said. We watched as a tow-headed ten-year-old who weighed about as much as broomstick neared the precipice, and was gone.

If Atlantis is a place of dream-like fantasy, then the Power Tower, a dark and imposing structure, was, to my mind, the stuff of nightmares—and an eyesore to boot. I can't figure out quite what they were thinking when they designed it. This, after all, is a land of benign beauty: Swordfish dance atop the regal coral towers, winding paths afford scenic views of waterfalls, exotic fish flicker beneath the surface of the lagoon. There's a different swimming pool for every day of the week. The Power Tower, by contrast, with its weathered iron façade and dark windows, looks like an evil cathedral, a haunted factory feeding on sunburned tourists, their high-pitched screams raising every hair on my arms.

While the physical thrill of a water slide is one way to kick your childlike instincts into play, another is to spend some time engaged in pure wonder. Earlier that day, we'd toured The Dig, a mock archeological excavation site at the resort where you can wander dimly-lit caverns, admire cave drawings (circa 2005), and peer through floor-to-ceiling glass walls at all manner of aquatic life. Silver schools of fish shimmer in the watery sunlight, restless sharks pace back and forth, and stingrays shudder along the bottom, lifting off like flying saucers. Behind them, a scene worthy of a Hollywood set: tumbled stones, rusted artifacts, crumbling staircases that lead nowhere. For a moment you could believe you are looking into the past, at the remnants of another age. And then you remember this is nothing more than an artfully cultivated relic—a reconstructed and imagined memory, calling to mind the classic poem by Marianne Moore, about "imaginary gardens with real toads in them."

That was where I encountered the largest and most stunning sea creature I had ever seen. He emerged from a dim corner of the lagoon, as if from the very depths of our collective imagination. With a wingspan of twelve feet, and weighing in at about 1,000 pounds (think of a SmartCar with wings), this mysterious manta ray, Zeus, was the king of this underwater lair, undulating past with incredible grace and ease, casting a shadow, and a kind of spell, over everyone and everything in its path.

The shrill whistle of an intimidating Bahamian lifeguard broke my reverie, and before I knew it, we were being pulled up the ticking conveyer belt toward the apex of the water slide. "Hold on tight," she warned, "and don't forget to lift your butt up!"

"Do what?" we yelled.

"Lift your *butt* up! Or else you'll hit the bottom." Needless to say, I did not appreciate receiving such critical information this late in the game. But there was no time to argue, and we had little choice but to face our fate with fists and butts clenched.

There was a long, yet imperceptible pause as we tipped over the edge, and gravity took hold, reminding me that for all our big ideas, we're little more than pieces of inert matter being shuttled along by unseen forces. Seconds expanded into one eternal moment as my body splintered and shook from sheer momentum. We plummeted down the steep camel-back drop at a heart-stopping rate, only to be shot *back* up the other side, then plunged into total blackness, careening around the unseen corners of what seemed like a large intestinal tract. This must be what it feels like to be digested, I thought, to be broken down into your most vital, simple parts. There's something incredibly liberating about being shaken loose from your surroundings, coming temporarily unglued and flying frictionless through the dark. I never stopped screaming—which, after a few seconds of the initial knee-jerk reaction, ironically kept me calm, like a terror-induced mantra. As long as I heard my own voice echoing back at me, I knew I was still there. I was a waterlogged bat sounding my way through the unknown.

Then, just as suddenly as it began, those long, strange moments collapsed, snapping shut like a telescope, and we were spat out the other end like so much waste. The end.

I climbed out of the pool, trembling with adrenaline and newfound pride, falling into breathless step with my sisters as we giddily padded our way over the white-hot pavement. We would go back a few more times before the end of the week, and by then, I could anticipate, even enjoy, the drop and swerve, the hapless hydroplaning. This in itself seemed an accomplishment of sorts: To learn to love a fearful thing for its own sake. To be, as the Buddhists teach, truly present. This is, of course, the essence of play. And while it's a native land for children, as an adult, you often need directions to find it again.

A week after I got back, I was checking my email before work and half-watching *The Today Show* when Meredith Vieira cut to a reporter on location in Atlantis. The man explained that the largest manta ray in captivity had been scraping the leading edge of his wings against the walls of the aquarium—a clear sign that he'd simply grown too large for the place. I watched in utter disbelief as Zeus was airlifted from the lagoon in something that looked like a giant diaphragm, and gently lowered into the open water. I was sad to watch him go, knowing that I'd never see him again. But I understood. Sure, it was fun being the big fish, but even in a place like Atlantis, things could probably get old after a while. As Zeus fluttered free of his net, I wondered what it felt like to return to your natural habitat, to stop swimming in circles and instead feel a whole world opening up ahead of you, a deep familiar pull drawing you home.

Terri Trespicio is a senior editor at Body+Soul *magazine and freelance writer. An award-winning poet, she earned her MFA in creative writing at Emerson College, and currently teaches in the publishing certificate program at Boston University. Her work has recently appeared in* Boston Magazine, Boston Globe *magazine, and* The Best Women's Travel Writing 2008. *She lives in Waltham, Massachusetts.*

❧ ❧ ❧

A Station on the Way

A handsome young Italian offers a grieving mother comfort. But could it last?

*T*he train, speeding past the station without stop-ping, pierced the tunnel entrance and plunged into black emptiness. *That certainly isn't the train from Rome,* I thought. *But it is 7:30. Where is it?* I didn't lose hope, for it wasn't unusual for a train in Italy to be thirty minutes late, especially in July when Italy is full of summer tourists. I continued to wait on the platform, pacing back and forth to subdue my apprehension.

For over three years, I had been meeting Antonio at the station in Formia, Italy. We'd meet every other Thursday after he finished work as one of Pope John Paul's body-guards. I had jumped up with butterflies when I heard the bell clang to announce the train that had just passed through. I wasn't able to understand the Italian announce-ment because the loudspeaker crackled.

Sauntering toward a large, concrete planter and bench near the entrance to the train platform, I waited. The azalea blossoms in the planter had reached their peak but seemed to be hanging on. The bench, decorated with curlicues along the edge could snag my stockings, so I sat down carefully. I had dressed in the Italian way for Antonio: A printed summer dress with a white sweater over my shoulders and sandals for comfort. Maybe I should have brought a jacket for the cool, summer breeze that chilled me.

Glancing toward my left, I noticed someone clad fashionably, a pretty girl leaning against a pillar with the heel of her boot bracing her. She wore a blouse-like leather jacket and blue jeans. Her burgundy pointed boots matched her jacket. A man approached her. He was not so elaborately dressed; he wore a light blue shirt and beige cotton pants. The flecks of gray in his otherwise black hair suggested a good ten years' difference. I watched them embrace. Warmth and excitement streamed through me when I thought of the bond Antonio and I shared.

I was jarred out of my reverie by the grinding gears, smoke, and smell of what sounded like ten motorcycles powering right onto the train tracks. I turned around to look behind me through the open doors of the station. Only two motorcycles actually blasted into the parking lot, braked and parked.

Cold sweat dripped down my back. *Here I go again*, I thought, *but at least I'm not shaking anymore. Maybe I'm slowly getting hold of myself.* The motorcycle scene brought back all I was trying to forget.

My older son, Dennis, had been killed on a motorcycle in the Northern California countryside where we lived. At eighteen he was so full of life that he thought nothing could stop him. A truck hit him. He flew eighteen feet, gasped once and his life was over. After many months of mourning, I ran away to Europe, still wearing a knee brace from trying to jog away my grief.

I found work with the U.S. Navy stationed in Gaeta, Italy. It is a beautiful resort town on a peninsula in Southern Italy, between Rome and Naples. Learning right along with them, I taught the Navy families how to adapt to living in a foreign country. Six months later, Antonio came into my life.

I had taken a bus from Gaeta to catch a train to Naples at the Formia Station, a few miles east of the peninsula. Once aboard, I peered out the window, enthralled with the walls formed by the ancient rocks and stones which sparkled in the sunlight. I held on tight, for this vehicle screeched at every stop, lurching forward when it accelerated. Across from where I was sitting, a sign brightly painted in greens and reds caught my eye. Below the sign, I noticed a young Italian man. He was watching me. I smiled. Not quite smiling back, he shifted a corner of his mouth, just like Dennis used to do. The bus screeched. All else was silent except for the engine growling now and then. I looked over at the young man. This time, raising his dark eyebrows, he grinned. I felt his gaze and quickly looked out the window. *He has probably been around these ancient rock walls all his life and they may mean nothing to him,* I thought. *They are so old and still beautiful.* The other passengers departed at different stops along the way, which left only the two of us on the bus.

"Are you American?" he had asked with a tone smooth as melted chocolate.

"Yes." I turned, sneaking a look at him out of the corner of my eye.

Though he was sitting, it was obvious he was tall by the way his legs extended away from the seat. He appeared to be in his early twenties. Daring to look up, I saw the beauty of his dark skin and square jaw. My heart caught in my throat and I had to catch my breath. I wanted to run away; I felt so exposed by his gaze.

"Where do you go now?" he asked.

"I'm on my way to the train station to go to Naples to meet a friend." I hoped I sounded nonchalant, not as uneasy as I felt. Then it crossed my mind *I'm much older than he is. He's probably young enough to be my son. I needn't feel so awkward. No reason I can't ask him the same.*

"Where are *you* going?" I ventured.

"I go to Rome to work. We both go to the train *ma apposto direzione*. Your train *parte fifteen minuti*. He paused a moment. "Will you take coffee with me?"

"Um, O.K.," I said, putting my fingers over my lips. *Oops.* Then arguing with myself, I came up with, *well, it'd be interesting to get more acquainted.* I peered out the window searching for those sunlit rocks and stones.

When the bus arrived at the train station, he helped me with my bag and we strolled to the coffee bar. I couldn't think of anything to say. Here I was with an attractive young man who had invited me to coffee. Never did I expect that my trip to Europe would lead to this kind of adventure.

At the bar, Antonio pulled out a cigarette and glanced around, then directly into my eyes. "Will you go out with me?" he said.

"What?"

"Will you go out with me next week when I come *da Roma*?"

"But I don't know you. I don't even know your name!"

"Well, I'll tell you. I am Antonio Ombra. I am from a town near Napoli. I go a Roma to work and stay there all week. Then I return to my home near Napoli." He smiled that same sweet smile I saw on the bus.

"I'm Bonnie."

We finished our coffee and Antonio took my arm, leading me to the ticket window. Though I was fiddling with my purse, a comfortable silence rested between us while we waited in line for a ticket. Then I started thinking. *What if he asked me again? I'd have to answer. I did want to say "yes," but I didn't know this man. What would people say if they saw me with him? He's so much younger than I am.* Antonio gazed at me, but didn't speak. I had to decide. If I said "no," I'd probably never see him again.

"So?" he asked.

"So, what?" I answered, knowing full well what he wanted.

"Will you go out with me?"

"But where? When?" I asked in confusion. The train pulled into the station.

"I'm here at the station by 7:30 in the evening on *Giovedi*, uh Thursday. You come?"

I hesitated, nodded. "All right. I'll come."

I watched the tension leave Antonio's face. He helped me onto the train with my bag. The whistle blew and the automatic door slammed shut. Thursday evening. 7:30. I was spinning in a whirlwind. It had happened so fast that we didn't even have time to say goodbye.

When I returned to my apartment in Gaeta late that night, I still churned with excitement. I longed to call home, but who would I call? Dennis? He wasn't there anymore. I slumped down in the chair thinking about him, like the times he'd lean on the refrigerator in the kitchen while I fixed dinner. And just before he died, how I finally said to him, "Hey, Den, I'd like to tell you something."

"What?" he said watching me stir the spaghetti.

I stopped, turned, wiped my hands and said, "Well, I know you know I love you, but I want you to know that I really like who you have become."

"Yeah, Mom." He walked off to watch TV. Within seconds he returned. "Thanks, Mom." he said. Two weeks later he was gone.

Oh dear, I was bringing back all that sadness tucked inside some pocket of my heart, only to lay me low once again. Dragging my sweater behind me, I buried myself in bed.

Antonio arrived at the Formia Station that next Thursday and neither of us had much to say. I remember thinking that he probably wouldn't expect me to meet him. When he arrived, I wanted to tell him in Italian that I was glad to see him, but I didn't know how. I searched for my Italian phrase book. A short silence came once again, and then Antonio pointed to a phrase.

"You come today."

I turned and glanced up at him. "*Si, si,* I came," I said, my blood rushing to my toes. *That's enough of this phrase book*, I thought. *I'd rather look at him than it. I'll try on my own. His eyes say what words don't, anyway.* I stuffed the book back into my bag.

Antonio stood up, and giving me his hand, said, "Let's go." I was impressed by his directness. We left the train station to stroll down the hill toward the sea.

"Where exactly do you live?" I asked.

"About forty kilometers from here *con la mia famiglia,*" he said, "with my mother and father and sister and brother." I breathed a sigh of relief. I had heard so much about Italian men and their mistresses, and I certainly didn't want to be involved with a married man.

"Do you know English very well?" I asked in Italian. He looked puzzled and then asked me, "What do you do?"

"I write," I said. "See those fishing boats over there with the fisherman just tying up his boat? That's what I like to write about, about people in places like this, far away." Again I tried Italian, and hoped I was being clear:

"*Da-gli'stati uniti* (from the United States)."

"Hey!" Antonio squeezed my arm. "You speak Italian and I speak English." He seemed to like that.

We ambled toward the fishing boats and he told me of his family. He spoke of life in this Latina Province where we lived. His deep voice resonated to my very core. A castle rose up in silhouette against the sky on the Gaeta peninsula out past the boats in the harbor, symbolic of kingdoms come and gone.

We took the same lurching bus on which we met to my apartment in Gaeta.

"Would you like some spaghetti?" I asked, not knowing what else to say when he marched in right after me.

"No, grazie."

We stood in the entry hall for some time. He gazed into my eyes. I tingled, not moving a muscle. He wrapped his hand around the side of my neck, leaning down to lay a kiss on my cheek, first one, and then the other. By the time he slid to my lips, sweet bells were ringing. But all of a sudden they stopped. Caution took me by surprise. I gently placed my hand on his chest to hold him back.

"Antonio. This is too fast for me. Please, don't."

He just nodded slowly, smiled and took a cigarette out of his pocket.

Whew. I could hardly breathe.

Ironically, I believe my reaction encouraged him. Over the months we did get to know each other. Those bells began ringing once more. I soon felt safe enough for Antonio to spend his weekends with me when he came to Formia on Thursdays, unless he had a special assignment with the Pope.

Just finishing lunch at a snack bar in Gaeta one Sunday, we walked to the bus that took him to his train. Suddenly, out of the blue, brakes screeched. I turned, terrified. A man in a cinquecento (a small Italian car) barely missed someone on a motorcycle on Lungomare. I stood there shaking.

"*Cosa succede?* (What's the matter?)" asked Antonio.

"The motorcycle. That car almost killed that man."

"But he didn't. *Non c'e problema adesso.* (No problem now.) Here." Antonio led me toward a bench near the sea where we sat down.

After a few moments, I turned toward Antonio and said, "I'm sorry. Give me a minute." He placed his hand on my shoulder. Shortly, I calmed down enough to say, "There are some things I haven't told you." Shaking my head, I mumbled softly, "That scared me because my son was killed on a motorcycle. I hate motorcycles. They're just too dangerous." Lowering my head, I tried to keep from making a spectacle of myself by revealing the tears welling up. Antonio quietly sat beside me with my hand in his lap. His kindness swept over me. I was hooked. I began planning my schedule around our times together.

Sometimes, when we were going to meet at the station, I'd get a ticket on the same train to go to Rome with him. His train to Rome would be arriving from Napoli. He'd lift up his window and in his deep voice, catch my attention, "Bonnie, *vieni qua*." I'd race to that particular car and climb up.

Other times on Thursdays, Market Day, we'd stroll through the vendors' stalls, viewing the castle on the peninsula in Gaeta. "In the castle," he explained one day, part in English and part in Italian, "two Germans are imprisoned. Even though the war is long over, the Italian people will not pardon them, due to the atrocities they commandeered toward the Italian people in Rome and in Monte Sole, a mountain town in Northern Italy."

Sauntering over to the shoes, I kept shaking my head, uneasy about those Germans in that castle remaining there forever.

All of a sudden Antonio grabbed my arm and led me away. He pretended to be calm, but I knew something was up.

"What's the matter, Antonio?"

"I explain to you later." He spoke with a tight voice.

"O.K., but you're hurting me!"

He let go of my arm, but kept his hand on my back to make sure we walked straight ahead. We returned to my apartment. I needed an explanation but was afraid to ask. He pulled out a cigarette and paced back and forth.

"What's the matter?"

"My sister was behind you."

"Is that all? You could have introduced us."

"Bonnie, you don't understand. My family cannot know about you. It would be bad for them and me. Even my cousins would talk."

"Why?"

"You are too old for me. I must marry someone soon since I am more than twenty-three, but she must be young. If my sister meets you, she will think I plan to marry you. It's the mentality here."

"Being together for over two years doesn't mean anything?"

"You don't understand. You have a different mentality."

"A different mentality? That's not a disease." All was quiet. Then I said, "Oh, I see. That's why you don't invite me home to meet your family, isn't it?" I shook my head in dismay. At that moment I realized that this Italian man was imprisoned in his history and culture so tight, just like the Germans in the palace, that there wasn't room for me. I wanted to strike back, but not knowing how, I merely recoiled in rejection.

"Go, Antonio. I have to think."

He slowly walked to the door. "I call you next week then. O.K.?"

I knew he was trying to console me, but I didn't answer. I just wanted him to leave. I opened the door and he stepped out, a whiff of cigarette smoke lingering in the air.

I dreamt that night of faces: Dennis's and Antonio's faces superimposed on each other's. Their corner smiles matched exactly. I woke up startled, moaning. I couldn't go back to sleep. I peered through the window at the dark, afraid I might see those overlaid faces again. Time stretched in two directions: Past and future. Immobilized, I remained at the window until doves outside sang to my canary's song.

Ten months later, approaching St. Peter's Cathedral where we were to meet, I turned left around the last corner; Antonio came around the same corner in the

opposite direction and bumped right into me. He had
to grab me to keep me from landing in the street. Then,
like a dancer grasping his prize, he swung me around.
Lacing his arm in mine, he led me toward St. Peter's.
We reached a small park near the Sistine Chapel around
the corner from the square and perched ourselves on a
concrete wall. I sighed, wondering what we were doing
there.

"I have something," Antonio said reaching into his
pocket. His tender enthusiasm caught me off guard. He
held a pastel package within my reach and handed it to
me as if he were giving me the world. Opening the small
gift box, I gazed at a delicate golden heart with a rose
embossed on its surface. Our eyes met. Feeling my heart
melt in the warmth and love surrounding the moment,
I sat quietly fingering the rose. Without a word, he
wrapped his arms around me.

"*Ecco*. (Here.)" He lifted up the necklace, unclasped it
and placed it around my neck. I couldn't see it too well
when I looked down, but could feel the tender token of
love with my fingertips.

"Do you hear those bells?" he asked. I smiled and
nodded. I saw them in his eyes, in his smile. I tingled
with their sound. The fullness and warmth of that
afternoon stayed with me for days. I began to think that
Antonio's feelings toward me were opening.

We dared once again to meet each other in Formia.
At first, we made plans just to meet at the train station
for a short time before he had to leave for Rome. When
I arrived, I found Antonio waiting on the train platform
watching some children playing with their shadows
formed on the columns. He walked toward me, and
nodding at the children ahead of them, he said, "In my
family I will have three." I smiled, wrapped my arm in

his and wandered along the platform with him.

In a few moments, Antonio stopped. "Bonnie, you won't have any of my children." He dropped his cigarette and stamped it out. His eyes pierced through me. I couldn't make a peep, not any kind of protest. What brought this up? Was his family pressuring him, or did he just want to end this?

"*Treno a Roma. Treno a Roma,*" bellowed over the loudspeaker. Antonio kissed me on one cheek and then the other. He grabbed a newspaper and climbed on the train. I stood there not quite comprehending. Like his cigarette, I felt crushed under the weight of his words. Maybe age *did* make a difference. After all, I wasn't childbearing age. Maybe this relationship could go no further. And there was nothing I could do. I was so deep in thought that I barely caught a glimpse of him when he pushed down a train window near me to mouth "Ciao."

Months had passed since the last time I had met him at the station. He called regularly, asking me to meet him. I'd say "no." *I'd like to try again, but our relationship wouldn't lead anywhere*, I kept telling myself. Then I wanted it to work out so badly, I'd think, W*ell, maybe it could—maybe.* Finally, I decided to telephone him, leaving a message that I would be at the station in Formia at the usual 7:30 on Thursday.

That Thursday, waiting on the curlicued, concrete bench, I heard the bell clang once again. I walked toward the stairs up which the arriving passengers came. Mothers gathered their children. In a few moments, like fans from a baseball stadium, throngs of people emerged. Heart pounding, I moved back toward the station's front door, a little to the left so Antonio could see me. People continued to flow up the stairs and out the door to catch taxis or buses and to meet friends. A few more minutes passed.

The crowd thinned. I nervously bit my lip and fingered my necklace. Unconsciously, I pulled too hard on it and the chain broke. I tried to catch the small golden heart, but it rolled away toward the stairs. Two young girls, about eight or nine years old, skipped around the azalea planter, watching the heart roll. They scurried to pick up the sparkle of gold they saw. "*Signora, signora,*" they cried. They wanted to return the charm to me. I gazed at the pretty young girls. For a moment, time stopped. I thought about the special love I had known evidenced by that heart and the chain pieces I still held in my hand.

"No. No. It's all right," I said in my best Italian. "You can keep it." They understood me and their eyes widened. "*Grazie, grazie, grazie,*" is all I heard as they ran back to their mother.

I glanced toward the dark tunnel from where the train had come, and slowly turned to leave. With a sigh, a pocket in my heart opened and emptied. Without a tear, I said to no one, "I think it's time to go home." The station's lights clicked on. I wound my way through the cars to my own car where I had left it a lifetime ago.

Bonnie Bruinsslot's travel stories have appeared in the Bodega Bay Navigator *and* Women's Voices of Sonoma County, California. *She is the author of two children's books,* The Fern Fairy Adventures *and* Katie in the Car. *Bonnie lives in Sebastopol, California and is currently at work on her travel memoirs.*

ॐ ॐ ॐ

Speaking the Same Language

A mother and her daughters learn Spanish—
and life lessons—in Mexico.

"Are you scared, Mommy?" whispered my seven-year-old daughter in the back seat of the battered Mexican taxi.

The driver accelerated, swerving into the left lane to pass a farm truck full of cows. The pale hazy sun slipped behind the mountains. Night was descending quickly as we roared through the desert toward San Miguel de Allende; it would be dark before we arrived.

More than the forced smile on my face, my queasy stomach spoke the truth. I was very nervous about our maniac driver, the lack of seatbelts, and how long it was taking us to get to San Miguel.

Annalyse, the seven-year-old, squeezed my hand, snuggling her head into my shoulder. She thinks I am invincible, I thought with a sense of irony. Her mom, the author of a book called *Gutsy Women*, felt like a wimp. I could be so brave when I was alone, but add the responsibility of traveling with my daughters and I was having an attack of insecurity.

I avoided an honest answer and rationally, if not confidently, responded, "Sweetie, whenever I travel somewhere I've never been before, I'm both excited and uncomfortable."

I explained, "I am just wondering what our host family will be like. During meals together will we be able to communicate? We don't know very much Spanish, do we? I bet they don't know much English either. I hope our teachers at the Language Institute will be as nice as your first-grade teacher this past year."

In the silence that filled the dark cab, I realized for the first time this trip wouldn't be easy. I wished there was another grown-up along to help me keep an eye on my exuberant, wandering blond daughters.

Why was I so insecure about going to Mexico alone with my kids? Before marriage and motherhood I had traveled alone around the world for two years. I used to be a confident traveler. Motherhood seemed to have made me wary and cautious.

At the Mexico City airport, we had held hands to stay together in the crowded terminals. News programs in the United States had warned us about the violent crime in and outside the city. Julieclaire and I wore our backpacks over our chests to thwart pickpockets and thieves.

Outside the terminal there were no benches for weary travelers at the curbside bus stop, so we stood waiting for over an hour for the bus to Querétaro. I was exhausted from watching our luggage, protecting my children and keeping them entertained.

Aboard the Primera Plus deluxe bus, Julieclaire and Annalyse napped. I nervously thumbed guidebooks during the four-hour trip. At the bus stop, we hailed a cab for the one-hour journey to our final destination, a Mexican home in San Miguel de Allende.

The scrubby countryside of the highlands of central Mexico ended abruptly as we drove into town. We passed tacky-looking shops and bars with men spilling onto the unpaved streets. Where were the traffic lights, the neon signs, and fast food establishments I saw in other Mexican towns?

Our cabbie stopped twice to ask for directions. Where were the narrow cobbled-stone streets and the charming colonial villas described in the guidebooks? When we careened around a corner into a dirt alley, I was sure we were lost or being taken for a ride. Our decrepit cab lurched to a stop as the driver pointed with pleasure at a messy hand-written sign on a whitewashed wall. It was the street address I had given him. I slumped back in stunned silence.

This neighborhood had no reassuring streetlights, no pedestrians, trees, or even a stray barking dog. It was deserted and dirty. Intimidated by the darkness, silence, and poverty of the scene, I didn't want to get out of the taxi.

The cabbie wanted no part of my hesitation or insecurities. He dumped our luggage on the street, grabbed his pesos, and sped off.

We pounded on the wooden door and hoped for the best. Annalyse's tiny warm hand found its way into my clammy fist. Julieclaire impatiently scuffed her foot in the dirt.

A short woman with charcoal-colored hair threw open the door, grabbed my free hand and pumped it in an energetic greeting. She wore a starched white apron over a somber black dress, and I guessed by her unlined face she was in her thirties.

She introduced herself as Lourdes, and wasted no time welcoming Annalyse and Julieclaire with hugs. Julieclaire, at ten-years old, was almost as tall as Lourdes. She took charge, leading us through an empty garage and into the main house, chattering non-stop in Spanish. Her monologue, none of which we understood, cheered us up as we stacked our heavy luggage in a corner of our new home for the next fifteen days.

Lourdes knew intuitively what we needed. My children were hungry and I wanted to be taken care of. She led us into a large, empty dining room and seated us at the only piece of furniture, a lace-covered table.

She brought in bowls of corn flakes and cold milk. Ah, reassuring corn flakes! I remembered another time, when I had been on the road for over nine months, alone. I discovered corn flakes on a restaurant menu in Southern India. I relished every bite, transported back to Ohio and childhood breakfast before school. Corn flakes had been my emotional link with home. And now, lifetimes later, my daughters also found a bowl of familiar cereal reassuring.

Removing her apron, Lourdes smoothed down her glossy hair, smiled, and sat down at the table with us. Little Patrick, her cheerful five-year-old son, climbed onto her lap and furtively glanced at the girls. He made funny faces to get their attention. Julieclaire made goofy faces in return and our laughter echoed through the bare rooms.

After our snack, Annalyse and Julieclaire argued over who would get the bigger drawer in the dresser for their clothes; and over who had to sleep with me on which bed in our tiny dark bedroom. Patrick peeked through the half-open door, fascinated by these two foreign girls who were squabbling as they pulled hair bows and games out of their bags.

Meanwhile, Lourdes gave me a tour of her three-bedroom, cement-block home, showing me what I would need to know—how to use the key to lock the front door, where to find purified water to refill our water bottles for drinking and brushing teeth.

We climbed up a narrow set of chipped cement stairs to the flat roof that served as the laundry. Lourdes showed me the clotheslines where we should hang our damp towels. A big, enamel washtub, with a wooden washboard and bars of soap stood in the corner. This is where I would hand wash our clothes and hang them up to dry.

Wooden clothespins held sheets and underwear on the clotheslines. They flapped in the balmy summer breeze. A crescent moon was pasted against the black velvet sky, myriad stars competing with each other for space in the heavens. I was awed by this nocturnal beauty but pleasure lay shrouded beneath fatigue and maternal responsibility.

Lourdes held back the corner of a drying sheet and motioned for me to follow her through the laundry to the other side of the open roof. I was unprepared for the sight that awaited me. Dominating the city's panorama was a pink Gothic cathedral with ornate steeples aglow with tiny lights.

We could hear the three children below, giggling together in the bedroom, playing peekaboo. I let out a sigh of relief.

Lourdes spoke to me in slow sentences, and my knowledge of French helped me to piece together her

Spanish words. Lourdes was divorced, living alone with her children. She supported them by taking in language students as boarders.

In addition to Patrick, she had a twenty-year-old son who worked the night shift in a dry cleaning factory and an eighteen-year-old daughter who was still in school and spent most of her time with her "*novio*," or boyfriend. With a shrug and resigned laugh, she explained that her older children were rarely at home.

Lourdes attended elementary school for four years and could read and write "*un poco*." She considered herself fortunate, because after her divorce, she kept the house but little else. Now I understood why the rooms were sparsely furnished. Julieclaire noticed there were no pictures on the walls and not a book to be seen in the home.

When Lourdes finished speaking I wanted to tell her about my family, my life. Many times in my travels I have confided in other women, often relative strangers. I have told them secrets about my loves, my losses, my insecurities. Under the regal moon, Lourdes and I stood in silent female communion and I tried to explain my fear.

I pointed to the dark, empty streets below and asked her in my schoolbook Spanish: "I am with my daughters. My husband, their Papa, is not with us. No other adult is with us. Is it possible to walk in the streets at night? We want to go after dinner to the main square, to sit on the park benches near the bandstand to watch people or hear the mariachis play, to see the peddlers offering candy and the old men get their shoes shined. But there are no lights here."

I motioned to the dark and deserted street below and continued, "No one is in the streets. I am afraid. Is it a problem? Are my girls safe? Is my purse safe?"

Lourdes reached out and looped her arm through mine. She was small but solid and smelled as fresh as her hand-scrubbed clothing that hung around us. As we stood arm in arm, amid the fluttering laundry, I knew she understood my distress.

She pointed to a nearby rooftop. I saw two women rocking in chairs quietly conversing as they watched the streets below. They were partially hidden by their own drying laundry. I was surprised. I hadn't noticed any other life in the neighborhood. She motioned to other roofs and open windows where women were together, witnesses to the dark and silent night. "No problem, Señora. Many women watch out for you. No problem to walk in the streets at night with no man," she assured me.

I had traveled to San Miguel to experience the customs and the language, but the lasting legacy of our journey was this female kinship, this reaffirmation of the bond our gender feels, worldwide, as we confide in and support each other.

During our two weeks in Mexico, my daughters and I learned some Spanish, shared in another family's life, walked confidently in the dark, laughed at ourselves, and ate too much ice cream. We returned home strengthened, surer of ourselves, and stretched, having touched other women with our spirits—and having been touched by theirs.

Marybeth Bond is a San Francisco author/editor of nine Travelers' Tales books, including the bestselling Gutsy Women *and* A Woman's World, *which won a Lowell Thomas Gold Medal for best travel book. She is also the author of two National Geographic books:* Best Girlfriends Getaways Worldwide *and* 50 Best Girlfriends Getaways in North America.

JOANNE ASTLEY

✍ ✍ ✍

Memories of Stone

In a Japanese temple, she stumbled upon small statues
dressed in baby clothes—but what did they mean?

As my feet touched the *tatami* flooring of my
concrete apartment, the woven rice stalks whispered. They encouraged me to wander, and I gladly
heeded their call. On a short train ride to the ancient
capital of Kamakura, I passed bright yellow straw
bundles drying in the rice fields. "That's it," they called,
"you're on your way."

In Kamakura, I observed the impressive forty-two-
foot bronze Great Buddha, who has sat in deep meditation for over 750 years. But the stalks murmured
again, and I found myself in the lesser-known Hesedera
temple. A tall and distinctly feminine statue of Kannon,
a Bodhisattva or enlightened being, greeted me with her
eleven faces. As my eyes wondered beyond hers, I found
what I'd clearly been led to see.

275

An army of little stone statues in red knit hats beckoned. As I stepped closer, more of these infant-sized Buddhas showed themselves. And then more. And more still. Some wore bibs, toys, or pearls around their necks, but all stood at attention, row upon row. Thousands of them.

The lack of explanation in my guidebook made me consider turning to my students for answers; surely, I thought, they would be the best source for my cultural education. The problem, however, was that my Japanese skills were virtually non-existent, and my students' level of English was so low that we were still working on basic grammar structures and vocabulary.

In fifteen-minute one-on-one lessons in my office just big enough for a desk, a chair, and a whiteboard, "the members" would flow in as if on a conveyer belt. All sixteen. Every day. Five days a week. If a member couldn't attend his or her session, he or she phoned the secretary, "Miss" Yoshida, who booked the English or *ego* lessons, and she would call another member to fill the open slot. "My dream," she told me on my first day at work, "is 100 percent attendance."

And her dream was achieved most days. After a speedy class with Mr. Tanaka from 9:00 to 9:15, I'd have a five-minute break that would end with Mr. Suzuki's arrival at 9:20. Once he'd returned to the factory, Miss Yoshida never failed to appear at 9:40. This process would repeat itself for a total of eight times in the morning, and then after an hour lunch break, the schedule would resume until quitting time at 5:00 P.M. Most of the members operated heavy machinery in the factory, except for two who were secretaries, and one of them was Miss Yoshida.

She would arrive very punctually for her *ego* lesson in her immaculate yellow polyester uniform, pull out her Hello Kitty pencil case, matching notebook, and sit very demurely in front of me. Having never taught before, and having limited resources at my disposal, I relied heavily on a book called *Side by Side*, which taught common conversation patterns using cartoons and speech bubbles.

As the clock ticked audibly, we practiced the dialogue first with the words written in the bubbles and then without. Like most students, Miss Yoshida could grasp this in the fifteen minutes.

Me: What are you doing?

Miss Yoshida: I'm walking

Me: What are you doing?

Miss Yoshida: I'm jumping

Me: Great job, Miss Yoshida.

Miss Yoshida: Thank you.

And Miss Yoshida would smile and look down, careful not to make too much direct eye contact, or to look too pleased with herself.

As the members' skills, and my Japanese, inched slowly forward, the hope of asking any students about the little stone statues faded. Since my time in Japan preceded the ubiquity of the Internet, and since no English books were to be had in my small town at the foot of Mt. Fuji, I resorted to querying co-workers.

My boss, Kyle, was a good source. He'd married a Japanese woman and spoke her mother tongue fluently. At six foot, three inches, and another inch of curly brown hair, he stood out more than the rest of us *gai-jin*, or foreigners, often bumping his head on the low doorways of more traditional Japanese buildings.

"Oh, those things," was his response when I asked him about the rows of little stone children.

"Yes, what are they?"

"Well, they're called Jizō statues. They're there so people can remember children they have lost."

"Lost children? You mean people whose children died?"

"Yeah, that's it."

"But there are so many of them. That many children have died?"

"Well, you have to include the aborted ones."

"Oh, O.K. I see, so aborted fetuses are included?"

"Very much so. In fact, that's mostly what they're for."

He then turned away and started chatting with our co-worker, Jan, about something completely unrelated, making it clear that he had no interest in continuing the conversation.

Further attempts at gaining information gave me jigsaw pieces of information. I soon learned that the foot-high Jizō statues, as well as abortion, were sensitive topics in Japanese culture, not ones to be idly discussed as my students acquired more English, or as I learned to speak Japanese. I recalled details from my orientation about the importance of harmony in Japanese culture, and how expressing one's opinions directly was frowned upon.

Zoë, another colleague, who was on her second stint teaching in Japan, told me that Japanese women could not easily obtain the birth-control pill because the medical establishment deemed it dangerous to their health. Instead, they relied on men to use condoms, and consequently, the unwanted pregnancy rate was higher than in Canada and the United States. Because of this, Zoë explained, women had trouble-free access to abortion, which had become like a backup method of birth control for Japanese women, many of whom had had multiple abortions.

"Ridiculous," Zoë hissed while shaking her head. "If women could just get the Pill, they wouldn't have to repeatedly go through these invasive medical procedures." Her upper lip curled in disdain as she spoke. "But people are so brainwashed into believing the Pill is dangerous that they keep going with this system."

I could see Zoë's point, but no matter how "ridiculous" it might seem to us that Japanese women didn't have the same right to a pill that had become synonymous with the "sexual revolution," at the very least they had straightforward access to a procedure that in 1991, in North America, was still controversial.

Prior to my departure for Japan in 1991, Dr. Henry Morgantaler had set up his abortion clinic in my old neighborhood near the University of Toronto. On my way to class, I saw protesters waving banners in an effort to block women from entering. They heckled Dr. Morgantaler and the nurses as they began their workday, despite a 1988 Supreme Court of Canada ruling that had essentially lifted any restrictions on abortion. Meanwhile, south of the border in the United States, the famous Roe v. Wade case had made abortion legal in 1973; however, some conservative Christians ensured that the right to an abortion was in question, and a significant number of abortion doctors lived in fear of their lives.

The talk with Zoë made me reflect on how in Canada, and especially in the United States, religious belief had clashed with the socio-political notions that women had the right to make their own choices in terms of the delivery of a child. My thoughts turned, once again, to the little stone Jizō statues, and I wondered what impact Buddhist thinking had had on abortion practices in Japan.

I hoped a visit to the *ego* section of a Tokyo bookstore would enlighten me further. A plethora of popular fiction and non-fiction books awaited me on the shelves, but, disappointingly, nothing about Jizō statues. I managed to find an overview of Buddhism, which illuminated the Buddhist thinking on taking a life, and explained that the first fundamental precept is "...to refrain from destroying living beings." It also pointed out that Japanese Buddhism has co-existed with Shinto, a pagan belief system, which preceded the introduction of Buddhism to Japan in the 6th century.

This, however, left me more puzzled. I wondered if Buddhism considered abortion to be "destroying a living being," and if so, why were temples offering Jizō statues for women to adorn? I wondered, too, if Shinto traditions had some influence here. I also questioned whether Jizō statues gave women the opportunity to come to terms with a choice that Buddhist or Shinto teaching supported, or whether women used the little monuments to express their dissatisfaction with a system that prevented access to all kinds of birth control. In a country where harmony among people was paramount, perhaps adorning miniature statues with children's clothing was a way for women to make their dissatisfaction *indirectly* heard?

Meanwhile, Miss Yoshida continued to be cheerful about regularly achieving her dream of 100 percent attendance, and was clearly pleased that she was moving onto more complex conversation patterns such as "Do you like?" such and such, "Yes, I do" or "No, I don't."

On one occasion, she brought a cute stuffed animal to class and stroked it while asking: "Do you like?" Another time, she branched out and asked: "Do foreigners like sushi?" and then giggled at her own daring attempt to connect with me. "Well, I don't know about other foreigners," I replied, "but I *love* sushi." At this, profuse giggles poured from her lips, which she blocked with her fingertips, as if to stop herself from any more outrageous outbursts.

From my box-like office the only view was the rows of desks where men smoked cigarettes while they worked. When Miss Yoshida finished her lesson, she joined the few other yellow uniformed dots in a smoky sea of men, who shuffled about in their beige pants and green jackets. I watched her find her place, farthest from Mr. Katō, the manager of our section, who sat at the "head" of the office with his back to me. Miss Yoshida knew, as did all her co-workers, that once she married—and it should be before age twenty-five—she would "retire" from the company to be a full-time homemaker and mother. She knew, too, that when walking through the office halls, she would do well to walk behind her male superiors.

This was the Japan I was to leave a year after my arrival, full of frustrations and unanswered questions. I returned to Toronto briefly in 1992, the same year that Dr. Morgentaler's clinic was firebombed. I moved on to Pittsburgh, Pennsylvania, where large pictures of fetuses on buses screamed "This is a child, not a choice." Pro-life protesters paced the streets on Sundays, shouting angry slogans. In 1993, the newspaper reported that an abortion doctor, David Gunn, was shot and killed in Pensacola, Florida, and only a year or so later, Dr. John Britton was also murdered in the same city. In 1998, Dr. Barnett Slepian met the same fate in his home in Amherst, New York. Meanwhile in Canada, attempts on the lives of abortion doctors occurred in 1994, 1995, 1997, and 2000.

In Pittsburgh I found a book, *Liquid Life: Abortion and Buddhism in Japan* by William Lafleur, which helped to finally answer my questions about the little stone children.

Adorning miniature statues with bibs, hats, or jewelry is a way to make offerings to Jizō, a Bodhisattva and guardian of children, as well as a way to memorialize a dead fetus or *mizuko*. The ritual, called *mizuko kuyō*, or quite literally "water child memorial service" was practiced more covertly prior to World War II when famine and poverty sometimes caused illegal infanticide and abortion. In 1948, abortion laws were liberalized in cases where the health of the mother necessitated it, and by 1952, the law was amended so that the decision was left solely to the discretion of the physician. Since there was no longer any accountability to a governing body to prove the "necessity" of an abortion, the procedure became easier to obtain.

Twenty years later, in the 1970s, while women in the West were starting to take the Pill, *mizuko kuyō* became particularly visible as temples—solely devoted to this ritual—promulgated the notion that if the *mizuko* was not properly apologized to, it would seek retribution or *tatari*. The temples suggested that by purchasing a Jizō statue, adorning it, and possibly paying for its care in perpetuity, women would prevent a host of problems that an avenging *mizuko* could cause. The threat of *tatari*, coupled with the reliance on abortion as the chief means of family planning, explained the sheer number of Jizō statues dotting the temple grounds.

Some Japanese Buddhists, such as Ochiai Seiko, have spoken out against the practice of *mizuko kuyō*, and the business-oriented temples that warn against *tatari*. She has called for a return to Buddha's original teachings, which reject the possibility of Shinto-influenced avenging spirits that prey upon the living, and stresses instead the notion of individual responsibility for one's own actions.

The Zen Buddhist master or *roshi*, Robert Aitken, also criticizes the idea of avenging *mizuko*, but does not reject the practice of *mizuko kuyō*, as he believes it can benefit the bereaved in much the same way that funerals do. And despite the first precept against "destroying living beings," Aitken emphasizes the importance of compassion for women who have made the arduous decision to terminate a pregnancy.

In the Japan I was to leave in 1992, women still did not have access to the Pill and continued to rely on less effective forms of birth control. Not surprisingly then, Japan had become known as an "abortion heaven." By 1999, however, restrictions on the Pill were lifted, but by 2007 only 1 in 100 women actually used it. Fears about its safety still persist, despite the fact that 100 million women worldwide use this form of contraception.

After I left Japan in 1992, a good friend of many years called me in Pittsburgh to tell me she was pregnant. She was in a crumbling relationship, and had made the wrenching decision to end the pregnancy, as she couldn't see herself managing as a single mother. She had set up an appointment near her home in Toronto, at Dr. Morgantaler's clinic.

I called my friend the evening after the abortion to see how she was.

"Oh, frazzled," she said with a laugh to disguise that she really was frazzled.

"I'm sorry you've had to go through this," I offered.

"Yeah, I know, it sucks," she said dryly. "I mean, I'm glad it's over. I had to do it; there was no other way, right now. But I feel like I've lost something, not a baby necessarily, but a part of myself. And it was so cold, so clinical…" her voice trailed off.

"I can imagine," I said, feeling useless. I thought she might feel bad about what she had done, so I said: "The time wasn't right, but it could be again at another time."

"I know, I know," she said, choking back the tears. "It's not so much that…it's just, what do I do now? I mean, I leave the office after it's over, and that's it. It's over. How do I process this feeling of loss?"

And, she was right, of course. How could she process this? There were no rituals in our culture to deal with this newly legalized medical procedure. In our drive for the right to choose, we had neglected to think of the after-effects. And no matter how sure she was of her decision before and after the procedure, how was she to deal with the fact that she had been in a clinical environment where some part of her had been removed? There were no quiet incense-filled temples for her to visit, no baby clothes for her to buy and place on small statues. No rituals in which members of the community and family surrounded her. No place for her to sit and, if necessary, grieve. Not even a Hallmark card with a sappy greeting that could, however briefly, soothe her.

I knew my friend liked sculpture and played around with clay for fun.

"You could make a little figurine," I suggested. "A memorial of your lost part. Place it on your shelf in your living room, and adorn it with jewelry or clothes or whatever you wish. You can talk to it and tell it your feelings."

As the words came out of my mouth, I thought she would cringe, or think I was crazy.

"That's a great idea," she said, her voice brightening.

As I hung up the phone, I wondered if *mizuko kuyō* could be just that: a quiet place for women to talk to their lost parts, their lost selves, to find them, embrace them, make sense of them, grieve, and finally, let them go.

꙳   ꙳   ꙳

Joanne Astley has made footprints in several continents. Born in the UK, she immigrated to Canada in the 1970s. After graduating from the University of Toronto, she taught English in Japan for fifteen months. From there, she moved to Pittsburgh and then Dallas, where she completed a Masters in English and Creative Writing at Southern Methodist University. She has since returned to Canada to live in Guelph, and is currently completing her first novel.

❧ ❧ ❧

Return

A quarter of a century later, a mother and daughter
relive the past in Barcelona.

I picked up my daughter at the airport, and the next
morning at 8:00 we left the village where I live
in Málaga province and headed for Barcelona, driving
north up the coast, first on the *autovia*, then along the
coast road that wound around bays and coves. Stone
cylindrical watchtowers perched on headlands and
rocky cliffs fell straight into the blue, September sea. We
had to make it in one day, spend two days in the city, and
then drive back in one day to meet my other daughter
and baby grandson at the same airport in Málaga. An
intense beginning to the visit. Neither Ana nor I had
been in Barcelona for twenty-six years—the last time we
were there as a family with her father and sisters. We'd
stopped there on our way out of Spain, after spending
most of the previous year in the village in the south

where I now live year-round. Ana was then only six years old.

This trip was my daughter's idea, and since I finally had a decent car, the road trip was feasible, if not practical. Ana wanted to see the countryside, which is beautiful all the way north, and especially the sea views while we were driving along the coast. So, through Almeria and the vast areas under plastic where three crops of fruits and vegetables can be produced a year and where the sea coasts are among the least developed in Spain, then Alicante, Murcia, and Valencia, where the orange groves stretch for many miles, and the palm trees. Somewhere in a town in Valencia province we stopped for a lunch of *raciones*—small portions of ham croquettes, roasted red pepper salad, Spanish omelette, and wine. Then we were back in the car and pushing north, Ana happy to be back and seeing this part of Spain for the first time as a young woman. I was also thrilled to return, remembering the landscape now, recalling what I had felt all those years ago when driving through with my family, when we were on our way out of the country after ten very intense months living in the village—a year that changed all of our lives forever.

We took turns driving. I was nervous about entering a big city after dark when we didn't really know where we were going or where we could park. I had booked a room in a hotel listed in my guidebook, which, when I saw the name and the Plaza it was on, and how close it was to the *Ramblas*, I thought, that's it. That is surely the little hotel we stayed in twenty-six years ago. When I talked to the man over the phone, asking about parking, he said that we could no longer drive a car into the Gothic Quarter and would have to park outside it—and that it would be expensive unless we could find something on the street—perhaps in *Montjuï*, off the *Avenida Parall-el*...perhaps.

We couldn't make it before dark—the trip was over six hundred miles—and darkness was falling as the traffic increased exponentially the closer we approached the great metropolis. Ana had taken over the wheel, and her experience driving in Los Angeles for several years was certainly a help here. We strained to see any signs mentioning *Montjuï* or *Avenida Parrall-el*. The cars and trucks all around us, and we ourselves, seemed to be being pulled faster, faster into the city, as if into a huge spinning vortex of light, energy, intensity. We saw the sign at the same instant and exited, immediately finding ourselves in a dark, strangely unpopulated area, where we drove about, turning up and down streets, ending up in the large, empty parking area of a huge warehouse. No, this wasn't right. We saw a man and stopped to ask about *Avenida Parrall-el* and *Montjuï*. "Ah," he said. "You have to return to where you came from and continue a bit and then you'll see it." We had gotten off the expressway too soon—easy to do in Spain, because they mark the exits so well and with such forewarning, that it is easy to respond too quickly. When we told him we hoped to find parking in the street, he looked at us with mild astonishment, then nodded and said it was *posible, pero...*

Our second attempt proved correct, and we eventually found ourselves very near the port, driving around the entrance to what seemed to be a large hotel, garden, and park, where I hoped to find a place to put the car. But no, there was no public parking area. We drove to where a large blue "P" marked an underground garage, but the man there said parking here was certainly not free, it was twenty-three euros a day, and if we thought we could find parking on the streets outside, good luck!

It was 8:30 and we were very tired, but we tried. We drove up and down the streets at the foot of *Montjuï*, but everywhere we saw a spot, either a red or blue or green triangle notified us (1) that under no circumstances could one park there, or (2) only residents of that street could park there, or (3) only handicapped persons or persons delivering or loading things could park there. As we sat in the car on a side street deliberating about what to do next, Ana saw a shady-looking character eyeing us, so we moved on and drove back to the unpleasant man in the parking garage and checked the car in. We asked him where we could easily find a taxi, because it was now almost 9:30 and we didn't know how far we were from the hotel, walking—fifteen minutes? Half an hour? People told us different things. The man seemed exasperated with these two obviously not wealthy, worn-out looking females. He gestured and turned away. We walked up out of the garage, followed by the Moroccan garage attendant who had observed the behaviour of his boss below. He was sympathetic to our plight and told us where we could get a taxi, then he saw one himself parked even closer by, and he directed us to it.

We told the driver where we wanted to go, showed him the street written down in the guidebook, asked the price—six euros—and off we went. In two minutes we were driving up one side of the famous *Ramblas* and in eight minutes we got out just around the corner from our hotel. We took our luggage, paid the kindly driver, wandered into the quarter, saw the stone walls of the hotel… then the plaza and its sycamore trees. Ana sucked in her breath. This is it, she said. I nodded. It was indeed the same hotel. Immediately recognizable. I felt twenty-six years fall away. I was that younger woman—all of the things that would happen had not happened yet.

After checking in, noting that our room was in the back, not overlooking the square as before, we washed up and went out to explore. Barcelona—the air seemed to vibrate. The *Ramblas*, the long series of esplanades that point like an arrow to the port, was full of people walking up and down, flower stalls, clothes and jewelry and souvenir stalls. We badly needed some refreshment and headed for a lovely wooden-beamed *tapas* bar for wine and tasty bits of sausage, chicken wings, potato salad, olives, and boiled shrimp. I knew it would be expensive since it was right on the *Ramblas*, but we would economize later. After that long drive we needed to pamper ourselves. Then we walked down all the way to the port and the statue of Christopher Columbus pointing west toward the New World. We looked at the water and the luxury restaurants and shops, all new since we had last been here, and we walked out the long pier, where people sat on benches and low walls. We walked and walked and then headed back to the hotel for a needed night's sleep.

The next morning we had breakfast at a café near the hotel and walked about the area, enjoying the wonderful shops full of temptations—shawls, leather boots and bags, a large gallery of ceramics from every part of Spain and Portugal, the shop where all styles of *alpargatas*, the Spanish rope-soled espadrilles, were made and sold. I bought Ana two pairs for her upcoming birthday, one pair the flat, white canvas and black-ribboned style so typical of the area that people have worn here for many generations. Twenty-six years ago I had bought myself a pair in this same shop. When he later saw me wearing them, an old man from my village told me that during the Spanish Civil War, when he was forcibly conscripted to fight for the rebel army, Franco's army, he was driving a mule provision wagon through the woods some-where when he saw six legs hanging down from a tree, on the feet were these same *alpargatas*. The men, Spanish Republicans, had been hanged.

Ana and I spent time on the *Ramblas* enjoying the mix of people from all over the world and the mimes, or living statues—one who appeared to be a warrior from Genghis Khan's army, glowering with his upheld sword. We walked and gazed, found little hidden squares with little cafés and churches. Ana was particularly enchanted with the ice-cream shops that offered such a multitude of flavors—one in particular held a stainless steel lazy Susan tilted toward the window, hypnotically turning its colorful wares around and around. She took a photograph of this marvel. We stopped later for wine and talked and talked—of life and history and our family's past and present.

In the porch of the church in the plaza where our hotel was situated, we saw a sign advertising a classical guitar concert to be held a few blocks away that evening and we bought tickets. That evening we entered the Palau de la Música Catalana, a splendid example of modernist architecture and design. The concert hall was decorated with mosaics and swaths of plaster vines and roses. Plaster horses emerged from the walls on either side of the stage. Concert goers could buy a glass of sherry or wine and a *tapa* or two before the concert, and we eagerly took advantage of this, enjoying the pleasure of being in a sophisticated city that had everything to offer, including, suddenly and surprisingly for us, this music of Albéniz, Rodriguez, Villa-Lobos, and others. We wouldn't have time to go the museums or see many of the sites, but next day we planned to visit La Sagrada Familia, the astonish-ing Gaudí-designed cathedral in the center of the city.

The following morning we had our usual breakfast:
toast, coffee, and freshly squeezed orange juice, and then
walked two and a half miles or more north to see the
cathedral, called a temple by Gaudí. The last time we had
been there, only four of the main spiralling towers had
been completed and we were able to walk up the inside
steps of one of them. Now there were eight. The plans
call for seventeen. Under construction since 1883, Gaudí
almost immediately took over as architect. More workmen were in evidence now than twenty-six years ago. We
had to wait forty-five minutes to take the elevator up one
of the towers because there were so many people, but the
wait was worth it. Some people find Gaudí's style overly
fantastical; others, myself included, find it glorious, joyful,
and profound. The mosaic-tiled baskets of fruit perched
atop the pinnacles, plaster animals, snails, birds clinging
to the facades, the curves and spiralling lines that seem
to lift the massive structure above the ground, as if it is
ascending into the sky. Four of the eight main towers
completed represent Christ's Nativity, massive realistic
figures depicting main aspects of this story covering the
facades. The other four towers, the newer ones, depict in
a more stylized fashion figures from and segments of the
story of Christ's Passion.

We walked all around the temple, gazing at the
details, feeling the effect. Workmen in hardhats kept
appearing in the gaps and openings high above the
street. We sat for a while in a park across the way where
we could look across a small pond at the structure and
the ongoing work, which would take many more years
to complete. We looked at the pigeons and sparrows,
like the workmen entering and exiting the many openings. We gazed at the temple's reflection in the water, at
the clouds drifting past the spires. The temple bell rang

out the hour, deep and sonorous. When we walked past again to begin our long walk back to the hotel, others on the sidewalk also walked, circling the huge structure, gazing up, gazing up. I remarked to Ana that so it must have always been when the great cathedrals of Europe were being built over a period of two or three hundred years: the people, including all of those who knew they would not live to see its completion, must have circled the growing mass when they were in the streets going about their business, gazing up, watching it rise. Many of those we saw that day were not tourists but native Barcelonans who happened to be in the area, drawn to look at the aspiring, inspiring temple, their gaze pulled up, up. Their faces seemed smoothed by the sight.

That last evening, tired from our full day and the walking, Ana and I had dinner in a restaurant off a hidden square where the owner warned us not to leave our bags in clear sight because of the numerous pickpockets drawn to unsuspecting visitors. I told Ana of how, twenty-six years previously, when we checked into our hotel, the proprietor had warned us of the "5,000 known pickpockets" who had entered the city to take advantage of all the people in the city for the World Cup. Then we walked back toward our hotel, finding more small, lovely plazas. We stopped for a final couple of glasses of wine in a little bar where the waiters gazed at Ana, commented on the obvious fact of our being mother and daughter, offered us little dishes of salted almonds freshly fried in olive oil, and smiled at us. We talked of our impressions of the city and of how moving it was to have returned after so long—not the entire family this time, but a mother and daughter, connecting in more complex ways and communicating what we felt, remembered, understood, wanted to share. Ana said she could imagine living in Barcelona for a year or two or...

The next morning we paid our bill and checked out. I told the young woman that we had been in this hotel twenty-six years ago. She looked at me, and I thought, "Ah, she wasn't even born yet." We shouldered our bags and walked down to the port and to the underground garage, where we found our car intact. Ana at the wheel to drive us out of the city, we maneuvered our way onto the motorway and began the long drive back, exiting the *autovía* at one point to wander a bit and buy supplies for a picnic in the delta of the Ebro River, where we dipped our toes in the water and watched the water birds. Then driving, driving, south to Málaga.

჻ ჻ ჻

Sharon Balentine has published short stories in The Missouri Review, Green's Magazine *(Canada),* The Tulane Review, Rosebud, Pangolin Papers *and* StoryQuarterly, *among others. Prose pieces have appeared in several* Travelers' Tales *anthologies:* Women in the Wild; A Woman's Path; *and* The Best Women's Travel Writing 2005, 2006, *and* 2008. *Her poetry has appeared in literary magazines such as* Borderlands: Texas Poetry Review, Stone Drum, Skylark, West Wind Review, Timbercreek Review, *and in the anthology* Terra Firma.

℘ ℘ ℘

Mexican Rain

In a town full of "whispered secrets,"
love and loss are inevitable.

*E*very encounter in San Miguel de Allende happens a bit like this: you see him walking across the *jardín* with the chestnut-haired woman. (Maybe they are just friends?) You see him at the tortilla stand on Barranca. (He lets you cut the line.) You see him at the Fuji-film shop. (You ask if he prefers black and white, or color.) You see him at *La Biblioteca* reading poetry. (You ask if he likes Sandra Cisneros. He says, "Who?" so you blush, and tell him about your favorite book, *Loose Woman*.) San Miguel is like this. He is here, there, and everywhere.

In Mexico, you simply decide what you want and it becomes a reality. Like when I looked up at the crescent moon and thought, "I am going to kiss someone tonight," and the bad boy with the dog and the motorcycle appeared. Poof!

It is the Friday night of my last weekend in San Miguel. My plane ticket is booked for Wednesday at 6:10 P.M., leaving out of Mexico City, four hours away by bus. If Angel falls in love with me tonight, I could extend this overdue vacation from my social work career. If not, I will die alone in an overpriced New York City hovel taking home the nightmares of my clients: abused children, "oppositional defiant" teenage boys, worn-down welfare mothers. Weekends, I can look forward to interrogations with my family at overwrought Madison Avenue restaurants. That and trying to meet the elusive American man. What am I supposed to do, wait for Prince Charming to drop from the roof of my subway car?

I don't see Angel at Mama Mía. Just the same beer-bellied gringos who warm these stools each night. They ogle me as if I were the next best thing after Bimbo bread. In New York, no one gives me a second glance, but here you'd think I was dressed for the Miss Mexico pageant.

"Hey baby, you're really hot," says an overweight bald guy in a weak imitation of the Mexican seduction.

"Give me a break," I order a margarita and touch the hem of my black mini dress making sure it hasn't crept up too far.

Usually, I enjoy the attention; it reaffirms my existence. But not tonight. I scan the room casually, as if I am meeting someone.

Then Angel walks in. I know his name because I heard it through the grapevine (a whisper in the *jardín*, an overheard conversation at the *farmacia*). He looks at me with sea-glass green eyes and I think *maybe there is a God*. He lights a cigarette from the bartender's out-stretched lighter.

"*¿Tienes cigaro?*" I ask, even though I don't smoke. Dying of lung cancer seems a small price to pay for the solace of male companionship.

He holds out a pack of Faros, the inexpensive Mexican brand bearing the little man looking at the lighthouse through a telescope. When his match meets cigarette, we are inches apart. I think, this is why people smoke: instant intimacy.

I inhale deeply and break into a coughing fit. Angel laughs and pats my back. I, who am always full of words and wit, am paralyzed by his touch. Angel's freshly-shaved head reminds me of what Noah (my last prince) did to himself when, six years ago, I broke his heart. I wept when I saw him, his beautiful black curls chopped off, his head naked and exposed like a hairless cat. I am now almost thirty, in a masochistic job and single, *soltera*.

"Did you see the gallery opening?" Angel asks in English, spiced with a soft accent.

"Oh no. How was it?" I finger a hole in the chair where splinters are forming.

"The usual. Indigenous women with babies on their backs. Beggars. *Tú sabes*. Clichés about Mexico. Are you an artist?"

"I wish I was."

"*Pues*, what's stopping you?" He makes it sound easy.

"Responsibility?" I say. "Duty? The fact that I worked my ass off to get a degree in social work." My career seems distinctly less appealing from the vantage point of San Miguel. Travel does this to you. You view your life as if looking down from an airplane; everything seems smaller, like moveable figures in a doll house.

Mexicans always seem impressed when I mention social work, unlike back home where people usually stare at their feet. "Social work is noble. But responsibility and duty, these are good things to wash away with tequila," he replies.

"I'm not really noble," I say.

"Noble *and* modest?"

"Compliments are a contagion around here." I chew on the end of my straw until it's ragged.

"What kind of artist would you want to be?"

"Writer. But I'd write something groundbreaking. Be a risk taker, like Frida Kahlo." I first learned about Frida while teaching fifth grade in Los Angeles, right after breaking up with Noah. Her poster hung above my bed: blood, thorns, and searing eyes. I trusted her to teach me how to get through it: survivor of a tram accident, multiple miscarriages, twenty-six operations and heartache—if not her, then who?

"Ah, Frida. Everyone loves Frida."

"I loved her before everyone else."

"Not before I did." Angel winks and my stomach flips. He glances at the vacant doorway.

Angel is a photographer who has lived in Paris, Havana, Rio, and Rome. Now, conveniently, he splits his time between San Miguel and New York. He is living the life I always imagined I might lead, back when I was ten and still believed anything was possible: I'd publish my first book when I was twenty-one, get married at twenty-seven, and have two kids, a boy and a girl.

"You must to excuse me. I'm in a bad mood tonight— my *novia* left me." Angel turns his face away. "*Hombre*, another drink, no?" He slides a twenty-peso coin toward the bartender and three shots appear on the counter: one red, one clear-ish white, and one green, like the Mexican flag. He throws his head back and swallows one at a time, slamming down the empty glasses. "Maybe you can explain American women?

They are so independent, not needing or wanting anything. What is that?"

Mexicans think that my traveling alone makes me independent, without needs. But I am no Isabella. Isabella is only twenty but according to Angel, she's *extremely* mature. He is thirty-six, but unafraid of marriage. *Novia* means girlfriend and fiancée, as if the two are always one and the same, as if you would never date someone you didn't intend to marry.

For the next hour, I listen while he talks. I want to draw him out of his sorrow as simply as my Daddy used to—making something from nothing—creating castles out of cardboard.

"You're sweet," he touches my hand.

My head is spinning from the cigarette, the liquor, and Angel. "I'm leaving in five days." I blurt it out like it's a national tragedy.

"San Miguel is like that. Every time you meet someone, it's their turn to go."

To me, San Miguel is a place where everything is new and shiny and needs to be grabbed instantly. I want to pull him back under the spell that San Miguel has cast on me.

The next day, en route to the mail center, my feet lead me past the *jardín* toward Ten Ten Pie. It's three blocks out of my way, but I pretend I'm just walking by.

He's playing chess over cigarettes and beer. "Come in," he waves. He is sitting with a group of scruffy men, who have the appearance of a pack of wolves. I slip into the seat next to him. Angel nudges my arm after making a good move. I am drunk on the nearness of him. A topless mermaid, surrounded by lecherous sailors, grins at me from a mural painted on the wall below the open kitchen. Above her, dark-skinned women with hairnets chop and sweat, slap tortillas, smash avocados, stir steaming pots of rice and beans.

Daddy tried to teach me chess, but it always seemed so rule-bound. Finally, one of the men jumps a queen over some knights. Angel takes my hand, "Let's go before I lose everything." He leads me toward the *jardín*, the center of everything. Thunder rumbles. Grey clouds hang heavily in the sky. The bells of the *parroquia* jangle. Blackbirds fly away in jagged triangles. People scurry under the archways of the buildings surrounding the *jardín*. The shoeshine men put away their rags. The fruit woman pushes her children under her rain tarp. Mariachis pile into trucks. The square is suddenly empty except for the two of us. Large drops of rain begin to fall. A flash of lightning illuminates the church; the sky is setting off its own fireworks to celebrate our reunion. He pulls me up under the gazebo. "We could go to my place. Have tea, warm up."

I say yes, not believing he is really asking me. Perhaps my amazement stems from years spent at an all-girls school, cloistered from the presence of men. Freud might say it is due to Daddy's departure when I was three. Regardless, in the presence of men my IQ plummets.

He leads me over slippery cobblestones. We duck beneath waterfalls cascading out of downspouts. The rain is like diamonds pouring out of the sky. He holds his coat over my head, plucks a white rose off someone's wall and hands it to me, keeping me hooked.

We arrive at a dead end: Calle de los Muertos. I should see it as an omen, but like the horses in Central Park all I can see is what's directly in front of me. My toes are numb, my hair is plastered to my head and mascara must be trailing down my cheeks, but I don't care.

The first thing I see upon entering the apartment is her breast. A vast blow up in black and white. The head is mysteriously cut off, so all you can see is her perfectly rounded voluptuous 36–D-cup. Probably one of his award-winning photos. My breasts would never merit any prizes. I try not to look too closely, although it is blinding.

Angel makes chamomile tea and quesadillas. How nurturing, I think, a man who cooks. On his infrequent visits, Daddy used to make these awful hamburgers filled with peanuts; he never remembered that I hated peanuts.

"Can I see your photos?" I warm my hands on a chipped teacup.

Angel pulls a dusty box from a shelf and sits down at the kitchen table next to me. There are old nails left in the walls. On some of them, you can see the shadow of missing picture frames.

"This was in Paris. It's a style I am experimenting with."

His photos are disjointed. A neck, an arm, half a face. His photos, like his apartment seem incomplete, the characters like puzzle pieces trying to find their matches.

"You like Mexican music?" he asks.

"I love it! I wish I knew how to dance better though." I have been diligently taking salsa lessons but I'm still clumsy, trying to remember where to put my feet, how to read the hand signals from my partner.

"I'm a terrible dancer, but a good listener. Come." He has an old-fashioned record player with real records. I haven't seen one of these since last setting foot in Noah's dorm room, the day he kicked me out. The day I told him I had a crush on someone else. Someone younger, someone not as nice.

"How can you be a real Latino and not know how to dance?" I joke. Noah hated dancing. He would sit in the corner and watch, the observing writer, hiding behind his words.

A melancholy ballad plays, the fuzzy sound of worn vinyl. If my life were a movie, this would be my soundtrack: imagine the most heartbreaking music you've ever heard.

"I *can* dance," says Angel. "I just choose not to, unless I am with someone I want to be closer to." He puts out his hand and I slip into his arms. We sway to the music, my heart bang-banging against his chest. Then he takes my jaw in his hand and kisses me.

It's this I live for: the forgetting that happens in the moment their lips press against mine, the warmth of their hands against my back, the heat of their breath against my neck, the smell of their sweat, the way they clutch and grope and want, want, want; in this moment, they want what I have and the longer I drag it out, the longer this feeling will last; I go from invisible to visible, and the fact that a man like this would want to be with me proves *something*.

Angel slides the straps of my dress off my shoulders and kisses my neck and shoulders gently, attentively. I run my fingers through the soft fuzz of his hair, the back of his neck, trying to forget, trying to make him forget.

We curl up on the couch (under the breast). When the record comes to the end, the needle gets jammed, and the same line repeats over and over, something about love. Up the narrow staircase, he pulls me, and I follow, even though I don't know where we are going.

The window shutters bang against the walls, rain streaming onto the floor. He pushes them shut and mops up the water with an old shirt. The bed is unmade, as if left in a hurry.

"Are you afraid of me?" he asks, patting the empty space beside him. "I'm not dangerous."

"Are you sure?" I sit tentatively, my knees tucked beneath my chin.

Angel pulls my dress over my head and runs his fingers over me like a sculptor examining his work. I wonder if he is comparing us: my bones to her softness, my flat chest to her voluptuousness. He takes off his damp T-shirt, kicks off his worn sneakers, but leaves on his khakis. His chest is pale, his tummy soft and smooth, like a boy's, like Noah's. I kiss his stomach, his chest, his collarbone.

"This is a nice curve," he runs his tongue over my hip bone, "and this, and this." He plays with the elastic on my underwear. Then his fingers pull away. He leans back, reaching for a cigarette. He taps one on the dresser and contemplates a match. Finally, he says, "I don't want to hurt you. Let's just sleep, O.K.?"

I let out a breath I hadn't realized I was holding. I can't decide whether to feel relieved or rejected. "Angel?"

"Yes?"

"If you didn't have anyone else, do you think you would want…uh, I'm such an idiot, forget it." The wind throws the windows open again, cool air rushes in.

"*Díme*. What? What?" He pulls my hands away from my face.

"I'm so bad at this thing with men, you know? I don't know how to do it at all."

"You are not so bad as you think, *neníta*." He wraps me into the curve of his body, our legs interwined. The rain has slowed to a pitter patter. At night when I was a little girl I loved listening to the sound of rain raging outside.

I lie awake listening to the sound of Angel's breathing. I am grateful that we haven't slept together because I think this will make it easier when he wakes up to discover that I am not Isabella. I know this will hurt later, and must have known it before we kissed, but none of this has been enough to protect me from the power of my longing.

It was night that was the hardest after Noah. For years afterward, I huddled on the right side of the bed (not realizing I was huddling) until a friend discovered me and said, "Why have you got yourself all squashed into the corner! Why don't you sleep in the middle, silly?" For six years I had been sleeping with a ghost.

Morning comes with its unfortunate predictability.

"Want to go for breakfast?" I ask, wrapping the sheet around my chest and patting down my electric-socket morning hair. Angel still has on his pants and is lighting up the day's first cigarette.

He kisses me on the forehead. He does not flee or toss me to the floor as I was expecting.

"I have to meet people for a job. Sorry." He starts getting dressed, his cigarette still dangling from his perfect lips.

"*Claro que sí.*" It's an expression I learned in Spanish class. I've practiced so often it almost sounds true: *of course, sure, whatever.*

"*Bueno*, I'll see you. O.K.?" he says. Last night's rose lies wilted on the floor.

"*Bueno.*" I hand it to him. "You know, she must be crazy."

He takes what is left of the rose and holds it between his teeth like a flamenco dancer. "We are all a little crazy, no?"

Everyone in San Miguel inevitably meets. It's a town full of whispered secrets. Standing in the doorway at Mama

Mía, a few days later, I see her. Someone tells me she's Angel's *novia*. Tonight she's on her own, but she does not lack for company. All the men have their eyes fixed on her, the chestnut-haired woman twirling in the arms of the reedy pianist who has stepped off the stage to dance with her during the band's break. She has on flat Mexican sandals that only someone beautiful can pull off, along with a floor-length lavender chiffon skirt, a white off-the-shoulder peasant blouse and gypsy earrings. Her feet move swiftly and sharply to the drumbeat. She clears the other couples off the floor. Spinning in circles beneath her partner's arm, her hips sway to the steady pounding of the salsa spun by the DJ. One by one men vie to dance with her. The pianist hands her off to the drummer, a short, round man with a dimpled grin. He pushes her hips this way, and that, their feet in sync, sailing back and forth. Despite his size he moves with inexplicable precision. Her hair flies about, her feet fly, her arms lift and fall: one, two, three, kick, then again, and again. The trumpet player cuts in, tapping the drummer out. The crowd roars with approval when the drummer refuses to let go.

A bearded man resembling Al Pacino stamps out his cigarette and nods at her. She glides into his open arms, leaving the trumpeter behind. The man pins one arm behind her back, the other draped down, swinging like the hand of a grandfather clock: tick-tock, tick-tock. They dance forehead to forehead, effortlessly. He pulls her close—then pushes her away, like a tease. She ends in a dip, neck and hair thrown back, one foot in the air. The crowd claps and she bows, a cool smile on her face.

This is not the cold discothèque solo grooving that I learned at Studio 54 when I was a teenager sneaking in on a fake ID. If only I could dance like this woman, the world would fall at my feet.

I slink off to the bathroom, past the line-up of drunks at the bar, past the flamenco guitar player who is offering melancholy songs to a bored crowd of tourists and couples eating greasy Italian food at wooden candlelit tables beneath colorful Chinese paper lanterns that hang from dormant bougainvillea branches. Everything that had seemed so bright and beautiful last week is already lost to me.

By Tuesday night, my bags are packed. I begin collecting excuses for Angel's silence: he is too depressed. He doesn't have a phone. He has forgotten where I am staying.

Shamelessly, I go to his house. In the light of day, it looks smaller, more run down. Isabella answers the door.

"I've seen you dance," I mumble. "You're good." A weak apology for trying to steal her life.

He stands behind her without a shirt on, still wearing kakhis. After she leaves he says, not unkindly, "But what did you expect?"

Back in my hotel room, the rain beats down steadily on the roof like the congas at Mama Mía. I flick on the TV that hangs from a corner of the ceiling. There's a movie on about a woman who photographs her lovers' shoes. Finally, she has an exhibit. The men are there. Her family is there. And the shoes: cowboy boots, Doc Martens, leather-tasseled businessman shoes, rag-tag sneakers with holes in them, loafers, riding boots, punk-rocker shoes, and more. Some are standing up, some lying down, some have socks hanging out of them, some still hang off feet. She has kept pieces of them; I have given away pieces of myself.

Before the airport I take a taxi to Frida Kahlo's Casa Azul in Coyocan. I have carried around her paintings in my head for so long: Frida with the broken column, Frida with Diego on her mind, the two Fridas holding hands, one clasping Diego's picture, the other the scissors that have sliced the vein to her heart. In the marketplace they sell more of her: Frida with thorns on your grocery bag, revolutionary Frida to wear around your neck, a coaster for your drink bearing the couple on their wedding day—tiny Frida next to giant Diego, paintbrushes in hand. It's Frida who has captured the heart of the world, not Diego; it's now that I get it: she never realized her own greatness, she gave it all away.

I pull out a pen and begin to write, bumpy lines on a crumpled napkin. With each word I begin to feel a tiny bit better. As I write, I begin to see my story with distance, the way I will look back at Mexico through the frame of the airplane window, as something beautiful I am pulling away from, the space between us allowing me a perspective I couldn't have from the ground.

Pamela Alma Bass earned her MFA in creative writing from the University of San Francisco. She has received two Gold Solas Awards from Traveler's Tales for her non-fiction and her work has appeared in various anthologies and magazines. She teaches humor writing in San Francisco. These days the only boys she chases after are her sixteen-month-old twins. Find her online at www.pamelaalmabass.com.

DIANA COHEN

Bread, Clay, and the Spanish Civil War

A potter in an Andalucían village shares his craft—
and secrets—from Spain's dark history.

$\mathcal{P}$epe and his pottery yard were both ramshackle and to the casual passerby may have looked dilapidated, even unpleasantly cobwebby. All that is true I suppose, but the eyes that turned away after only a superficial glance would have missed a small, self-contained world, teeming with life and rich with history. The hub around which everything pivoted was Pepe himself, young and burnished bronze from the hours he spent muscling clay under the scorching Andalucían sun.

Discovering the pottery was like stumbling into a little community, revealed by my chance tumble down a dim corridor and out into the sun-drenched yard behind. I first saw Isabel, a roly-poly woman swaddled in an old apron, who lived in a few rooms that opened into the pottery yard.

"*Ven, ven*" she called, beckoning me insistently with that characteristic Spanish imperative of fingers pointing down at the ground and a little scooping of the hand. So I ducked under her hanging sheets and ample underpants flapping in the Mediterranean breeze and found myself in the middle of a dusty yard of clay pots laid out on wooden planks, drying in the morning heat. Isabel had an incandescent smile and chestnut eyes that danced with so much hidden mischief that I would have followed her anywhere. At the time, due to my limited Spanish and her non-existent English, we communicated almost entirely by smiles and hand-signals. Even then I understood that the language barrier was a blessing. Since I couldn't talk much I could completely relax. I didn't have to say anything and didn't have to spin lies and false truths and didn't have anyone asking questions about my life in California, a life I pretended had never been. I could just get by on my smile.

Isabel was as staunch and sturdy as the trunk of one of the old olive trees that grew on the fringes of town. Her slight young husband rode a motorbike that made an eardrum-piercing racket when he fired it up. When I first met Isabel she was especially round, pregnant with her fourth child. Shortly before the baby was born her husband was killed in an accident, but I never knew how, since at the time I spoke about enough Spanish to ask for a drink of water. I did, however, understand the finality of the word "*muerto*." The new baby, a second girl, was born with a wandering eye that gave her tiny face a sweetly skewed expression. And for a long while Isabel lost the magic of her smile. It never occurred to me to make the connection between her life and my own young husband's accidental death when I too was pregnant, since I was too busy forgetting and shoving my past into the shadows. Unconsciously searching for a place to hide away from loss, I had fled California for Spain, alone with my three young children. What I couldn't have guessed was that Spain was the perfect place for hiding secrets, hiding as it was from its own painful past.

But the treasure of the place was Pepe. Pepe the Potter, as our family came to call him, to distinguish him from a whole town full of men called Pepe. On that first morning he was in his shed, seated on a board at ground level with his legs dangling in a pit below, spinning a mound of red clay. His smile was simply a sunbeam. The man was hospitable to kids and cats, fishermen who built boats in his yard, elderly señoras dressed in black who shuffled in wearing their bedroom slippers, seeking his advice or a hand with this or that. He was also kind to the Gypsies camped on the other side of the cinder-block wall that separated their world from the universe of the pottery.

"*Hombre* Diana!" he would exclaim with surprise when he would see me walk in through the dust after I too became one of the creatures who called the pottery "home." If his hands were covered with the goo of wet clay, as they almost always were, he would invariably offer me his forearm to shake.

"*Hombre* Diana," I can still hear him say it and know that I would be welcomed back no matter how long I'd been gone. A few days, a few years, it is always the same smile of pleasure as he puts down the cigarette glued to his lips—always a Ducado, the blackest of the black tobacco—and thrusts out his arm.

If you closed your eyes and conjured up any figure, any shape, Pepe could quickly make it appear from the mound spinning between his fingers. Sometimes he'd have to cut it free to finish the details: the handles of a Greek urn or the ear-lobes of a Mayan mask, but the primary shape was always born there on his wheel. Once Pepe threw a long slender cylinder, then coiled it into a clay trumpet, finishing it with intricate scales and the head of a fish. That coiled clay trumpet hung in the hallway of our old house for years, until our time in Spain had run out. The man could make magic with his hands and a lump of clay he called *barro*.

The intricacies of glazing and painting fine designs eluded him however. If there is truly a goddess in the kiln during firing—potters will tell you that once the pots are in the kiln they're in the hands of the gods—those deities of glazing never did smile down on Pepe. Even the omnipresent ghosts of all the men who had worked at this pottery over the generations, loading and unloading the big kiln, were no help when it came to the glazing. Their spirits might still be lurking about, but what did they know of fancy glazes? This was a pottery that had produced the roof tiles for the church in the *plaza*, casserole dishes for preserving meat in salt when ice was still delivered on a cart by Salvador and his mule, Pepito, flowerpots and the two-handled coffee mugs called *pucheros*. This was a place that produced the utilitarian objects that people needed for their daily lives, not decorative pots with fancy glazes.

But Pepe was a dreamer. When I first became a regular, he was working with a young Parisian artist who had imported powdered glazes and was decorating Pepe's pots in the style of Italian majolica. When they opened the door of the big old white-domed kiln that Pepe called an *horno* after he had stayed up all night shoveling debris and discarded wood into the flames below, they must have been seriously disappointed. The glazes had run and jumped spots and thoroughly mis-behaved. It had to be discouraging to these two artists who had dreamed of making beautiful pottery to sell to the tourists who were starting to wander the streets. So Pepe was doomed to throwing endless flowerpots, ash-trays and casserole dishes and never did figure out how to fully express all his creativity. Yet his pottery yard remained the central address for anything made of red clay in the region, just as it had been for over a hundred years.

Meanwhile, Pepe had to support his growing family: his wife, Carmela, their five daughters and Carmela's mother, Carmen. And that was before José Antonio was born, and then Rebecca two years later. Carmela, always industrious and inventive, began selling clams, mussels, and other shellfish on a damp burlap sack in front of the morning market. By this time Pepe had bought a car and took driving lessons so that he could get up before sunrise and drive into the wholesale fish market in Málaga, almost an hour's drive east. Then Carmela and her elderly mother would resell at their little spot what-ever Pepe had bought that day. And, if they didn't sell it all, they could always take it home and eat it for lunch.

When I was at the pottery I could just be me, word-less and inarticulate. Nobody asked any more than that. I loved the silence and sitting and watching him work. I loved the whole troop of people who called the pottery home: Isabel in her apron, watering her scarlet gera-niums, hanging out her washing, Antonio, who could neither read nor write, building his fishing boat, using only a plane, a chisel and a hand saw. I can still hear his deeply sonorous voice as he announced his arrival each morning:

"Pepe, Pepe," until his friend's name floated like a particle of dust in the shafts of sunlight.

"*Voy, voy*," Pepe would call back, hopping up from his place at the wheel to welcome his friend. I liked the ginger-colored cats that would sit around watching Pepe work. Between the fish heads and innards that Isabel tossed them each day when she cleaned fish for lunch and the detritus from the gypsy camp, they survived but had no trouble maintaining their sleek figures.

At any time there might be one or more of our many young daughters, sometimes two or three of Pepe's, Isabel's two and my two girls, playing together out in the yard.

"Mariquita," Pepe would sing out genially from his spot at the wheel, drawing out the "quita" like an opera diva holding a long trilling note. None of them were named Mariquita, but the girls heeded the warning none-the-less, knowing that Mariquita was the mythical naughty girl who had strayed too close to the clay pots drying in the sun. Especially in the afternoon sunlight they'd play around in the dust until Pepe finally swung the sagging wooden door of the shed shut and he and his girls would walk home in the dwindling twilight to Carmela and supper.

After that first day I began going back, occasionally at the beginning and then almost every day and every free moment. I tried hard to visualize my hands and fingers working Pepe's magic with the clay. The cats and I would watch him sloshing around in the big pit where he dumped the raw clay and worked it using his bare, wide feet and the powerful muscles of his short brown legs. Every so often he would pull up a bucket of water from the old whitewashed well where the frogs lived amid the ferns, and throw the water into the pit, droplets of crystal scattering into the sunlight. Then he'd hop back in, stomping methodically back and forth until the mixture was smooth and the consistency of pancake batter. It would rest there in the pit for days while the sun sucked out its excess moisture. Then, when it had just the right consistency, he would carve it into big slabs, like cutting up a giant milk chocolate sheet cake.

By this time he had built a second potter's wheel for any aspiring potters-to-be, like me and another young woman from Italy who worked there at the beginning. Clearly he relished our company. He was also was a patient teacher, especially when I had so much trouble mastering the art of the wheel. Those damp red lumps would wobble and tilt and were forever spinning off center. Still I stuck with it, perhaps more from cussed determination than anything else. And sometimes Pepe would throw a big cylinder of wet clay and hand it over for me to decorate. This I could do, and I'd lose myself in the work while he sat at his wheel smoking, spinning out ashtrays and casserole dishes and telling me his stories of his boyhood growing up in the years following the Spanish Civil War, fought from 1936 to 1939.

Pepe was the magnifying lens through which I came to understand the town of Fuengirola and her history, especially the terrible years of hunger after the war. During the years I lived there and for many years after, the Spaniards were engaged in a collective pact of amnesia regarding anything having to do with their Civil War. Nobody said anything, not even in whispers. Except Pepe. Except to me. But I noticed how he always lowered his voice to avoid being overheard and risk being denounced to the fearsome Guardia Civil. I started carrying a small notebook and ballpoint pen faithfully back and forth from our apartment to the pottery. On those clay smudged pages I would jot down the bones of his stories in Spanish so that I could capture their essence. By then I understood a fair amount but still spoke only meager Spanish, so I would often have to stop him to ask what a word meant. In that old notebook I recorded not only Pepe's stories but the stories his father had told him when he was a young boy, squatting in the dust, listening as his father too worked the clay.

"Diana," he would say, his voice dropping to a conspiratorial whisper, "there wasn't a dog or cat or even a songbird around for years. They either died from starvation or disappeared into some cooking pot. Even the rats and mice got eaten."

"I was born in 1932," he said, inhaling deeply as a big curl of cigarette ash dropped off the end of his Ducado. "Of course I have no memory of the beginning of the war. But my father always said it was a time that turned families, neighbors and even brothers against each other. He used to tell me how the German planes bombed our province of mostly poor *campesinos*—people whose only crime was trying to scratch a living from their small plots of land. So by early in the war Málaga was cut off from the rest of Spain. And that was just the beginning of the hunger. By the time the war was over and Franco had won, a third of the population was dead, disappeared, or had fled to France. That's what happened to Carmela's father: One day he started walking toward France and kept right on going—he was afraid if he stayed that he'd be taken out at night and shot. He never came back to live permanently with his family again. But the worst was yet to come." He paused to light another Ducado, took a long drag and let the smoke out slowly.

"Meanwhile, the rest of the world had their own war, World War II, and who had time to remember the people in Spain?" He shrugged his shoulders and opened his damp hands with resignation. "Our animals were dead and the *fincas*, the farms, abandoned. There was no wheat to grind for flour and no bread. Many men and women had been killed or fled or they'd been rounded up and disappeared into prison. And the ones who were left, mostly the young and the very old, slowly starved. And the rest of the world forgot us.

"Diana,"—he always pronounced my name Deeana— "you have to understand that to a Spaniard, *comer sin pan es imposible,* a meal without bread is not a meal. Even if there had been food, which there wasn't, without bread it's as though we haven't eaten. By this time I was about ten, so I remember the Moor who would regularly come by boat from North Africa accompanied by his silent black bodyguard. He'd come to take back as much pottery as my father could make. At the time, money had no value since there was nothing to buy. My father would barter his *cerámica* for olive oil and sacks of flour and rice that would keep our family from starving. The next night my father would fire up the little clay oven—*el joven* Pepe, the young Pepe, he named it after me—and bake the bread late at night so the smell of baking bread would be carried out to sea rather than torture a hungry town. But early the next morning the women with their string bags and large, pleading eyes, were always waiting quietly at the gate.

"There were young women that dirt, hunger, and despair had turned old, skinny women whose ragged clothing barely covered their naked bodies. There were skinny babies perched on their mothers' boney hips with another silent child or two, their noses always yellow with snot, clutching her skirt hem. There were Gypsy women, skinny as sticks, young and old, but you couldn't tell the difference. Almost all the women wore black—*en luto*—mourning the husbands, fathers, and brothers who'd died.

"With tired dark eyes and faces deeply lined from too much work, too much sun and too much hardship, they'd crowd at the gate of the pottery, hoping to trade a little salt or a few vegetables grown in the hard dirt, a couple of dried figs, or with nothing—*contra toda esperanza*—hoping that my father would share a few bits of bread out of compassion for the children. And after the women had gone, my father was left with six loaves or so for our own family of eight: my father and mother, my five sisters and me, the youngest and only boy."

He reached out to the white clay *botijo* that was always sitting on the ground beside him and lifted it in the air. As he tilted his head back a thin gurgle of cool water arched elegantly out and into his open mouth. (When I tried drinking from this water jar I invariably splashed my chin and drenched the front of my shirt, to Pepe's frequent amusement. But I was getting better at it.)

"Hunger, deprivation and separation from their men left the women of our town so vulnerable," he wiped his mouth and narrow mustache on the short sleeve of his shirt and picked up the thread of his story. "My father once told me how the captain of our town's contingent of Guardia Civil treated the wives of the men he had imprisoned. When the women would come for a visit, perhaps bringing a small packet of food, the *jefe*—the chief—would force them to strip naked. He'd rape the younger women before he allowed them a visit." Pepe shook his head in what I understood to be his attempt to understand what seemed beyond understanding. "*Las mujeres son un botín de guerra.*"

"Pepe, what does it mean '*un botín de guerra*'?"

"Women are the spoils of war," he explained. "The cruelest way of punishing your enemy is to *violar* their women. Fuengirola wasn't the only town where this happened my father told me, but in my opinion it's partly why people still hate the Guardia. Diana, surely you've felt it yourself when the Guardia pass?" I nodded my head in mute agreement.

"*Mi padre* once told me how, despite the awfulness of those years, out in the *campo*—the countryside—the old orange trees continued to blossom and bear fruit abundantly. One day, underneath a tree, my father discovered the bodies of a man and woman whose guts had exploded from gorging on too much fruit."

At the beginning I had been drawn to the pottery by the challenge of mastering the potter's wheel, but now it was the power of Pepe's stories that drew me back day after day. Besides learning to use the wheel, I was absorbing the language and getting a history lesson about Spain and this village as seen through his eyes.

After listening to this story I understood why Spaniards of Pepe's generation were so short—in his case the top of his head may just have reached up to the tip of my nose. He seldom wore anything on his feet other than a pair of beat-up old sandals that he could slip in and out of with ease. He was bow-legged as though he had spent his life on the back of a horse rather than kicking a heavy wooden potter's wheel and he almost always wore holey old shorts that accentuated his sturdy bowed-out legs. Whatever it was about him, however, whether it was his broad smile and unflappable disposition, his luminous dark eyes full of the delight of a kid, or his generosity, always quick to share whatever he had, Pepe had some quality that drew people to him magnetically. He seemed enormously content with his place in the world despite his voracious curiosity about life beyond this village. Each of the assortment of people who found their way to the pottery seemed to expand the boundaries of Pepe's life. And irresistibly, we all fell in love with him, each in our own way.

♫ ♫ ♫

Diana Cohen lived for many years in Andalucía, Spain, working as a potter, teaching English to Spanish children, and studying the rejoneo, *the artful bullfight from horseback. She wrote a cover story for* Lookout, *an English language magazine published in Spain on the centuries old religious pilgrimage, the Romería del Rocío. A graduate of Mills College and the recipient of a 1983 Coro Fellowship in Public Affairs, she lives in San Francisco and is finishing a memoir on raising a family during the last years of Franco's Fascist Spain. Visit her online at www.donaquijote.com.*

Passport Past

Her old adventurous self lives on.

The passport officer had to search for a page with enough room to add his stamp, which he did, with the familiar thump of the tool of his trade. Then he pushed the worn little blue book back to me. That was all. No comment. No fanfare. I stepped away from the window so the next traveler could step up, but marked the occasion in my mind. My passport would expire the next day. With this unsmiling officer and this inauspicious moment in Toronto, it was officially retired.

These days I don't have the opportunity to travel as much as I once did. I have a new passport now, but it isn't filling with exotic stamps as quickly as the old one did. It might not even be full when its ten years come up. Life slows down. I've slowed down. My passport is four years old and still looks almost new. How sad, I sometimes think. How restful, I think at other times.

   Still, before tucking my old passport away, I leafed through it, recalling an adventure with every stamp. I remember the hassle of getting visas for the Baltic states, blushing my way through a phallus-filled museum of erotica in Japan, decorating my hotel rooms with fistfuls of colorful wildflowers in Norway, sleeping in a bitterly cold hut constructed of teak in the hills of Thailand, being interrogated by Netherlands passport control over a stamp from Malta, slogging through an ill-conceived and grueling train trip across five Alpine countries in two weeks. I called that journey "The Alpine Death March," but at least it got me a stamp from Slovenia—the kind of place the makes me think "whodathunkit?" Before the fact, I could easily imagine someday visiting France. Slovenia? Never crossed my mind until I was there. And there I was. And I had the stamp to prove it.

   From time to time, I like to study the photograph of myself, so many years younger. Jokes about the horror of passport photographs are trite, but this photo is different. It is, in fact, one of the best photographs ever taken of me. My hair is long, my eyes come-hither, my skin unwrinkled, my smile Mona Lisa mysterious. Passport officers invariably seemed disappointed when they looked up from the photograph to view me in person, in all my jet-lagged glory. Once, a young security guard at JFK airport looked at the photo, then at me, and with the air of sharing a confidence, leaned in with some advice. "You should wear your hair long again," he said.

   I hated to let this old passport go, this little book containing a beautiful, adventurous me and all my journeys.

   Of course, I now have a new passport with a new photo. It's an O.K. photo. My hair is shorter, but still long. I have a friendly smile, and character lines (allow me the euphemism) have gathered in the corners of my eyes. Sure, it's a nice enough photo, but it doesn't cause anyone to glance up hopefully, looking for the traveling beauty. And the pages are filling slowly. I have stamps from Mexico, Brussels, Italy. But nothing too terribly far-flung, nothing with the scent of adventure. Shall I return to Slovenia just for the stamp?

The exotic woman who carried my old passport may not exist anymore. Maybe she never did, not really. But I have posted her on the bulletin board above my desk, so that I can look at her now and then and remember. At least she lives on in the pages of the worn little blue book. And she'll live forever, among my souvenirs.

Sophia Dembling is author of The Yankee Chick's Survival Guide to Texas. *A freelance writer based in Dallas, she still resembles her new passport photo.*

ACKNOWLEDGMENTS

Editing these books is nothing less than a privilege, and every year I marvel at my good fortune at having bumped into the likes of Larry Habegger and James O'Reilly, Travelers' Tales founders. Many thanks as well to the whole gang at Solas House for finessing the many details on the editorial and production side, especially Susan Brady, Sean O'Reilly, and Christy Quinto, as well as my intern Amy Krynak, Travelers' Tales intern Shannon Bowman-Sarkisian, typesetter Melanie Haage, and cover designer Stefan Gutermuth.

About the Editor

Lucy McCauley's travel
essays have appeared
in such publications as
*The Atlantic Monthly,
The Los Angeles Times,
Fast Company Magazine,
Harvard Review*, *Science
& Spirit*, and Salon.

Photo by Gail E. Atwater

com. She is series editor of the annual *Best Women's
Travel Writing*, and editor of three other Travelers' Tales
anthologies—*Spain*, *Women in the Wild*, and *A Woman's
Path* (coedited with Amy G. Carlson and Jennifer Leo).
In addition, she has written case studies in Latin America
for Harvard's Kennedy School of Government, and now
works as a developmental editor for publishers such as
Harvard Business School Press. She lives with her hus-
band, Charles Bambach, and their daughter, Hannah, in
Dallas—with frequent returns to Boston.